Praise for
Walking Tall in Babylon

"Hats off to Connie Neal for this realistic road map for leading children through the perils of a pagan society. As a parent of two daughters, I am grateful Connie has provided a guide to protecting our children from moral shipwreck while also inspiring them to hold out the light of God's truth in a dark world."

—DR. ROBERT JEFFRESS, pastor of Wichita Falls First Baptist Church
and author of *I Want More!* and *The Solomon Secrets*

"*Walking Tall in Babylon* is the book parents—and especially fathers—have been waiting for. Connie is an author who can speak to a man's heart in his own language. Not just for moms, Connie's latest book will help men take the lead in training their children to be godly and wise."

—LYNDI AND BILL MCCARTNEY, founder and president of Promise Keepers

"Connie Neal does an incredible job of helping readers teach their children the interplay between moral absolutes, consequences, mercy, and grace found in Scripture, giving kids a grid for making moral decisions. Great biblical exposition and terrific practical tips as well. I can't wait to start practicing these principles with my own kids!"

—WILL PENNER, editor of *Youthworker Journal,* director of youth
ministries at East Brentwood Presbyterian Church in Nashville,
Tennessee, and father of three

"Connie Neal offers real, biblically based tools for nurturing our children's faith in a world full of threats. But rather than focusing on the evils, Neal points out the more insidious danger of losing touch with the world our children live in. She shows parents how to help children tackle negative influences with a strong faith as they seek to impact their generation for Christ."

—CARLA BARNHILL, editor of *Christian Parenting Today* magazine
and author of *Blessings Every Day*

"*Walking Tall in Babylon* starts strong and gets stronger as it goes; I especially enjoyed the chapter about preparing our children to be in the world without becoming worldly. I wish I had this book through the years of rearing my children."

>—CHUCK SMITH, JR., senior pastor of Capo Beach Calvary and author of *Epiphany*

"Most of our children go to school every day in Babylon, and Connie Neal teaches us how we can lead them through safely and securely in Christ."

>—VICKI CARUANA, founder of America's Teacher and author
>of *Apples & Chalkdust* and *Prayers from a Teacher's Heart*

"Terrorism, school violence, moral decay, and a corrupt culture... Help! Connie Neal gives us the biblical backup we need to help mentor our children to adulthood. Armed with God's Word and Connie's practical application, we can parent our children in the new millennium with confidence."

>—CHRISTINE FIELD, author of *Help for the Harried Homeschooler*
>and *Life Skills for Kids*

"*Walking Tall in Babylon* is an inspiring handbook for any parent who desires to raise godly children in today's world. Connie Neal skillfully shows us how to touch the hearts of our children and challenge them to live as Daniel did in a hostile and dangerous society."

>—JOANNE MILLER, RN, BSN, cofounder of the National Center for Biblical
>Parenting and coauthor of *Say Goodbye to Whining, Complaining, and*
>*Bad Attitudes* and *Good and Angry*

"This book is a must-read for any parent committed to raising children to withstand the negative influences of our culture today. With this manual, parents can train their children to understand God, recognize the fallacies in their culture, and know when and how to take a stand for what's right."

>—DR. SCOTT TURANSKY, cofounder of the National Center for Biblical
>Parenting and coauthor of *Say Goodbye to Whining, Complaining,*
>*and Bad Attitudes* and *Good and Angry*

WALKING TALL IN BABYLON

RAISING CHILDREN TO BE GODLY
AND WISE IN A PERILOUS WORLD

Connie Neal

WATERBROOK
PRESS

WALKING TALL IN BABYLON
PUBLISHED BY WATERBROOK PRESS
2375 Telstar Drive, Suite 160
Colorado Springs, Colorado 80920
A division of Random House, Inc.

All Scripture quotations, unless otherwise indicated, are taken from the *Holy Bible,*
New International Version®. NIV®. Copyright © 1973, 1978, 1984 by International
Bible Society. Used by permission of Zondervan Publishing House. All rights reserved.
Scripture quotations marked (NASB) are taken from the *New American Standard Bible*®.
© Copyright The Lockman Foundation 1960, 1962, 1963, 1968, 1971, 1972, 1973, 1975,
1977, 1995. Used by permission. (www.Lockman.org). Scripture quotations marked (NKJV)
are taken from the *New King James Version*. Copyright © 1982 by Thomas Nelson, Inc.
Used by permission. All rights reserved. Scripture quotations marked (NLT) are taken
from the *Holy Bible, New Living Translation,* copyright © 1996. Used by permission
of Tyndale House Publishers, Inc., Wheaton, Illinois 60189. All rights reserved.

Italics in Scripture quotations reflect the author's added emphasis.

ISBN 1-57856-580-4

Published in association with Yates & Yates, LLP, Literary Agents, Orange, California.

Library of Congress Cataloging-in-Publication Data

Neal, C. W. (Connie W.), 1958–
        Walking tall in Babylon / Connie Neal.— 1st ed.
            p. cm.
Includes bibliographical references.
        ISBN 1-57856-580-4
    1. Child rearing—Religious aspects—Christianity. 2. Daniel (Biblical figure) I. Title.
        BV4529.N43 2003
        248.8'45—dc21

                                                                            2003004784

Printed in the United States of America
2003—First Edition

10 9 8 7 6 5 4 3 2 1

To all parents hoping to keep life safe and good for their children,
who want their children to grow up to be godly and wise in these perilous times…
and who are willing to hear the Word of God,
and walk in His ways to bring that about.

CONTENTS

ACKNOWLEDGMENTS

More than any book I've written, this one was shaped by people and events influencing me during the writing process. Lindy Beam, youth culture analyst for *Plugged-In* magazine planted the idea in my mind. Her interest in and questions about how my husband and I are raising our children to be in the world but not *of* it made me reflect deeply on the biblical beliefs foundational to our parenting. Her quote on what should be the goal of parents today captures my hope for those who read this book: "…to grow kids who are wise, thoughtful, culturally literate, pure, God-fearing, and who can make a positive impact in their world." Thanks, Lindy, for your encouragement, prayers, and pointing out the need for such a book in today's world.

Thanks to WaterBrook Press: Dan Rich, Don Pape, Brian McGinley, Laura Barker, and the team that initiated this project and offered valuable input along the way. Kudos to John Hamilton for the cover design, which I loved at first sight.

Special thanks and appreciation are due my primary editor, Erin Healy of WordWright Editorial Services. Her vision to see where I was aiming to go before I made it clear, her excellent guidance as to how to communicate what I hoped the reader would come to understand, and her patient reworking of the text to bring the message across in a way that would be of most benefit to the reader were vital on this project. Again she has earned my deepest gratitude and admiration.

Thanks are also due to the following people:

Sealy and Susan Yates, my agents for this book.

Carla Barnhill and Camerin Courtney, whose reactions to ideas I shared with them caused me to think further on some points before solidifying my conclusions in print.

Nina Perry, my mom, who let me use her home to seclude myself to write.

My husband, Patrick, and children, Casey, Taylor, and Haley, for allowing me to share some aspects of their lives—and for their patience as I rewrote the manuscript.

The women of the Sioux City, Iowa / Nebraska 2003 Compel Conference, who let me test the message with them and clarify it one last time during the editing process.

Thomas Mockabee, who helped me focus my role as author and the greatest needs of my readers.

As always, thanks to my friend Kim Roberts (along with her husband, Rick, and parents, Charles and Betty Kelly) for their prayers that covered me while I wrote.

ONE

WHERE DO WE BEGIN TO KEEP LIFE SAFE AND GOOD FOR OUR CHILDREN?

As the mother of three, I find it a challenge to get back into the swing of things as the school year begins. Last fall our son, Taylor, became a leader in his junior-high group at church. Part of his commitment was to read a daily selection from the *One Year Bible*. On the morning he was to begin, I couldn't even find the *One Year Bible*. I found the *Daily Bible* and figured we'd stay with the spirit of his commitment, even though the passage we would read differed from what the rest of the group was reading that day. Taylor, thirteen, our daughter Casey, sixteen, and I sat down at our kitchen table and opened to the passage assigned for that date. It was from Amos, one of the minor prophets, starting in chapter 8. We didn't have time before school to study the context of the prophecy, so we jumped right in. Little did we realize how differently the text would appear to us by dinnertime.

Here are some highlights of what we read:

"In that day," declares the Sovereign LORD, "the songs in the temple
will turn to wailing. Many, many bodies—flung everywhere! Silence!

"In that day," declares the Sovereign LORD,
"I will make the sun go down at noon
     and darken the earth in broad daylight.
I will turn your religious feasts into mourning
     and all your singing into weeping.

I will make all of you wear sackcloth
    and shave your heads.
I will make that time like mourning for an only son
    and the end of it like a bitter day."

I saw the Lord standing by the altar, and he said:

"Strike the tops of the pillars
    so that the thresholds shake.
Bring them down on the heads of all the people;
    those who are left I will kill with the sword.
Not one will get away,
    none will escape." (Amos 8:3,9-10; 9:1)

So much for jumping into Scripture at random! I recall saying, "Can you imagine such a thing?" Of course, we couldn't. I made a mental note to study the book of Amos so I could put these terrifying, although seemingly irrelevant, verses into a context that would make sense for our lives today. No time for that now. We had to rush out the door to get the kids to school. After I dropped them off, I turned on the radio news. It was the morning of September 11, 2001.

When I arrived home twenty minutes later, I raced to turn on the television. As I watched the terrible events transpire, I was astounded by how what I was seeing reminded me of the cataclysmic events described by Amos: dead bodies everywhere. The dead being carried out of the city. Stunned silence. That phrase about the sun going down at noon and the earth going dark in broad daylight came to life as I watched a terrified cameraman running from one of the collapsing towers and being overtaken by a cloud of debris until the picture went black. It was as if I were in the darkness with him. That day our celebrations turned to mourning and our songs of joy to weeping. Signs of sorrow were everywhere. Our nation and much of the world wept as one weeping for an only child. Indeed, in the end it was a bitter day.

Perhaps the Old Testament prophets have more relevance for us today than we realized. According to the apostle Peter, we are supposed to pay close attention to them:

> Dear friends, this is now my second letter to you. I have written both of them as reminders to stimulate you to wholesome thinking. I want you to recall the words spoken in the past by the holy prophets and the command given by our Lord and Savior through your apostles. (2 Peter 3:1-2)

The shaking of our world that bright autumn morning shook me as a parent and a Christian. I was already committed to write this book before 9/11. I had already been focusing on a message of hope and encouragement for those parenting in perilous times. But after 9/11, I found that the questions I would need to address in order to authenticate that hope went deeper and felt more urgent. Something happened inside me that was elusive at first.

It's hard to assess fully how the terrorist attacks of 9/11 changed our lives. We all seem to be casting about for a new approach to keep life safe and good, even though we live with a new realization of the constant threat of danger. Without neglecting the everyday concerns close to home, we also have to deal with the emotional impact of seeing such devastation come on our nation and fellow citizens so suddenly. Ongoing threats call us to live in a heightened state of alertness. These new concerns all have to be managed along with all the concerns we had before that dreadful morning. We still want the best for our children.

Have you thought about how you have changed since then? Do you try to ignore the threats? Do you find yourself obsessing about them at times? Have you noticed increased stress taking its toll on you? Are you aware of changes in your priorities? Researchers say Americans are seeking help with stress symptoms at rates more than double those preceding 9/11. Dr. Mary Manz Simon, an expert in child development and authority on trends in

Christian resources for children, says that the aftermath of Columbine and the terrorist attacks of 9/11 are the driving force behind many parents and grandparents who are searching for answers in books and resources. We're urgently seeking help to keep life safe and good for our children and ourselves, while bracing ourselves for whatever may come.

For me, the attacks of 9/11 also symbolize the incursion of immorality into the sanctity of our homes. The unforgettable images of those planes bursting into the offices of unsuspecting workers reminded me of the "flaming arrows of the evil one" mentioned in Ephesians 6:16. There we are told, "In addition to all this, take up the shield of faith, with which you can extinguish all the flaming arrows of the evil one." It seems that the spiritual forces of evil arrayed against us have crossed a new barrier, forcing themselves into our lives in ways that were unthinkable not so long ago. No longer is it enough to keep ourselves and our kids away from places where we know there is danger, whether physical or moral. The enemy is attacking with aggressive immorality that comes unbidden, intruding into formerly "safe" places where our families study, work, play, and live. It's not enough to keep ourselves and our children safely within the walls of our homes and churches. Recent revelations of fraudulent practices, cheating, sexual abuse, pornography, and other forms of unrighteousness threaten to bring down the very structures we thought secure enough to protect our lives, our minds, our retirement accounts, our very souls. It appears that the assault of aggressive immorality is trying to engulf us everywhere at every moment. We all are being forced to live in a state of continual alertness; as concerned parents we do this for ourselves and our children.

According to Scripture, we should have been living on alert all along, but I recently noticed that a major shift in my inner life had occurred. This realization came in May 2002, when I received a letter from Focus on the Family. I have long been a supporter of that organization and so have received many similar letters, but this particular one prompted an inner wrestling with my role as a parent. In it Dr. James Dobson addressed our culture's moral decline and the hesitancy of some Christians to speak out against unrighteousness. Dr. Dobson outlined his primary concerns, writing, "Despite the relentless attacks by homosexual activists on the institution of marriage, and of 'safe-sex' ideology, pro-abortion sentiment, and other forms of immorality that are engulfing us, there are those within the church who remain convinced that it isn't our place to make our voices heard on these issues. In their estimation, controversy about sexuality, the sanctity of human life, and the traditional family are 'political' in nature and therefore unworthy of our attention."[1] Dr. Dobson challenged those who "choose to remain silent in response to the moral free fall we are experiencing" not to neglect using political means to address moral issues that affect our lives, especially the lives of our children. He took issue with those who opted to sidestep political means of reform in favor of just preaching the gospel by saying, "Engaging the culture and sharing the gospel message are not two distinct things; rather they are inexorably intertwined."

Dr. Dobson continued, "The world into which today's children are born has become a very dangerous place. It has changed tremendously.... But now, the culture is at war with parents. It is very difficult to get kids safely through the minefield of adolescence." My head was nodding. *That's for sure!* I read further, "We're seeing a relentless attack on childhood today. There are many people in the activist community who hate the Judeo-Christian system of values, and recognize that if they can gain control of children, they can change the entire culture in one generation. That's why there is a tsunami of propaganda flooding over our culture." I had to agree.

Dr. Dobson then gave a review of significant assaults in public policy that had taken place in a single two-week period regarding the issues he had previously laid out as important. I could almost hear the frustration and irritation behind the words in Dr. Dobson's familiar voice. He focused in on legislation related to the advancement of a pro-homosexual agenda in California's public schools, which my children attend. He concluded, "Sadly, the majority of parents either didn't notice or didn't seem to care, because the legislation passed with too little resistance. Where are the moms and dads who are supposed to be looking out for the welfare of their kids? Why was there not an avalanche of opposition in response? Perhaps it is because Christians have been told that public policy issues, even those that affect their children, are not their concern."

I so resonate with Dr. Dobson's passionate call for parents to be involved in shaping public policies that affect our families. But even as I read his letter, I became increasingly aware that, while I want to impact the culture on a national level, my day-to-day energies are consumed in equipping my children to deal with our culture in settings much closer to home.

I felt compelled to put my thoughts on paper in the form of a letter to this man I so deeply admire. I share this with you because it brought to light for me how dramatically I—and the world as I perceived it—have changed in this past year. Perhaps it will do the same for you.

Dear Dr. Dobson,

You asked, "Where are the moms and dads who are supposed to be looking out for the welfare of their kids? Why was there not an avalanche of opposition in response" to the legislation you mentioned? In posing these questions about parents of children in California's public schools, you are speaking about me and the parents of my children's friends. So, let me try to answer your questions....

You recounted the significant events you saw as negatively affecting and threatening our children in a two-week period in the arena of public policy. Let me share with you the significant events I saw as negatively affecting and threatening my children—more directly—in a two-week period around the time I received your letter. All these events related to the well-being of my family, as I experienced and perceived them....

As a part of my normal routine, I now start the morning by deleting the unsolicited pornographic or inappropriate e-mails that somehow slip through our filters. Sometimes the titles are identifiable, although altered to evade detection like R*A*P*E S*E*X; other times they are veiled with descriptions like Live Show or Barnyard Fun! which was a lure to a Web site on bestiality. When I try to delete some of these, I'm sometimes taken—unwillingly—to photos of graphic nudity, sexually provocative poses of teen girls, or to pornographic Internet sites I cannot exit without turning off the computer. This bombardment of smut increases after my son visits sites related to his hobby of building robots (a favorite of teen boys). This assault never hits me without a profound emotional impact. My husband opts to stay away from the computer altogether to avoid such aggressive temptations. After dumping these vile transmissions from my in box, I return to find an urgent alert asking me to help fight against unsolicited pornographic Internet spam. I go to their Web site, add my name to their petition, and alert some of my friends. Before I can start work, I check the history and temporary Internet files to see exactly what has been viewed on my computer.

News stories that first week included the abduction of fourteen-year-old Elizabeth Smart from her second-story bedroom. I prayed for her and her family while getting up to double-check the lock in my daughter Haley's upstairs bedroom window to make sure it was still secure. The man accused of abducting and murdering seven-year-old Danielle van Dam had come to trial. I wondered about my new neighbors. We live in a nice neighborhood full of kids and culs-de-sac. What seemed like the perfect place for us to raise our children was recast in my mind as a child molester's paradise. *Mental note to self: Check out new neighbors. And you still haven't gone to the sheriff's department to view the list of known sex offenders in our area.* The Danielle van Dam case touched close to the heart for Haley and me because we were at a children's ministry conference in San Diego when the little girl went missing in that same city. We had prayed for her when we heard the newscast.

Many of the news shows that week featured Child Protection Experts (a growing business, no doubt) being interviewed about abductions and sexual assaults of children. They told us to talk to our children to reassure them that stranger abductions are rare; only five or six

American children are abducted each week. (That's supposed to comfort me?) One expert said nine- to thirteen-year-old girls are at greatest risk. My Haley, age eleven, wonders why I won't let her and her friend walk to the park despite her persistent pleas. We're told to empower our kids, encourage them to communicate about their fears, supervise them closely, teach them to try to get away from an abductor, stay in groups, and tell a trusted adult if anything feels wrong to them.

That interview was followed closely by reports of rampant sexual abuse of children by highly trusted priests. Even more highly trusted church officials kept this danger secret from the parents whose children were entrusted to their care. These pedophiliac priests were reassigned to other parishes. Even those with repeated accusations of sexual abuse of minors were sent to work with unsuspecting families in other parishes. So, when it comes to "telling a trusted adult," whom can we trust?

Some Protestant or nondenominational Christians might console themselves by compartmentalizing this scandal within the Catholic Church. I can't do that. I have known of several Protestant churches where child molestation or sex between a minister and a teen has been quietly covered up until unwillingly disclosed. (None of these remain secret and have been dealt with by appropriate authorities.)

With the proliferation of Internet pornography, it's difficult to know who may have been corrupted by it. In one case I was asked to consult on,[2] a popular and trusted children's pastor was accused by his wife of being seriously addicted to pornography. She was so convinced that his depth of immersion in this kind of smut put the children at risk that she separated from him in an attempt to force him to deal honestly with his sin. She urged the church staff to remove him from direct ministry with kids. He was allowed to keep his position, over her protests. However, she was removed from her ministry position on the same staff for being too angry and unforgiving. Many months later, the depth of his depravity and deception was fully uncovered and understood by church leadership. He was finally removed from ministry with children.

I have seen these kinds of cases all across the country, where *trusted* ministers were corrupted by sexual impurity that could turn God's people into prey. These were all people we used to be able to trust.

During that same two-week period, *Headline News* noted that it had been one year since Andrea Yates, the Christian mother who homeschooled her children, got up one morning and systematically drowned all five of them in the family bathtub of their Christian home. In trying to explain this to my children, it did not help that—when it happened—her husband and father of the five dead children went on television to say, "The Lord gives and the Lord takes away, blessed be the name of the Lord."

The report a year later says Mr. Yates complains that his wife is being treated as a hardened serial killer when, he says, she should be seen as "a loving mother who became seriously ill." Granted, she may have been mentally ill, but the fact that she was a Christian mother requires me to help my kids process this terrible act in a way that draws necessary distinctions. They joked it off, relieved that they're old enough to bathe themselves. But I noticed Taylor paid attention to the news report, so I asked what he was thinking. He answered, "I think she is a hardened killer. She's not a loving mother. Even if you went crazy, you can't go crazy in one night. She made a conscious decision." Odd, how he changed from "she" to "even if *you* went crazy," then back to "she."

That confirmed what I felt I needed to monitor. Could my children hear how that "loving Christian mother" murdered her children and wonder if something like that could happen to them? Kids tend to personalize everything they hear. Their mom is a "loving Christian mother" too, and sometimes I'm so stressed out it might make them wonder if I'm going crazy. While Taylor's comparison of Andrea Yates and his mother may not cover the complexities of mental illness, it assures me that the title of "loving mother" retains its sacred meaning and that my son feels safe with me. I'm glad I was there to notice his

change of expression and help him process that in a way that keeps
the sense of security in our Christian home intact.

Do you also feel a need to be more sensitive to how your children are per-
sonalizing formerly unthinkable things that are bombarding them in current
events?

In a breaking news alert, an American was apprehended for plotting to
make and detonate a "dirty bomb"—one with radioactive matter—
somewhere in America. The same day, a government official released a
statement, saying, "Global terror networks are going to get their hands
on nuclear weapons and use them against us." Another official in the
Defense Department announced, "It will take anywhere from one year
to five or ten years until they have a dirty bomb, and they are preparing
to use them."

An Al-Qaeda spokesman said, "America should be prepared. It
should be ready. We are coming to them where they do not expect it."[3]
The war against terrorism requires us to bear in mind that covert terrorists are still at large in our country, plotting our destruction. I found
the news that terrorists overseas were caught with surveillance video
of Disneyland particularly disturbing. Meanwhile, debate continues
over whether to reinstate smallpox vaccinations in light of bioterrorist
threats. My kids fear the shot more than the threatened pestilence,
but it still troubles them. When Taylor noted the connection to Bible
prophecies citing pestilence as a sign of end times, Haley said she
doesn't want the Lord to come back until she's had time to grow up.
My husband and I had to help them both sort through it over dinner.
The term "weapons of mass destruction" is becoming commonplace,
but nonetheless disturbing. I think, *How do we help our kids not be
overshadowed by fear?* For the moment, I opt for turning off the news
and letting Haley turn on *The Cosby Show.*

How I wish the dangers were all "out there" in the big bad world rather than in and around my home. Bear in mind, we live in a nice neighborhood with a strong moral influence in local government, churches, and schools. However, that week while driving Casey and Taylor to an evening performance at their school, we had to detour around several police cars, a news van, and an ambulance in front of a home cordoned off with crime-scene tape, less than a mile from where we live. I put it out of my mind while I enjoyed the performance. On the way home I congratulated Casey and Taylor on their good work, then we finished their homework before bed. I later learned that an estranged husband had shot and killed his wife and one of her friends, and shot and seriously injured two children.

The following week our local news interrupted regular programming with an alert to help locate a suspect in a rape and attempted rape in our area. The man, in his early twenties, attacked a fifteen-year-old girl sitting at a bus stop outside a local high school in the middle of the day. He pulled her into the bushes and ripped off her blouse, but she was able to fight him off. I paid special attention because some of the girls who were in my Bible study group attend that high school. The attacker was apparently intent on gratifying his perverse lusts. He drove about two miles, saw a forty-year-old woman watering her lawn and asked to use her phone. When she said no, he forced her back into her home and raped her. The news alert warned that he was most likely a serial rapist, undeterred by risk, still at large in our vicinity. *No, Haley, you cannot go to the park with your friend, and I can't take you right now.* I wonder how I can get across the real danger without destroying her innocence. I do my best, but I decide I should have my daughters look at the composite sketch so they can run if they see anyone fitting the description. Such are the decisions fathers and mothers have to make these days, even in "good neighborhoods."

As I walked speedily to my mailbox down the block, I noticed a familiar truck backed up to the garage of my neighbor's house. She and her family are fellow Christians. We weren't close friends, but we were friendly. Her husband left her for another woman and is filing for divorce. Although she has two teenagers, she can't afford the house without his income, so they had to sell. I realize the truck must be her husband's; he's there to get his stuff. I wondered how she's bearing up. The last time I saw her she was in tears. I've been meaning to stop by to give her some support and feel a twinge of guilt that I haven't had time. I prayed for her as I hurried home, recalling that the serial rapist hadn't been caught yet.

I've spent these two weeks juggling a deadline for this book and filling out a stack of forms that must be turned in to accept the scholarships and awards Casey has been granted for the Christian college she's planning to attend next fall. My husband and I are grappling with serious financial pressures, due in large part to working for a "Christian" company that broke our contract without paying me. I'm sure we'll be okay, but I decided to call a friend and my pastor's wife for prayer support. Then I thanked God that I could finally close the door to my home office and get back to writing.

Haley finally got to go outside to play with her friend, Jessica, because her dad could go with them. I heard the doorbell. Casey came running in, "Mom, Jessica's dad is at the door. Haley fell off her scooter and broke her arm." I raced out to the car to find Haley crying and moaning in pain. One look at her forearm told me I couldn't look again. We rushed her to the hospital, where the emergency room triage nurse confirmed that her arm was broken. With my goal accomplished, I became aware that I wasn't feeling so well. I have an aversion to being in medical settings, and before I could find a place to lie down, I fainted and hit my face on the bottom of an office chair. The doctor gave me medication for pain and anxiety, then prescribed that I avoid stress. We all had a good laugh—despite the pain.

At that point I stopped writing my letter to Dr. Dobson, realizing that my "venting" had served to crystallize my own thoughts regarding the dangers facing my family. I didn't send the letter, but it made me give serious thought to how much I have changed since the events of 9/11. Let me share a few concluding reflections that may help you, too.

Some of the stress we parents face daily comes from feeling overtaxed by all the worthy appeals to help with good causes and deal with truly important issues. I spend a considerable amount of time driving everyone where they need to go. While driving I listen to morally uplifting radio programs. Very often I am presented with important stands I am called to take to stem the tide of immorality cresting over our culture and to protect our children from its terrible effects. These requests come from Christian broadcasters, church, parachurch organizations, phone solicitors, e-mail alerts, and our local schools. I don't write down numbers while I'm driving, but I often go to related Web sites later and do what I can to help.

Continually fending off pressing dangers and being alerted to a host of potentially negative influences in our culture come along with the basic duties of life: grocery shopping, driving in the carpool, having neighborhood kids over who need loving attention, games that require a referee, trying to maintain an intimate and loving relationship with my husband (who needs my encouragement, and I his), laundry, keeping the house livable, volunteering at church, and on it goes.

Most of the parents I know are conscientious; we are busy, doing our best to protect our kids in the world Dr. Dobson rightly described as growing far more dangerous. We are not unconcerned; if anything, we are overly concerned about too much. Our parental radar screen has become overrun with blips of danger. We are actively trying to raise our children with healthy, positive, and godly influences. We don't want to let go of our desire for them to enjoy the blessings, fun, and innocence of childhood, but we are forced to confront new realities in this world where our children will grow up. The center of our child-protection radar screens has shifted drastically to focus on imminent dangers.

Do you relate to some of this? Are you, too, uncomfortably burdened with a sense of imminent danger that distracts you from what would have held your attention a few years ago? Have your priorities changed? Have you been robbed of peace and joy as a parent? Do you find that approaches to protecting our kids that seemed right in the year 2000 seem insufficient today? Does yesterday's strategy for keeping life safe and good for ourselves and our children call for review?

Before 9/11, I was already planning to write a book explaining the parenting principles that guide my husband and me as we raise our children. Our approach is rooted in lessons we've gleaned from Daniel's generation. The message remains, but my urgency has intensified, my focus sharpened. I appreciate and support Dr. Dobson's efforts on behalf of families and his calling to use the influence of Focus on the Family to set public policy that protects children—mine included. And while I share his concerns, I've come to recognize my own calling as a parent prompts me to respond in ways far beyond writing to my congressman or signing a petition. In response to Dr. Dobson's question, "Where are the moms and dads who are supposed to be looking out for the welfare of their kids?" I have concluded that my lack of action on those important issues simply bears evidence that my parental priorities were forcibly shifted by recent events. I was fully occupied looking out for the welfare of my kids, just closer to home than the California legislature. I pray God gives all of us wisdom as we continue to support needed legislative reforms while figuring out how best to look out for the welfare of our children. I hope this book helps us all work out a fresh, biblically based strategy that will work in today's perilous world.

The strategy I came to lay out in these pages can be traced through a story in the Old Testament, affirmed in the commands of Christ, reiterated in the teachings of the apostles, and preached by Old Testament prophets. Of these, the apostle Peter wrote,

> And we have the word of the prophets made more certain, and you will
> do well to pay attention to it, as to a light shining in a dark place, until
> the day dawns and the morning star rises in your hearts. Above all, you
> must understand that no prophecy of Scripture came about by the
> prophet's own interpretation. For prophecy never had its origin in the

will of man, but men spoke from God as they were carried along by
the Holy Spirit. (2 Peter 1:19-21)

As I relate the story of what happened in that long-ago generation, the parallels to our own generation and the implications may sound alarms for you. Who likes to hear sounds of alarm? Certainly no one welcomes danger. And yet, when real dangers are at hand, we need to deal with them appropriately.

I often fly on commercial airlines. I don't like listening to the safety features of the aircraft, but I listen more attentively these days. God forbid that some emergency would ever make the plane go dark so I'd have to follow the lights along the aisle to an exit. However, if that were to happen, which would be the best response: to sit there in denial thinking, *This can't be happening,* to be paralyzed with fear, to lapse into hysteria, to collapse in overwhelming anxiety? Or to follow the lighted path out *through the dangers* to a place of safety?

Alarms are sounding all around us. This book is meant to be like a lighted path, along which we can lead our children through danger and into the blessed life God wants them to live. Different people react to danger with differing emotions. However we may feel, what matters in these perilous times is that we follow the light of God's Word, which is a lamp to our feet and a light to our path. In the Word we will also find an additional source of hope and encouragement, because in the tale of Daniel, God has given us a panoramic story of real parents and real children who succeeded in perilous times. As their story unfolds, you can judge for yourself what kinds of implications can be drawn from the astounding parallels between their situation and our own. I will focus on the tremendous power we can have as parents to raise our children to pass through the dangerous times in which we live. We can influence these kids to be among those who grow up to be godly and wise, blessed and a blessing, rather than defiled or destroyed.

WHEN REFORMS AND LIMITS ARE NOT ENOUGH

Our story begins about 640 years before Christ, when the kingdom of Judah and a remnant of Israel were all that remained of God's kingdom on earth. It is the story of a good king doing his best to overcome the moral decay and corruption evident in his land, threats of destruction, and impending judgment of God. Of this king it is recorded in 2 Chronicles 34 (NASB),

> Josiah was eight years old when he became king, and he reigned thirty-one years in Jerusalem. He did right in the sight of the LORD, and walked in the ways of his father David and did not turn aside to the right or to the left." (verses 1-2)

So, we see a king with a heart turned toward God, doing right in the sight of the Lord. During Josiah's rule, much of what consumed his energies involved tearing down idols, making righteous societal reforms, and legislating morality that was more in keeping with God's ways than what had gone before him. Josiah held political, religious, and societal power and used all God put at his command to do good. Scripture tells us,

> For in the eighth year of his reign while he was still a youth [about age sixteen], he began to seek the God of his father David; and in the twelfth year he began to purge Judah and Jerusalem of the high places, the Asherim, the carved images and the molten images. They tore down

the altars of the Baals in his presence, and the incense altars that were high above them he chopped down; also the Asherim, the carved images and the molten images he broke in pieces and ground to powder and scattered it on the graves of those who had sacrificed to them. Then he burned the bones of the priests on their altars and purged Judah and Jerusalem. In the cities of Manasseh, Ephraim, Simeon, even as far as Naphtali [what had been Northern Israel], in their surrounding ruins, he also tore down the altars and beat the Asherim and the carved images into powder, and chopped down all the incense altars throughout the land of Israel. Then he returned to Jerusalem. (verses 3-7)

King Josiah had several sons, and would eventually come to have many grandchildren. He left his sons inside the protective walls of Jerusalem while he went out to accomplish his work of tearing down idols, overthrowing those who were leading people away from right worship of the one true God, closing down secret places where people mingled their sexual lusts with their worship. Josiah's efforts were commendable, but his sons were not as protected from the evil all around them as he might've hoped. The corruption the king battled *outside* Jerusalem had permeated life *inside* God's holy city. Corruption and sexual immorality—heterosexual and homosexual—were an accepted part of life in Jerusalem, even within the courts and inner chambers of the temple. In the end, the king's enforced external reforms did not remedy the nation's deepest moral problems.

External reforms and boundaries are fine and sometimes necessary. Unfortunately, they are never enough to regenerate human hearts. When external reforms and limits are not accompanied by an inner work of God in the hearts of people, they don't last. Consider Josiah's legacy:

Josiah removed all the abominations from all the lands belonging to the sons of Israel, and *made* all who were present in Israel to serve the LORD their God. *Throughout his lifetime* they did not turn from following the LORD God of their fathers. (verse 33)

As soon as Josiah died, the people of Israel and Judah immediately turned from the Lord. Why? In spite of all the good he did, King Josiah left something undone: He neglected to raise his own children to be godly and wise, with obedience flowing from hearts of love for God. That which he left undone proved to be the undoing of all the good he had done. The evil that was dormant in their unregenerate hearts broke out in rampant rebellion as soon as the external limits were lifted. Over the course of this generation's story, as I'll present it to you in this book, you will see how this seemingly small lapse (small in comparison with the larger societal issues that took precedence) led to the destruction of Josiah's sons, grandchildren, and the kingdom he had hoped his reforms would save.

Before my husband and I had our own children, I had the privilege to serve for ten years as a youth pastor to the children of many other parents. I learned much during that time that I promised myself not to forget when I became a parent. I observed some parents who put tremendous stock in external reforms of their children's environment. They set strict limitations on what their children heard, watched, listened to, and read as well as on how they behaved and with whom they socialized. These children knew how to *perform* up to the Christian standard that had been offered them through "Christian role models" in music, videos, and reading material. They made friends within the limited Christian circles where they were allowed to move: only Christian schools, only church youth-group functions, only approved entertainment options.

I was disturbed to see that many of these kids whom I cared for and had taught God's Word—kids whose parents were vigilant in imposing external limits, who stood with the rest of the youth group to make a vow of purity until marriage when that was called for—threw off the external reforms imposed by their parents as soon as they were out of Mom and Dad's direct control. The plaid skirts and navy trousers of the Christian school uniform came off as readily as gothic black in situations of sexual temptation. Many of these kids took up the ways of the world, including sexual immorality, drinking, drug use, materialism, and foul language as soon as they were out of their parents' house—or even in their parents' house while their parents were out.

Some dipped into worldliness with far more energy and intensity than their peers who had not had such restrictions in their formative years. Some tried to keep their ungodly practices hidden from their parents, whom they still wanted to please; others made no attempt to hide their behavior and seemed to comfortably reconcile unholy living with a profession of faith in Jesus Christ.

I agreed at the time that the external reforms and limits set by these kids' parents were basically good. But I also realized that limits were obviously not *enough* to accomplish what any sincere Christian parent hopes to see happen in the lives of their children.

When I made the switch from youth ministry to parenting, my husband and I began to seek God about what was missing that could make a difference. We prayed that God would help us raise our children to be godly and wise, and that their righteous behavior would flow from their *own* heart of love for God. We haven't neglected to set and enforce wise limits, but we understand that boundaries merely give us the protected time and opportunity to nurture our children's hearts for God. We have launched our oldest child into the world, and she seems to be following the Lord as we have prayed she would. We have two others who are eleven and thirteen, so we're certainly not gloating here; we—probably like most parents—are alert to the dangers and risks all kids face without presuming our kids will skate through surely and easily.

In spite of the challenges our children may face, we are peaceful and hopeful for their future. We have entrusted them to a faithful and all-powerful God even while we do all we can to align our parenting with his directions for raising kids who will be protected from curses and who will live to follow him and be blessed. We have developed much of this strategy and confidence from the important lessons we have learned from the lives of Daniel and his godly friends, who were of the same generation as Josiah's sons.

A stark contrast exists between the majority of children who fell to evil and those few who stood for God during the reign of King Josiah. All the youth of that generation grew up in a common environment. They all lived with wars, threats of war, political upheaval, uncertainty, religious apostasy, blatant idolatry, corruption in government, tolerance of infanticide, and a major shift in the balance of world powers. When looking specifically at Josiah's sons compared to Daniel and Friends, I discovered they were all of the same social class, all members of the royal family of Judah. They faced the same cultural influences, the same national enemies, the same moral restrictions imposed by Josiah's righteous reforms. They faced the same kinds of temptations. They heard the same prophets and priests, celebrated the same national holidays and religious rituals, and probably worshiped side by side in God's temple in Jerusalem. But their lives took dramatically different paths, leading to outcomes that were as different as curses are from blessings.

In this story, the stakes included spiritual and moral preservation but were ultimately higher than that. Most of that generation fell away from God or never knew him. The fates of those who fell were marked by family disintegration, famine, starvation, the ravages of disease, and destruction at the hands of merciless enemies. They met their ends in a variety of terrible ways that had been prophesied in regard to those who forgot God's Word and rejected his ways and his plan of redemption. Most of that generation died without ever experiencing the blessings God wanted his people to enjoy.

Out of that generation of youth, only a remnant even survived. Of those, God chose to introduce us in great detail to *the few* who were the cream of the crop. Those few grew up to be godly and wise, protected, blessed, honored, successful, beacons of God's truth and power shining brilliantly in a dark, pagan, and depraved world. Their story can serve as an example for us. Given all the examples God provides in his Word, we would be much better off to learn from and follow those examples.

The four young men God highlights for us grew up to be heroes of the Bible. They were brave and true when most of their generation were desperately afraid. They remained holy when their contemporaries gave in to temptation, were defiled, and ultimately were destroyed. Instead of falling under the judgment of God, these few escaped and were blessed by God. At the same time the Babylonians were slaughtering their peers, Daniel and Friends were given every advantage in the courts of the king of Babylon. They were provided the best education in the world at the time. They were promoted to excellent jobs. They became culturally literate, influential, rose to positions of power, and acquired the wealth that came with those positions. They remained devoted to God and were not defiled by the corruption all around them. Because of their unyielding devotion to God and their faithful service in the community in which they lived and worked, they shone as bright lights in a dark world, bringing the light of God into their pagan culture and offering a powerful witness of the one true God. They encouraged other believers and converted unbelievers. Among the first to be taken captive to Babylon, they went *into the world,* and the Lord their God went with them to accomplish his purposes. It is from their lives and example I draw the title *Walking Tall in Babylon.*

Which group would we want our children to be part of if we could influence the outcome? Of course we would want them to be in the camp of Daniel and Friends. Let's look briefly at a summary of what we can see in their lives that distinguished them from the sons of King Josiah and their peers.

DANIEL AND FRIENDS' SEVEN CHARACTERISTICS OF WALKING TALL IN BABYLON

1. They knew God's Law and accepted God's commands as *the* absolute moral standard and personally as *their* absolute moral standard. They listened carefully to God's Word with a heart *to obey* it, so they *desired* to walk in his ways.
2. While well educated in general and always at the top of their class, they were also fully educated to live productively in the pagan world. However, they were personally determined not to become participants with their pagan neighbors in their sinful practices. Their personal relationships with God and their knowledge of his Word, his ways, his requirements, and the consequences of disobedience were strong enough to withstand the temptations of a pagan culture.
3. They developed relationships with "faith-full" friends who also accepted the Law of God as their absolute moral standard. They

sought God together in times of need, helped one another, and encouraged one another to stand firm in their determination to obey God, no matter what.

4. Their devotion to prayer was part of their daily lives. They lived dependent on God, with a right attitude that allowed two-way communication with him. When they prayed, they expected God to answer their prayers. When they called for help, they expected God to rescue them.

5. They sought and experienced God's supernatural power in their lives. They grew in their knowledge and awareness of the spiritual battle between the Lord and the spiritual forces of evil that were behind the false gods. They engaged in spiritual battles through their defiance of evil in the natural realm, through their prayers, and through the use of supernatural gifts God gave them to use for his glory.

6. They lived attuned to the unfolding fulfillment of prophecies in their lifetime. They regularly studied God's Word and the writings of the true prophets of God, believed them to be true, looked forward to prophecies being fulfilled, prayed, and acted accordingly. They knew God's Word well enough to recognize and dismiss false prophets and false diviners.

7. Their lives showed that they loved the Lord their God with all their hearts, and all their souls, and all their strength. Their courage demonstrated they would rather die than defile themselves or dishonor the Lord by bowing to an idol or by ceasing to bow daily in devotion to God, whom they firmly believed to be the *only* true God. They also showed their love for God by loving and serving their pagan neighbors, and by being a blessing in their workplaces and communities, while revealing the power and glory of God to those who had never known him.

Who among us wouldn't want our children to grow up to have those seven characteristics? Who wouldn't want our children to live lives that bring them all the benefits and blessings Daniel and his friends enjoyed? No one. Certainly, Daniel and Company offer excellent role models for anyone to follow; this is not a new idea. But *how* did Daniel and his friends become such heroes? Just by following good role models? By reading and hearing stories about heroes who did things God's way? Or did something else influence them? Knowing *how* they grew into godly and wise people who walked tall when others fell is key to helping our children follow their path. If we can identify the biblical principles employed by the parents of Daniel and Friends that influenced them to be among the few who rose above the dangers of their day, perhaps therein we will find ways to powerfully influence our children to remain rooted in God even after they leave our homes.

There has been a strong trend among my peer group of Christian parents and experts that seems (to me) to overemphasize external controls as the best way to influence our children to embrace lifelong godliness. I do not believe we should abdicate our responsibility to impose godly limits. I support righteous cultural reforms. Such external reforms and limits are necessary. Indeed, it is our parental responsibility to shield our kids from exposure to immoral displays, to forbid sinful behavior, to consistently discipline willful disobedience, and to restrict potentially harmful influences that bombard them. If we parents don't set such protective limits for our own children and support public policy that extends that protection to the larger community, certainly no one else will care enough to do it for them. So setting protective limits—as God leads—along biblical, righteous moral guidelines is right, needed, and good.

If that is all we do, however, we may be making the same kind of mistake good King Josiah made with his children. We certainly don't want the same kind of outcome we will see in their lives as our story unfolds. Therefore, the question of *how* Daniel's parents positively influenced their son to become godly and wise, to stand tall when his generation fell, is vital. A wrong assumption on this point could cause us to expend enormous energy to no good purpose in the ultimate outcome of their lives.

Dr. James Dobson made a good point when he noted in his May 2002 letter (see chapter 1) that, "There are many people in the activist community who hate the Judeo-Christian system of values, and recognize that if they can gain control of children, they can change the entire culture in one generation. That's why there is a tsunami of propaganda flooding over our culture." I agree that the key to changing the entire culture in one generation is to reach the children. The question we must answer properly is, How does one "gain control" of children for God's purposes? I'm not talking about other people's children, but our own.

Do we really change the hearts of children by changing their environment? Do we make our children godly and wise by making the environment around them more godly? Or might we make the environment more godly by first influencing a change of heart within each of our children? A popular idea going around these days is that if we reform the culture, we will create an environment where people will not only become safer but also more righteous. This would be fine if all we were concerned about is cosmetic change. Josiah commanded his people to serve the Lord, and they did so, as long as he forced them to. The outside of their cup was sparkling, but inside it was full of corruption.

Think about it!

So, how much does external reform have to do with reaching our children's hearts? Will environment make a difference in whether our children obey God? Let's briefly review a couple of Bible stories. Adam and Eve had the perfect environment (and the perfect parent for that matter), but that didn't keep them from falling into temptation and sin. Cain and Abel were raised in the same nearly perfect environment with the same parents, but one turned to evil and murdered his brother, who worshiped God. The difference between them lay in their hearts. When God tried to turn Cain away from evil and the curse it would bring on him, God reasoned with him and sought to deal with the sin that was crouching at the door of his heart.

Scripture does not teach that we become righteous and withstand the corruption of culture by making the culture less corrupt. Righteous behavior is evidence that we're reaching our ultimate goal, but getting our kids to *perform* well is not the point. God opted to aim for Cain's heart; that would seem to be our best primary aim as well.

So, in general, as a matter of principle, we should make it a priority to get insight into our children's hearts. We need to make sufficient time in our daily lives for the relationship building that will enable us to become familiar with what's going on in the innermost parts of each of them. While we do that, we can prayerfully determine how to enforce or adjust boundaries.

Of course, God gives free will to everyone—even the kids we love and want to *make* serve the Lord. We cannot *make* our children turn out like Daniel and Friends. Even God opted not to *make* Cain be good. We parents can only do our best. We are called to reach our children's hearts with the gospel of Christ and the Word of God so that they "may become blameless and pure, children of God without fault in a crooked and depraved generation." In such a generation they can shine like stars in the universe as they hold out the word of life—in order that we may boast on the day of Christ that we did not run or labor for nothing (see Philippians 2:15-16). We labor to reach the heart with the saving gospel of Jesus Christ and to teach God's Word to each individual to make disciples. Only God can transform their hearts and minds by the power of his Spirit. Then they can go out into the culture to change the world, regardless of how dark that world may be.

Given this clarity of our aim, dare we believe that we can be a significant influence in the lives of our children? Yes! In fact, the more I looked into *how* Daniel and Friends became the heroes they were, the more convinced I became that their parents were their primary influencers. Studying the lives of their parents (although they are never mentioned by name) and the times in which they lived, we can discover ways to effect whether our children fall or rise up to walk tall in Babylon.

STRATEGIC SOURCES OF INFLUENCE

The cover story of *Christianity Today's* August 5, 2002, issue reported that George Barna, evangelicalism's most quoted pollster, is in search of what he calls the SSI, or Strategic Sources of Influence, needed to bring about critical righteous reforms in our country and culture. He has spent the past ten years compiling research data on the state of Christianity and the church in America. He has traversed the land, trying to get the church to wake up to where they are falling short and to change. The article states, "God had called Barna 'to serve as a catalyst for moral and spiritual revolution in America.' He had hoped to push church leaders to revitalize the church, to make it as beautiful and powerful as God meant it to be."[1] He concluded recently that his ten-year campaign had failed. The *Christianity Today* story says Barna has given up on expecting the church to bring about dramatic change in the culture. He is reported to be "more fed up with the church than ever." This being so, the article asks, "What's next?" The answer: "Having concluded that today's church can't make a difference, his next question is, *What can?* He's doing research to identify the top influences on Americans' lives. He already knows the church isn't on the list. Movies, television, contemporary music, the Internet, books, parents, and politicians are. In the short term, he's looking for ways to affect what he calls the SSI, or Strategic Sources of Influence."[2]

When I read those words, I saw it immediately. You and I—parents of today's children—are strategic sources of influence, not only *in* our children's lives, but *on* our world, through the influence our children can grow up to have on it. If we are willing to receive God's message and follow his light for our path, we can help them live to love and follow the One who said, "Be of good cheer, I have overcome the world" (John 16:33, NKJV). In so doing, we help them overcome the corruption of the culture.

How does the Bible say people can "escape the corruption that is in the world"? Peter addressed this:

Grace and peace be yours in abundance *through the knowledge of God and of Jesus our Lord.* His divine power has given us everything we need for life and godliness *through our knowledge of him who* called us by his own glory and goodness. Through these he has given us *his very great and precious promises, so that through them* you may *participate in the*

divine nature and escape the corruption in the world caused by evil
desires. (2 Peter 1:2-4)

We want our children to escape the corruption of the world. This passage
doesn't tell us to read them stories of "good role models," as if seeing good role
models has any power to help them become good. Human effort cannot gen-
erate that power; it comes only from God's divine nature working in us. What
do we need for life and godliness? *Knowledge of God and learning to appropriate his very great and precious promises.* That is the primary and foundational
process for raising kids to escape the corruption in the world caused by evil
desires—which we and our children all have.

We do well to hold up good role models in life and literature. But if we
do not also help our children learn to appropriate the power of God in everyday life, we will set them up for discouragement and frustration. This power
comes from the person of the Holy Spirit working in us and them, through
our knowledge of God, and through appropriating God's great and precious
promises. If you, like me, realize that you have not focused on this to the
extent your children need, the rest of the book will help you do that. Also note
that the passage above begins with God's grace. Let us, too, rest in God's
grace—unearned favor—as we proceed seeking more knowledge of God and
his precious promises through which we can help our kids live a blessed life.

Only after the foundation described in verses 2-4 above is laid can we
begin the process of working out our character and behaviors.

For this very reason, make every effort to add to your faith goodness;
and to goodness, knowledge; and to knowledge, self-control; and to self-
control, perseverance; and to perseverance, godliness; and to godliness,
brotherly kindness; and to brotherly kindness, love. (2 Peter 1:5-7)

When we begin with the right foundation, and *then* use external limits
wisely, we can raise our children to be godly and wise as they build their
lives.

NO MATTER WHAT OTHERS DO OR WHAT THE WORLD MAY THROW AT US

God offered the parents of Daniel and his godly friends a way to appropriate God's blessings for themselves and their children, regardless of what others chose to do. During their lifetimes, God used King Josiah—as he uses righteous reformers today—to try to save their entire nation. God gave the parents of that generation (and gives us) a way to protect and bless their kids even when the moral reforms didn't hold. Their success was not dependent on enforcing external boundaries. It was not dependent on whether the walls built to protect them held up under siege. It wasn't dependent on their ability to completely shelter their children from the world. It was not dependent on the world's getting considerably better before their children grew up.

The same encouraging principles apply to us today. God's plan for us to raise our children to be like Daniel and Friends is not dependent upon holiness in the church, business, politics, the schools, our nation, or the streets. Rather, if we are willing to follow the godly example of those long-ago parents, and heed the message they heeded, we will discover how to respond to God and his Word, unhindered by the secular environment in which we live. God allows all parents to make choices that will directly influence their children's safety, future blessing, and their potential to be powerful agents for good in the world and to advance the kingdom of God. The rest of the book will explore how those parents in Daniel's time put these principles to work in their lives, and how we can do the same in ours.

THREE

DUSTING OFF
THE WORD OF GOD

Even though the Book of God's Law had been missing for over a generation before Josiah took the throne, no one seemed to mind. People relied on priests, interpretive teachers, and prophets to explain what God had said. These religious leaders taught selectively and interpreted what they knew of God's Word liberally, turning a blind eye to sins that had become socially acceptable among them—but who knew? The people were comforted by flattering prophets who proclaimed pleasant messages and assured them of God's protection; after all, they had the temple of the Lord and the sacrifices that took place there to counteract any pangs of conscience. By the time Josiah became king, neither priest, nor prophet, nor the people had examined their lives in the undiminished light of God's written Word for many, many years. They had drifted so far from God's holy standards as to set up idol worship, nature worship, male and female prostitutes, along with all manner of social injustice and corrupt dealings right in God's temple. Who would dare challenge the priests and prophets? They held power. They were the ones dispensing God's teachings to the people.

REDISCOVERING THE BOOK OF GOD'S LAW

In the eighteenth year of King Josiah's reign, when he was about twenty-six, he set about to repair and refurbish the temple, which had become run-down and damaged by neglect. Josiah raised money to renovate the house of the

Lord. People throughout Judah, and the remnant of Israel, gladly contributed. The public funds were delivered into the hands of faithful workers and builders who stood ready to begin the work.

"When they were bringing out the money which had been brought into the house of the LORD, Hilkiah the priest found the book of the law of the LORD given by Moses" (2 Chronicles 34:14, NASB). Scholars believe this book included all of Deuteronomy and perhaps additional selections from the five books of Moses, which make up the first five books of our Old Testament.

So, Shaphan, the king's scribe, brought the book to the immediate attention of the king. When the scribe read the book aloud to Josiah, it precipitated a crisis. Imagine Josiah's position: He was trying to do right in God's eyes as best he knew how. He was trying to undo generations of moral decay, corruption, and idolatry, but he had never been exactly sure what God had to say because the actual written Book of God's Law had been misplaced. Josiah must have felt conflicting emotions, a mix of hope and anxiety, as he awaited clear and definitive instruction from God's written Word.

King Josiah knew enough of what had been passed on through oral traditions to know things had not been right in his kingdom. That's why he had dedicated a good portion of his reign to eradicating that which he knew was immoral. What he had sensed was made starkly clear as he listened attentively to his scribe read the still-dusty scroll. These words had been spoken by Moses before God's people crossed the Jordan River to enter the Promised Land! The clarity of God's commands, and the realization of how far the nation of Judah had fallen short, must have been staggering for Josiah.

A PIVOTAL EVENT FOR JOSIAH'S GENERATION

Certain singular events change the course of history for individuals, families, and nations. Often those pivotal moments aren't recognized at the time; only in retrospect can we identify the event that would alter the entire course of the future. Hilkiah's rediscovering the Book of God's Law was a pivotal event for the nation. As word spread like wildfire that God's Law had been rediscovered, few realized the monumental impact that dusting off the Word of God would have on their lives. It would change the course of history for the nation of Judah; it would do the same for a particular couple who lovingly smiled over their new baby boy. Their lives and their baby's future would hinge on that amazing discovery and how they chose to respond to God's Word.

Repeatedly, God connected knowledge of and obedience to his written Word with the path of life and the well-being of the nation's children.

Oh, that their hearts would be inclined to fear me and keep all my commands always, *so that it might go well with them and their children forever!* (Deuteronomy 5:29)

These are the commands, decrees and laws the LORD your God directed me to teach you to observe in the land that you are crossing the Jordan to possess, *so that you, your children and their children after them may fear the LORD your God as long as you live by keeping all his decrees and commands that I give you, and so that you may enjoy long life.* Hear, O Israel, and be careful to obey so *that it may go well with you* and that you may increase greatly in a land flowing with milk and honey, just as the LORD, the God of your fathers, promised you. (Deuteronomy 6:1-3)

The Book of the Law documented critical points in the nation's history, which Josiah's generation had clearly forgotten. God's Word was specific about the judgments that would befall them and their children if they drifted away from his written Word and the godly life he wanted them to lead. The ancient ominous text read like a newspaper—if there had been such a thing at the time—clearly describing what was going on in their corrupt culture and apostate religious establishment. What Josiah heard covered the breadth of Israel's spiritual and national history. In the light of God's Word, it appeared clear even to the untrained observer that they teetered on the brink of a prophetic precipice, and the lives of their children and grandchildren were in immediate danger. No wonder King Josiah tore his robes and wept before the Lord (see 2 Kings 22:19).

So the king immediately sent a delegation to inquire of the Lord through the prophetess Huldah, who lived there in Jerusalem, saying, "Go, inquire of the LORD for me and the people and all Judah concerning the words of this book that has been found, for great is the wrath of the LORD that burns against us, because our fathers have not listened to the words of this book, to do according to all that is written concerning us" (2 Kings 22:13, NASB). The prophetess confirmed what common sense and God's written Word had already plainly told the king: They were in big trouble.

When King Josiah's delegation went to speak to the prophetess, she told them,

> This is what the LORD, the God of Israel, says: Tell the man who sent
> you to me, "This is what the LORD says: I am going to bring disaster
> on this place and its people, according to everything written in the
> book the king of Judah has read. Because they have forsaken me and
> burned incense to other gods and provoked me to anger by all the idols
> their hands have made, my anger will burn against this place and will
> not be quenched." Tell the king of Judah, who sent you to inquire of
> the LORD, "This is what the LORD, the God of Israel, says concerning
> the words you heard: Because your heart was responsive and you
> humbled yourself before the LORD when you heard what I have spo-
> ken against this place and its people, that they would become accursed
> and laid waste, and because you tore your robes and wept in my pres-
> ence, I have heard you, declares the LORD. Therefore I will gather you
> to your fathers, and you will be buried in peace. Your eyes will not see
> all the disaster I am going to bring on this place." So they took her
> answer back to the king. (2 Kings 22:15-20)

When Huldah's prophecy was delivered, the royal family and people of Judah had varying reactions. Some brushed it off, as they were used to doing with any prophecy that condemned their way of life. Some mocked Huldah, dismissing her as being out of step with the prophets they preferred, who spoke favorably of Judah. Some, like the couple we shall come to know better, simply held their children close and prayed God would show them a way to spare their children from the judgment at hand. That way was laid out clearly in the written document God had given them.

Knowing what God had written and responding to it lay at the root of the way Daniel and his friends were raised and the good fruit their lives eventually bore. If we hope to grow the same kind of good fruit in the lives of our children, we must also nurture the good roots from which such fruit can grow. Daniel's blessings in adolescence and adulthood are rooted in his parents' response to the rediscovery of God's written Word. I aim to convince you that dusting off the Word of God is essential for our well-being and that of our children also.

FOR THE SAKE OF OUR CHILDREN: A PIVOTAL CHOICE TODAY

The scroll the scribe read to King Josiah contained a specific message of judgment. Anyone who read it could see God had given explicit instructions on what they needed to do for their children and grandchildren to be blessed. It also foretold, in stark detail, the path the nation would take that would lead to judgment—and specifically how that would impact their children. The priest who found the Book of the Law was not judging them, nor was the scribe who dusted it off and carried it to the king, nor was the king. The written words themselves stood as judge over them.

Likewise, Jesus made it clear that the written Word of God, including the words he spoke from God, will be that by which every one of us will be judged. Jesus said,

> As for the person who hears my words but does not keep them, I do
> not judge him. For I did not come to judge the world, but to save it.
> There is a judge for the one who rejects me and does not accept my

words; that very word which I spoke will condemn him at the last day. For I did not speak of my own accord, but the Father who sent me commanded me what to say and how to say it. I know that his command leads to eternal life. So whatever I say is just what the Father has told me to say. (John 12:47-50)

Jesus' goal was to lead us to eternal life and protect us from judgment. God's written Word clearly shows us the way. The one who dares to dust off God's Word and read it will clearly see in advance what brings judgment, how to be protected from that judgment, and how to receive eternal life.

The Book of the Law made this point for Josiah's generation:

He humbled you, causing you to hunger and then feeding you with manna, which neither you nor your fathers had known, to teach you that man does not live on bread alone but on every word that comes from the mouth of the LORD. (Deuteronomy 8:3)

Jesus reiterated it for ours:

Jesus answered, "It is written: 'Man does not live on bread alone, but on every word that comes from the mouth of God.'" (Matthew 4:4)

WE HAVE A DISTINCT ADVANTAGE AND RESPONSIBILITY

Our generation has access to God's Word as no other generation in history. Consider this statement from George Barna:

The Christian faith is not based on oral tradition alone. The core doctrine of the faith is drawn from its foundational document, the Bible. We know that the Bible remains the best-selling book of all-time, and continues to sell millions of copies in the U.S. every year. There are more than 1500 different versions, translations and editions of the

Bible available for purchase in the U.S. More than nine out of ten Americans own at least one copy of the Bible. About six out of ten adults read from the Bible sometime during the course of the year.[1]

We have been given much more access to God's Word; therefore, we have a greater responsibility to read it. Saying "But I didn't know" will not get us off the hook, especially when God's Word is so readily available to us.

WHAT'S IN THIS FOR US AND OUR CHILDREN?

There are considerable benefits promised in the Bible to those who will hear the Word of God and let it change their lives from the inside out. Consider these benefits found in Psalm 19:7-11:

> The law of the LORD is perfect,
> > *reviving the soul.*
> The statutes of the LORD are trustworthy,
> > *making wise the simple.*
> The precepts of the LORD are right,
> > *giving joy to the heart.*
> The commands of the LORD are radiant,
> > *giving light to the eyes.*
> The fear of the LORD is pure,
> > enduring forever.
> *The ordinances of the LORD are sure*
> > and altogether righteous.
> They are *more precious than gold,*
> > than much pure gold;
> they are *sweeter than honey,*
> > than honey from the comb.
> *By them is your servant warned;*
> > *in keeping them there is great reward.*

There is also evidence that kids who know and believe the Word of God are protected from the negative effect of lacking a biblical belief system. Consider these statistics reported by Josh McDowell on his Web site BeyondBelief.com:

> Research consistently shows that what a person believes translates into behavior. Perhaps nowhere has that been more dramatically shown than in our survey of over 3,700 kids (all of whom were involved in an evangelical church). That study reveals that, compared to kids who possess a solid, biblical belief system, young people who lack such basic biblical beliefs are:
>> 225% more likely to be angry with life
>> 216% more likely to be resentful
>> 210% more likely to lack purpose in life
>> 200% more likely to be disappointed in life
>> 200% more likely to steal
>> 200% more likely to physically hurt someone
>> 300% more likely to use illegal drugs
>> 600% more likely to attempt suicide[2]

"JUST DO IT!" WON'T DO IT

Last week I flew to Sioux City, Iowa, from my home in California to speak at a women's conference. They requested that I speak on this topic, which is fresh on my heart. As the plane approached Omaha, Nebraska, the captain announced that the temperature would be zero degrees. That's thirty-two degrees below freezing to anyone born and raised in California. I caught myself wondering why I was going to Iowa in mid-January. And what did I know about Iowa anyway? All that came to mind was that Iowa was where the first presidential primaries take place, the first place political messages are tested in order to get a read on the heart of the nation. A thought came to me that perhaps the Lord was allowing me to deliver this message first in the heartland of America because it's a message we need to take to heart.

The only other things that came to mind when I thought about Iowa were cold winters and endless fields of corn. In my first job out of college as an employment counselor, I interviewed a young woman from Iowa whose summer job had been to ride a tractor into a corn field and taste ears of corn to see if they were sweet enough for the Jolly Green Giant. This train of thought reminded me of an old slogan for Kellogg's Corn Flakes: "Taste 'em again for the first time." That ad campaign actually prompted me to buy Kellogg's Corn Flakes on my next shopping trip.

Rarely does a slogan have such a desirable effect. If it were that easy, all I'd have to say in this chapter would be, "God's Word: Read It Again for the First Time" or "Just Do It!" and you'd rush to dust off your Bible and start reading it to your children regularly. But a slogan isn't enough to get us going; even warnings of judgment and promises of blessing weren't enough to get Josiah's generation going. Why? There are good reasons.

Picture the rubble in the temple at Jerusalem during King Josiah's reign. He had to bring in carpenters, builders, masons, and stonecutters to overcome generations' worth of neglect. The renovations required heavy lifting and the tedious work of picking through the rubble, not knowing what one might find.

I'm reminded of the feeling I have about venturing into Taylor's bedroom after it's become unlivable through accumulated clutter, numerous unfinished projects, and several end-of-semester backpack-emptying sessions. It's like an archeological dig where God only knows what I might unearth, and I'm not eager to make the discoveries. Besides, just letting it get to that condition doesn't reflect well on anyone, so we've been known to close the door for a time and pretend that room doesn't exist.

In the temple, once the renovations began and someone unearthed the Book of God's Law, everyone had good reasons to prefer the status quo:

- *For King Josiah:* God's Word precipitated a personal and national crisis.
- *For the priests, teachers of God's Law, and religious leaders:* God's Word embarrassed them. It pointed out their failure to do their

jobs—that is, not to let the people forget God's Word—on a grand scale. God's Word indicted them before their flock.

- *For the people:* God's Word warned of danger, pointing out their personal and national sins. It delivered much bad news, even though it also pointed to a way of escape.

These reasons may not be too different from our own when it comes to dusting off the Word of God in our own lives. If we want to get beyond the disheartening rubble, however, and clear a way of escape for our children by actively informing them how to live according to God's Word, we'll need to overcome a few obstacles.

WHY NOT DUST OFF THE WORD? FOUR TYPICAL REPLIES

1. "Yeah, I Already Know It. I've Heard It All My Life."

The hearts of Josiah's people may have been inclined toward God, their attendance at temple regular, even their willingness to obey sincere. Nonetheless, since they'd already heard it and were living by what they already believed, they didn't want to be told anything that would force them to rethink all their beliefs and would demand a radical change.

Danger for the people of Judah: What they "knew" with self-assurance was inaccurate or incomplete. Believing they knew the Word caused them to be complacent at the very time they needed to take action. Even the danger of judgment failed to move them when they had a chance to choose their destiny.

Parallel for us: When I was in Iowa, the hostess of the event dropped me off at the hotel and told me when she would be picking me up in the morning. I heard her say 8:45; I felt no need to have her write it down or tell me again. I scheduled my wake-up call and planned my morning routine accordingly. She had actually told me to be ready by 7:45, but I hadn't heard it or registered it correctly. I was complacently going about my normal routine, happily "on schedule" when the knock came at the door at 7:45. Even though I was intending to comply, I couldn't.

If we assume we already know the Bible, but we really only know it partially or with some degree of inaccuracy, we could be going about our lives blithely thinking we are complying with God's Word when in reality we are not. When the time comes, what we *thought* we heard from God's Word will not matter; only what the Bible actually declares will hold any weight. We would do well to double-check what we've heard or thought we've heard with what is actually written.

Overcoming the obstacles: What gets in the way of our *really* knowing God's Word? Pride, being oblivious to our need for action, and misplaced self-confidence top the list. We can, however, remove this rubble and overcome these obstacles by choosing to double-check everything we hear—and periodically, what we have come to believe—against God's written Word on the subject, even if we don't think it's necessary. What would it hurt? The apostle Luke commended the people of Berea for taking this approach:

> Now the Bereans were of more noble character than the Thessalonians,
> for they received the message with great eagerness and examined the
> Scriptures every day to see if what Paul said was true. (Acts 17:11)

2. "It's Not Relevant to Me Today. It's Ancient History."

The people of Judah could have reasonably thought that the message of Deuteronomy wasn't for them. For some, it was merely a written record of the message Moses gave to their ancestors centuries before. Anyone who took that attitude wouldn't have believed the message applied to them personally.

Danger for the people of Judah: What if it were not merely ancient history, but a current warning for their times—which it was—that they were missing? Their belief that it was not relevant did not change the truth; it merely caused them to be inattentive. They missed their opportunity to repent while they still had time to save their kids' lives.

Parallel for us: People who read the Bible as only a record of ancient history would commend themselves for gaining knowledge. What they don't see is that God wants the knowledge to prompt action, even today. Some prophecies in the Bible have yet to be fulfilled; what if we respond to them the same way Josiah's generation responded to the prophecies of Jeremiah? What if Peter's admonition to pay closer attention to the Old Testament prophets as the day of Christ's return nears (see 2 Peter 1:19-21) means that the prophecies are still relevant and warrant our direct response? If we fail to see the relevance, could we leave our children unprotected? I think so.

If we heard someone reading numbers at random from a phone directory, we would probably hear the information but not do anything with it. How would we listen to those same numbers differently if they were the serial numbers of a recalled, dangerous baby carseat like we had just purchased? Our sense that the information was directly relevant to the well-being of our child would cause us to listen attentively, determined to get every number right and to take immediate action.

Overcoming the obstacles: In order to overcome the disinterest that results from an inability to see how the various parts of the Bible apply to us today and personally, it's important to ask questions and apply the principles. We must *test* the relevance before we dismiss it! It is crucial that we read God's Word again with an eye to see how we might be making the same mistakes as previous generations, then seek God's guidance to help us avoid repeating their mistakes.

3. "I Can't Understand It. I'm Too Far Behind to Start Learning It Now."

Scripture makes it clear that Josiah's people gave up trying to live righteously. Even after hearing the Word of God, they continued in their sin until it was too late. Rather than rely on the Book of the Law, they depended on teachers, religious leaders, and prophets who had their own agendas.

Danger for the people of Judah: These religious leaders led the people astray and left them in grave danger. Even though the people did not know God's Word, God made it available to them: Josiah read it aloud, and God held them responsible to seek to understand and to teach it to their own children. When they didn't dedicate themselves to learn and apply themselves to understand God's Word, they could not be protected by it. They and their children were eventually destroyed, although God made repeated efforts to get his Word to them. God sent his Word verbally *and* in writing, but they did not pay attention (see Jeremiah 25:4). It would not have been too late for them to change if only they had listened while God still offered the opportunity.

Parallel for us: Today's generation of American parents grew up in an era when most people were biblically illiterate. Even though there are a proliferation of Bibles, our culture has deemed the Bible irrelevant. Even the spell-check feature on most computers doesn't recognize the names of the books of the Bible. Some of the following insights about our biblically illiterate culture may make you laugh and grimace at the same time. These come from the book *Soul Tsunami* by Dr. Leonard Sweet, who writes of our generation,

> The Bible isn't closed—it's unknown. Biblical illiteracy is such that 12% of the American people think Joan of Arc was married to Noah. Eight out of 10 US adults claim to be "Christian," but they are hazy and lazy about their faith. Four out of 10 Christians are unable to name the four gospels.[3] Only half of those who claim to be "born again" read the Scripture during the week.
>
> Jay Leno periodically does "man-on-the-street" interviews. One night he asked questions about the Bible. "Can you name one of the Ten Commandments?" he asked two college-age women. One replied, "Freedom of speech?" Leno then asked the other student: "Complete this sentence: Let he who is without sin…" "Have a good time" was her response. Leno then turned to a young man and asked, "Who, according to the Bible, was eaten by a whale?" The confident answer was, "Pinocchio."[4]

Overcoming the obstacles: Those who have never learned the Bible may need to overcome the shame and embarrassment of not knowing where or how to start, or having to depend on teachers because they don't know how to check out for themselves what others say. We need to take an active role in testing popular messages, but that may require us to improve our ability to think critically. If this requires practice on your part, you're not alone. Many people in our generation know little or nothing of the Bible. Be encouraged: Daniel's parents' generation started from nothing and were able to learn enough to put God's Word into practice in raising their son. Besides, we have access to our own copy of God's Word. Determine to dust off the Word of God—literally, if you have to. No matter how old you are or how much you have to learn, God will reveal his truth to you if you begin to read and study his Word in earnestness.

4. "I Don't Like What I Do Understand of It. God's Law Is Impossible to Obey, So Why Torment Us with Threats of Judgment When We Are Hopeless to Measure Up?"

Some people will say, "I don't read the Bible because I just don't understand it." I've heard popular speaker Zig Ziglar point out in one of his talks that it's unlikely people are bothered by the parts of the Bible they don't understand. Most of us are bothered by the parts we do understand.

Danger for the people of Judah: Many people in Josiah's generation could see that God's Word pointed out specific and obvious sins. They stubbornly held to their sinful ways and complacency because they believed they had no hope of change and felt locked into a destiny of destruction—but that attitude was what brought their destruction. They adhered to faith in false prophets even when common sense showed them that what God had written and what Jeremiah's prophecies affirmed was coming true right before their eyes. Their obstinate refusal to let go of their sins, unfounded beliefs, and false hopes, even when these contradicted many reasonable warnings that warranted their attention, gave them temporary delusional comfort but *caused* their eventual destruction. Personally, I think this is the most dangerous attitude of all. Look at how bluntly God spoke to them through Jeremiah:

> Now therefore say to the people of Judah and those living in Jerusalem,
> "This is what the LORD says: Look! I am preparing a disaster for you
> and devising a plan against you. So turn from your evil ways, each one

of you, and reform your ways and your actions." But they will reply, "It's no use. We will continue with our own plans; each of us will follow the stubbornness of his evil heart." (Jeremiah 18:11-12)

How can we possibly understand why parents and grandparents who heard the hideous warnings of Deuteronomy 27 and 28 did nothing to change their behavior? I don't believe they didn't care about their own lives or the lives of their children and grandchildren. Rather, I think they believed a lie, which rendered them immobile in the face of danger too terrible to dare contemplate.

Remember the analogy I used in chapter 1 referring to my hope that this book be like the lighted pathway in an airplane during an emergency? I asked a flight attendant how people react during real emergencies when those lights are activated. She said, "Some get hysterical; some become alert to hear and obey the commands I give to help get everyone out. But some sit there with blank expressions as if what is happening is too terrible to take in, so they disconnect. It wouldn't matter what I said to them; I can see in their eyes that their minds aren't receiving anything. Sometimes we just have to pick those people up and move them out of the way." That's how I understand the people in this fourth group. Even though they love their kids—perhaps *because* they love their kids—they can't bear the thought of God's wrath possibly falling on them.

They may not have read much of the Bible, but what they have read or heard includes threats of eternal damnation too terrible to contemplate. God's Word includes commands they feel powerless to obey, so they disconnect. They don't read the Bible because they, too, think they know what it will say, but they aren't smugly complacent. They think it might tell them that they are sinners who are bound for hell and the only way out is to give up all their pleasures (or the addictions and sins that enslave them), which they don't think they could give up if they tried. They may even have tried to change their lives (without the power of God operating in them to do so) and failed, so they conclude it's hopeless. It's no use! In order to block out the clear signs that there is a real emergency, they do whatever they can to keep themselves distracted; they deaden their perceptions of reality (overwork, drugs, alcohol, sex, sports, philanthropy—any obsession does the job). It makes sense that the last thing they would willingly do would be to dust off God's Word and see what it really says.

My brother-in-law, Kelly, is a good man who obviously loves his grown children and grandchildren. For thirty years I have been trying to get him to hear the gospel and receive Christ. I pray for his salvation and ask God to bring our conversations around to eternal matters. During one such opportunity, Kelly offered me his view on eternity.

Paraphrased, he stated that everybody figures we've got three options: There's heaven (where we all hope and assume we're going when we die), there's nothing (which doesn't make much sense or hold much appeal, but it's better than…the other place), then—he paused—there's hell (which is too horrible to even think about, so we don't). He said he was pretty sure there wasn't a hell, or that if there was, he and the people he loved wouldn't go there. He said to me, "It's not like I've ever sold my soul to the devil. I mean, I work hard, I love my kids and my wife and my grandkids. I do what I can to help people out. So if this God is as loving as everyone says, then I don't believe he would send people to hell."

I said, "Kelly, what if you don't have to sell your soul to the devil? What if you're already living in danger of hell—which is what the Bible says is true of everyone who has never had their sins washed away? If the devil already has the deed to every human soul because all have sinned, the surest way to damn you to hell is to keep you distracted until it's too late. The devil would not do anything overt. He'll distract you as easily with good things as with mind-numbing things until time runs out. Why would you even risk hell without being willing to at least read the Bible and see how God says you can escape it?"

That made him shake his head and lean into the conversation. My ideas clearly took him aback. He eventually replied, "Repeat that! What did you say? All he has to do is keep me distracted until time runs out? Write that down! Now that is something you should write in a book. That would make people stop to think."

I was amazed. It did make him stop to think. It made him start asking me many questions about God and the Bible. But it did not make him commit to read the gospel of John I gave him. Perhaps the fear of hell and conviction that he could never keep God's Law prompts his avoidance of what God has written. Instead, he opts to continue hoping he's going to heaven or that there is nothing after death. Somehow that judgment and eternal punishment part of the message is so terrifying as to be unthinkable. So people would rather believe a lie and console themselves with vague, unfounded hopes. The danger: Time is ticking away and God's Word is true. Such an immobilizing fear of judgment is the tool Satan uses to bring about that which is most feared.

Overcoming the obstacles: Believe the angel's message: "Do not be afraid. I bring you good news of great joy that will be for all the people" (Luke 2:10). Our antidote for immobilizing fear that keeps us from dusting off God's Word is believing that the gospel is *good news* of *great joy* for *all people.* That's what gives us courage to push past the rubble of all our fears. Even followers of God, even Christians, can overcome their hesitation to get into God's Word by realizing that God never commands us to do anything without also pointing the way and providing the supernatural power to do it. Reading the Bible regularly is how we discover the way and connect with the One who gives us the power to obey God's commands, escape God's wrath, and enjoy God's blessings.

To overcome this obstacle we follow Josiah's example: He did have to face the reality that "great is the wrath of the LORD that burns against us, because our fathers have not listened to the words of this book, to do according to all that is written concerning us" (2 Kings 22:13, NASB). We, too, need to give up (or at least doubt) our erroneous, if comforting, false beliefs and exchange them for true but tough warnings from God. We need to overcome any self-delusion that leaves us and our kids at risk. When we acknowledge the true severity of our situation, keep reading God's Word, and seek God as Josiah did, we, too, will discover under the rubble a message of true hope and salvation.

Whatever you choose to believe will require faith: It takes faith to believe everything is going to be fine when the world is obviously not fine; it takes faith to believe the Bible and obey its guidance in order to find safety in this life and for all eternity. Most betting men wouldn't bet as little as a lunch on a sporting event without at least checking out the track record of the teams. Dusting off the Word of God to read the basics of what God has written is like checking out God's—and humanity's—track record. The stakes are high; they include the future of our children and even our very souls. I hope and pray the stakes will motivate all of us to overcome whatever discomfort we have and actually *read* God's written Word. Indeed, this is what will make the difference between a life that stands tall in Babylon and one that does not (see Matthew 7:24-27).

HOW CAN WE CLEAR AWAY THE RUBBLE TOO HEAVY FOR US TO LIFT?

For me, one key understanding gets me through all the rubble and past the obstacles that might cause me to avoid the Word of God. Any one of the afore-mentioned reasons for not dusting off God's Word might discourage me if— once I read the Bible's commands—I believed I somehow had to meet its demands or even follow its wisdom in my own strength, or raise my kids well by my own wisdom. God's Word could be right in front of me, but I would grow weary of the burden of trying to sift through the rubble on my own. I would grow weary if I discovered the Book of the Law but didn't have the power to obey it. But we do! If we think we have to do what God says is right without his power to help us, we miss the point. Jesus told the religious lead-ers of his day,

> You diligently study the Scriptures because you think that by them you possess eternal life. These are the Scriptures that testify about me, yet you refuse to come to me to have life. (John 5:39-40)

Galatians 3:19-25 explains the purpose of God's Law, which was not only to show us the right way to live but also to expose our need for God's help to do it. It leads us to the only One who can empower us to live according to God's Law.

So the law was put in charge to lead us to Christ that we might be justified by faith. Now that faith has come, we are no longer under the supervision of the law. (verses 24-25)

The Bible gives good news for people in every category of hesitation! It heralds help in the words of Jeremiah that were fulfilled in Jesus:

This is what the LORD says:

"Stand at the crossroads and look;
    ask for the ancient paths,
ask where the good way is, and walk in it,
    and *you will find rest for your souls.*
    But you said, 'We will not walk in it.'"
    (Jeremiah 6:16)

God offered them rest for their souls, but most of that generation refused to receive it. Our generation needs to dust off the Word of God so we and our children can have the benefits of following the good way and escape the dangers of going our own way. That doesn't mean just going to the Bible and trying to do what it says in our own strength. We go to the Bible to find the Law. That shows us how far short we all come when our lives are compared to God's standards. We see our needs, our inability to do that which is most important, which includes raising our children the way they need to be raised. That realization and the effort of trying to live up to those standards on our own makes us weary. That's when we come to Jesus. Then he can guide us to the ancient paths, which he has walked perfectly, and take us through the rubble to the fulfillment of the blessings God wants for us and our children. Jesus said (and the written invitation is preserved in God's Word),

Come to me, all you who are weary and burdened, and I will give you rest. Take my yoke upon you and learn from me, for I am gentle and humble in heart, and you will find rest for your souls. For my yoke is easy and my burden is light. (Matthew 11:28-30)

Raising children to be godly and wise in perilous times could be a burden. We could easily grow weary, trudging along without the strength to take the steps we know we need to take. But Jesus offers us rest even while we grow in righteousness. Jesus doesn't just point out the way we need to go. Jesus offers to partner with us and bear the burden, indeed, to take the weight of it on himself. The way we receive this rest is by *coming to him* and *learning from him.*

I hope and pray that something in this chapter has persuaded you to actually dust off the written Word of God—the Bible—and read it again as if for the first time. I hope some of what I have offered in the way of benefits and blessings, warnings, and an appeal to avert dangers of every kind will persuade you. If not, please, do it anyway. Dusting off the Word of God is the pivotal event that will most influence the future for ourselves and our children.

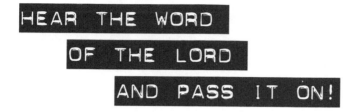

FOUR

HEAR THE WORD
OF THE LORD
AND PASS IT ON!

There was no shortage of opinions at court as to why King Josiah had torn his robes after he heard the Book of the Law read to him, although even the royal family did not know what the book said. King Josiah remedied that. He sent and gathered all the elders of Judah and Jerusalem.

> He went up to the temple of the LORD with the men of Judah, the people of Jerusalem, the priests and the Levites—all the people from the least to the greatest. He read in their hearing all the words of the Book of the Covenant, which had been found in the temple of the LORD. (2 Chronicles 34:30)

Imagine yourself there among that anxious assembly, abuzz with gossip, conjecture, and solemn concerns as they awaited King Josiah. In the coming passages, I'll ask you to imagine a young couple, taking turns holding their infant son, Daniel. His mother had to keep him close, since he was still nursing. Among the assembly were the prophet Jeremiah and Huldah the prophetess, sitting with others who loved the Lord. All the families of the royal line were there, among them Daniel's parents and parents of infants Hananiah, Azariah, and Mishael. King Josiah's sons were with their mother, Hamutal, but boys of ten and twelve aren't known to sit still and listen for long.

THE READING OF THE BOOK

King Josiah read the Book of the Law to his people. He recounted the history of the Hebrews' being led out of Egypt by Moses when God delivered them from slavery with mighty miracles. He read of their rebellion while Moses was still on the mountain receiving the Ten Commandments, of their forty years of wandering that ensued because they did not trust God's promise, and of their conquests in battle.

God repeatedly urged them to obey his Law and listen to his Word—*to perform it.* They were not to add to or take away from what God had written. Daniel's young parents must have listened attentively, recognizing how far their people had fallen short. They were told to remember the day God's people stood before the Lord at another great assembly, where the Lord said to Moses,

> Assemble the people to Me, that I may let them hear My words so they
> may learn to fear Me all the days they live on the earth, and that they
> may teach their children. (Deuteronomy 4:10, NASB)

Daniel slept in his mother's arms; her husband caught her eye. Both nodded in silent agreement before her gaze returned to baby Daniel.

King Josiah read the Ten Commandments. He recited how Moses interceded for the people when they were afraid to hear the voice of God any longer. The Lord's promise to Moses at that time lifted many hearts.

> Oh, that their hearts would be inclined to fear me and keep all my
> commands always, so that it might go well with them and their chil-
> dren forever! (Deuteronomy 5:29, NKJV)

There was hope! God declared his concern for them and for their children. The next section also addressed parents. The young couple paid close attention.

Hear, O Israel! The LORD is our God, the LORD is one! You shall
love the LORD your God with all your heart and with all your soul
and with all your might. These words, which I am commanding you
today, shall be on your heart. You shall teach them diligently to your
sons—

King Josiah's voice boomed! Daniel was startled awake. He grasped at his
mother's hair, then settled as she rocked him.

—and shall talk of them when you sit in your house and when you
walk by the way and when you lie down and when you rise up.
(Deuteronomy 6:4-7, NASB)

Soon came the warnings. King Josiah's eyes scanned the assembly.

Now, Israel, what does the LORD your God require from you—

His eyes met those of Daniel's father and mother, as if sensing their readi-
ness to do what God required.

—but to fear the LORD your God, to walk in all His ways and love
Him, and to serve the LORD your God with all your heart and with all
your soul, and to keep the LORD's commandments and His statutes
which I am commanding you today *for your good?* (Deuteronomy
10:12-13, NASB)

The book repeated God's persistent command that parents pass his Word
on to their own children. Those seeking some way to escape what Huldah
prophesied sensed urgency in the command. Granted, I am assuming this
kind of parental response based on my own love for my children, the protective instinct that went into operation when my children were babies, and
imagining what it would have been like to hear such a dire prophecy while

nursing any one of them. However, these assumptions are also based on the clear burden God placed on parents specifically to pass his Word and teachings on to their own children.

King Josiah's voice rang out:

> You shall therefore impress these words of mine on your heart and on
> your soul; and you shall bind them as a sign on your hand, and they
> shall be as frontals on your forehead. You shall teach them to your
> sons, talking of them when you sit in your house and when you walk
> along the road and when you lie down and when you rise up. You
> shall write them on the doorposts of your house and on your gates,
> so that your days and the days of your sons may be multiplied on the
> land which the LORD swore to your fathers to give them, as long as
> the heavens remain above the earth. (Deuteronomy 11:18-21, NASB)

This is a glimmer of hope. We can surmise that at least Daniel's father or mother determined to seize God's offer of blessing by determining to obey. The promise was for "as long as the heavens remain…" Even though Daniel's family faced dark times, there remained a way of blessing for those choosing to obey. Perhaps their son would have a chance.

A BLESSING OR A CURSE?

God's promise of blessings was counterbalanced with warnings. God made it plain:

> See, I am setting before you today a blessing and a curse: the blessing,
> *if you listen* to the commandments of the LORD your God, which I am
> commanding you today; and the curse, *if you do not listen* to the com-
> mandments of the LORD your God, but turn aside from the way which
> I am commanding you today, by following other gods which you have
> not known. (Deuteronomy 11:26-28, NASB)

As King Josiah finished reading, he recited the song of Moses, then a final admonition:

> Take to your heart all the words with which I am warning you today, which you shall command your sons to observe carefully, even all the words of this law.
>
> For it is not an idle word for you; indeed it is your life. And by this word you will prolong your days in the land. (Deuteronomy 32:46-47, NASB)

The young couple determined to teach their precious son for as many days as God granted them. The dire warnings were beyond terrifying, and their nation seemed to qualify for the curses (see Deuteronomy 27–28). According to Huldah's prophecy, judgment would be postponed throughout the lifetime of King Josiah. No doubt the nation had sincere wishes of long life for their king. Daniel's parents were grateful God had given them a window of opportunity—as long as King Josiah lived—in which to teach his Word to their son and command him to observe God's laws carefully. They didn't know how long they had, but they intended to make the most of their time.

BEGINNINGS OF GODLINESS

Since you're reading this book, I take it that you want your children to become godly and wise. By definition, *god*liness must be measured by God's standard. God's Word defines and helps us measure godliness. More essentially, the Bible also teaches us how to access the power we need to become godly. According to the Bible, there is no other source but him. There are other religious traditions and so-called holy books, but God says his Word is *holy*. Daniel's parents accepted that the Lord is the only God and his Word is the only divine revelation. Therefore, our starting point for teaching our children godliness is to hear or read the Bible.

BEGINNINGS OF WISDOM

Twice the Bible tells us the starting point for wisdom:

> The fear of the LORD is the beginning of wisdom;
>> all who follow his precepts have good understanding.
>>> (Psalm 111:10)

> The fear of the LORD is the beginning of wisdom,
>> and knowledge of the Holy One is understanding.
> For through me [wisdom] your days will be many,
>> and years will be added to your life. (Proverbs 9:10-11)

In both instances we see that God's precepts, gaining understanding, and knowledge of the Holy One are foundational to wisdom. These nurture the fear of the Lord. If you have read the book of Deuteronomy, which Daniel's parents heard, you'd think any parent in the room would experience the fear of the Lord and change their ways. Daniel and Friends' parents seem to have responded that way, but apparently most of the others did not. They heard, but they did not hear. They certainly did not listen to obey.

God's judgment was already being seen on the nation, in that they had become unable to hear and understand. God told Isaiah,

> He said, "Go and tell this people:
>> " 'Be ever hearing, but never understanding;
>> be ever seeing, but never perceiving.'
> Make the heart of this people calloused;
>> make their ears dull
>> and close their eyes.
> Otherwise they might see with their eyes,
>> hear with their ears,
>> understand with their hearts,
> and turn and be healed." (Isaiah 6:9-10)

This inability to hear and perceive what should be plain can be an indicator that God has already given the people over to a depraved mind (see Romans 1). Idolatry may have brought them to the point where God had taken away their spiritual perception and given them over to their own lusts. Indeed, this inability to truly hear and see often accompanies God's judgment in Scripture. Consider the number of times Jesus said to his audience, "He who has ears to hear, let him hear." Those who lack spiritual conviction and are unmoved by God's warnings should earnestly pray that God *give them ears to hear.*

It could be that we don't hear or listen to obey God's Word because we respond in one of the ways mentioned in the previous chapter. Perhaps we think we've already heard it (but we haven't heard *to obey*), or consider it irrelevant, or assume we can't understand it, or we refuse to accept responsibility for what we do understand but assume it's no use trying because obedience is out of reach. Whatever the reason, if we are not obedient to God's commands to pass on his Word to our children, we dare not leave it at that! Think seriously about the implications of these words from Jesus in this light:

Not everyone who says to me, "Lord, Lord," will enter the kingdom of heaven, but only he who does the will of my Father who is in heaven. Many will say to me on that day, "Lord, Lord, did we not prophesy in your name, and in your name drive out demons and perform many miracles?" Then I will tell them plainly, "I never knew you. Away from me, you evildoers!"… Everyone who hears these words of mine and does not put them into practice is like a foolish man who built his house on sand. The rain came down, the streams rose, and the winds blew and beat against that house, and it fell with a great crash. (Matthew 7:21-23,26)

The parents of Daniel and Friends heard and decided to teach God's Word to their children. This was what made the difference between whether their children were among those who survived or those who were destroyed. You may be thinking, *How do we know all that? The Bible doesn't give those details.* True. We arrive at that conclusion by deductive reasoning; all the facts the Bible does reveal fit together logically. My characterization of Daniel's parents is contrived. The following facts, however, are not: Daniel's family was among the royalty of Judah. Therefore, their presence at the reading of the Law was mandatory. Historical and biblical accounts agree that Daniel and his friends were born at that time. God decreed certain blessings and protection would come to those who obeyed these commands with regard to their children. Daniel and his friends grew up to be among the few who received those specific blessings. Therefore, one can logically deduce that their parents (or grandparents) must have met God's requirements. We will also see later, when we meet Daniel and his friends as teens, that they demonstrated a thorough knowledge of God's Word, were practicing it, and had supernatural support in doing so. Given the historical and biblical accounts, they wouldn't have learned this from the religious establishment or culture.

THE POINT OF DECISION

It's encouraging to note that their parents started with very little. They were challenged to make a decision (see Deuteronomy 4:10). Would they or would they not...

1. hear God's words?
2. learn to fear God all the days they live on earth?
3. teach their children?

We, too, must come to a decision, a volitional choice, on each of these questions. Will we commit ourselves to read/hear the Word of the Lord and teach it to our children so that they can learn the fear of the Lord?

You may have some of these common hesitations: *I'm willing, but I don't know anything about the Bible. What if I don't have much faith? What if I'm not sure I believe the Bible?* Those are reasonable questions, but not good reasons to put off this decision. Let's look at each one.

First Peter 2:2 tells us, "Like newborn babies, crave pure spiritual milk [the Word of God], so that by it you may grow up in your salvation." Therefore, starting like a newborn baby is the right attitude to have toward God's Word. How much does a newborn know? You don't have to know anything to start. The Bible says faith comes by hearing the Word of God (see Romans 10:17).

So if you have not heard the Word of God, you lack a basis for faith. A lack of faith is not reason not to read the Bible; rather, not reading the Bible may explain your lack of faith. As to having doubts, how could you believe the Bible if you don't know what it actually says?

So, the place to start is with a decision. Will you commit yourself to read/hear God's Word and pass it on to your children?

WHAT'S OUR MOTIVATION?

We all need motivation to carry out even what we know is right. God provided motivation of every flavor to help us:

Fear motivation: We fear raising kids who lack the moral clarity God's Word provides. Kids who become amoral, or immoral, follow the wrong crowd instead of developing the strength of character needed to do what's right. We know that kids who do wrong live with far greater risks, not to mention becoming destructive to others. God says we are to teach his Word to our children and command them to observe it carefully (see Deuteronomy 32:47, NASB) because "it is your life." We certainly don't want the opposite, which is death! Many deaths among young people (through drug overdoses, drag racing, drunk driving, homicide, and so on) are often the result of behavior God clearly declares to be wrong. Such fear motivates us to provide our children with the source of *life*.

Love and hope motivation: God's promises fill us with hope "that it might go well with [our] children forever!"—"forever" meaning all generations. Bottom line: We commit ourselves to do many things because we love our children, and we hope this will contribute to the best life possible for them.

Reward motivation: God holds out the promise of rewards, rewards any parent would want their children to have (see Deuteronomy 28:1-14, particularly verse 4). God tells us his commands are "for your good." He also implies the reward of long life, "that your days and the days of your sons may be multiplied," and "by this word you shall prolong your days."

Duty motivation: We should teach our children because God said we should. It is our God-given duty and responsibility. I draw this conclusion from Deuteronomy 4:10; 6:7; and 11:19-21. But might these just be Old

Testament commands for Old Testament times? No, the New Testament reiterates and addresses these commands specifically to fathers:

> Fathers, do not provoke your children to anger, but bring them up in
> the discipline and instruction of the Lord. (Ephesians 6:4, NASB)

These days duty has lost the power it once carried to motivate other generations. In addition, the idea that it is our responsibility to *personally* pass on God's Word is not widely accepted today—even by church-going parents. Most of us have delegated this responsibility to our spouse, the Sunday-school teacher, or others to whom God has not directly assigned this duty, perhaps without realizing we are disobeying God by neglecting it.

IT'S OUR RESPONSIBILITY

Search the Scriptures all you like; you'll not find a single verse that says God will hold Sunday-school teachers responsible to teach our children and grandchildren his Word. I'm deeply grateful for the ministry of wonderful Sunday-school teachers who taught me God's Word when my parents did not. I thank God for the wonderful people who work in the children's ministry of our church, as well as those who've taught and ministered to my kids through clubs or parachurch ministries. They've had a tremendous influence. But their ministry does not diminish God's command to my husband and me to pass his teachings on to our own kids and teach them *diligently.* The ministry of the church is part of how we can teach our children God's Word, but it should be secondary to our own efforts at home.

We've answered the "why" of teaching our children God's Word; Deuteronomy 6:6-7 tells us the who, what, when, where, and how:

Who will teach them? You shall!

What will you teach them? God's commandments!

When and where will you teach them? When you sit in your house and when you walk by the way and when you lie down and when you rise up.

How will you teach them? Diligently! Not haphazardly.

Don't feel bad if this is not your present approach. This idea is foreign to most people in our culture. Even dedicated Christians struggle with this particular command. Israel and Judah were agricultural societies where parents spent all day with their children. We live in a compartmentalized culture where many parents spend little time with their children. God knew cultures would change, but he didn't withdraw his command.

First-century Ephesus was more metropolitan than ancient Judah, but God did not excuse Ephesian parents from this duty. Just because this practice is not common in our culture doesn't mean it is not our God-given responsibility. Later, in chapter 10, we will look at how to train kids in morality and godly living. There are nuances beyond just teaching them the Law, rules, and commands. However, kids need a foundation of clear commands and rules. During the elementary school years, kids want rules for everything. They need the rules to be firm as a foundation for later learning on how to navigate complex moral decision making. However, in our generation, even among churched families, it is not unusual to find that this parental duty has been sadly neglected.

When I began to focus on this command to parents, I quizzed a man who I know to be godly. He's active in youth ministry, a leader in men's ministry, and in charge of men's accountability groups. I wanted to know if the men he led held one another accountable to teach God's commands to their kids. Since I regarded him highly and knew he was serving God in many ways, I figured if he didn't get this, most other men might not either.

So I asked him, "Do the men in the accountability groups hold one another accountable to pass God's Word on to their own children?" He looked at me with a puzzled expression.

"What?"

I repeated the question. He shook his head as he said, "No, not really."

"Why?" I asked.

He replied, "Well, I don't really see that as my job."

"Then whose job is it?" I asked.

"My wife's, I guess. We keep them involved in the children's ministry. So it gets done. It's just that I don't do it myself."

I don't mean to be too hard on the men. After writing this book, I was convicted that I had fallen short in passing on God's Word to my own kids, especially my youngest, Haley. So she and I began reading the gospel of Luke together. Actually, she's reading it aloud to me to get credit for her school reading Olympics. Last week as we were reading, she asked me about the reference Jesus made to the widow of Zarephath when he gave his first sermon in Nazareth. I launched into an elaborate retelling of the story of how the widow sent her children out to gather as many containers as possible in response to Elijah's command, and how God continued filling all the vessels with oil until the last one was filled. Then we continued reading. A few days later, I happened to hear a radio Bible study on the widow of Zarephath (see 1 Kings 17). I had told the wrong story! The story I told was about another Old Testament widow. I was so sure I knew it that I would have missed my mistake if the Lord hadn't corrected me. So, I myself, a mom who earnestly tries to pass on God's Word, have no room to boast. We all need to check again and make sure we are fulfilling our duty to pass God's Word on to our kids. Haley actually got a kick out of my mistake and willingly listened as I told her the right story. At least she knew I cared enough to try to pass God's Word on to her.

DARE WE NEGLECT SUCH AN IMPORTANT DUTY?

I doubt any of us would want to one day learn that our neglect of a God-given responsibility has been a spiritual hindrance to our children. This is especially true if we are among those who share God's Word with others. When I told one of my neighbors what I was writing about, this point attracted her attention. Her father was a minister and teacher at a Christian college. As a teen she was required to *behave* as a Christian, and she was punished if she didn't behave as was expected of a minister's daughter. If she did something wrong, her punishment was to stay home on Friday night and read her Bible. She said with a sarcastic laugh, "You can guess how much that made me fond of reading the Bible." When I mentioned my point that God commanded fathers to personally pass on God's Word to their children, she exclaimed, "You know what? Now that you mention it, my father never taught me the Bible! He never taught me what he believed and why he wanted me to behave a certain way. He just assumed that growing up around church I would catch on. He spent his life teaching other people the Bible. He was even a missionary for a while. But he never, never once, that I can recall, taught me the Bible."

Dads and moms, whether ministers or not, I pray that will never be said of us by our children. My neighbor and her husband do not attend church regularly. As it turns out, she has a lot to overcome.

My curiosity and concern led me further. I called someone working on the *Heritage Builders* products for Focus on the Family. This line of resources is designed specifically to help Christian parents pass God's Word on to their kids. The statistics I learned were not surprising. Ninety-two percent of the buyers of *Heritage Builders* resources are women. With all the goal-setting that gets done in business, with all the men's Bible studies, with all the accountability groups, it's troubling that few fathers are holding one another accountable to pass on God's Word to their own kids.

This phenomenon isn't new to our generation. In the first-century church, two women (a mother and grandmother) are mentioned by name for their fine job of raising Timothy, a young pastor, to know God's Word. You go, girls! But the guys need to catch up!

I had some fun razzing Bill McCartney, founder of Promise Keepers, that the women were doing a better job in this particular area than the men. When I brought it to his attention that 92 percent of the people buying *Heritage Builders* materials were women, he wanted the men to challenge women to a race to see who could get the job done to pass God's Word on to their kids. I jokingly pointed out that women had already lapped the men so many times, it would be hard to know how to judge such a competition.

Kidding aside, Coach McCartney and I agree that this is a very serious and important matter. If men summoned the energy I saw in Bill's reaction to the statistics, they could make dramatic progress. I asked Coach McCartney if he would like to say something to the men reading this book. He sent me a note and asked me to pass it along to fathers. He began by quoting Isaiah 38:19: "The father shall make known Your truth to the children" (NKJV). Then he wrote,

Almighty God has mandated that He will hold the father in the home responsible for communicating the truth of Scripture to his offspring. The man who stands by and depends upon his wife or church to divide the Word misses and violates the heart of his heavenly Father.

—Bill McCartney, founder and president of Promise Keepers

If you are a mom reading this book alone, perhaps you should share this part with Dad.

My suggested competition was merely for fun: God doesn't want fathers and mothers set against each other, but working together to fulfill their duty. If all fathers and mothers, grandfathers and grandmothers took this on as if it were their personal responsibility (and it is), they can be sure that together we would excel in this God-given duty.

GETTING STARTED PASSING ON GOD'S WORD

The first thing to do if you want your children to know the Word of God is to accept that teaching it to your children is your responsibility. If you're a single parent, it's your responsibility alone, though you'll need to rely more heavily (than those in a two-parent home) on your church family to help and to equip you to fulfill your responsibility. If you're married, you have the benefit of a team effort. If you're a grandparent and you know your grandchildren aren't receiving God's Word from their parents, you are called by God to pick up the slack. If you are the only parent who is a believer, so be it. God can use you, and maybe you can get the support of another relative or friend who also believes to help you convey God's Word to your children. (That's how Timothy in the Bible received God's Word, from his godly mother and grandmother. His father was not a believer.)

Second, as we discussed in chapter 3, you have to read or hear the Word of God first. Start reading the Bible, even if it's the first time. If you've read it, now read it with your attention on what you will want to share with your kids when opportunities arise throughout the day.

Here are some tips:

- Find a translation you can understand. If you don't read very well, get the *New International Readers Version,* translated at a third-grade reading level. I recommend *The Kids' Devotional Bible* by Zonderkidz. This will make it easy for you to immediately start sharing the Bible with your kids (ages 6 to 10) in kid-sized bits that are relevant to their lives.
- Pray and ask God's Holy Spirit to help you understand what his Word says.
- Declare your commitment, make it specific (for example, "I'm going to read a chapter a day until I get through the New Testament"), and make yourself accountable to another person or group.

Don't know where to begin? Here's a list of helps to assist your reading experience:

- I highly recommend *What the Bible Is All About Bible Handbook* by Henrietta Mears. Ranked as one of the best-selling Bible handbooks with more than four million copies in print, this handbook has now been updated for a new generation of Bible readers. Billy Graham said of this book, "One of the greatest needs in the church today is to come back to the Scriptures as the basis of authority, and to study them prayerfully in dependence on the Holy Spirit. This book will help make the reading and study of God's Word interesting, challenging and useful." There is also a children's version called *What the Bible Is All About for Young Explorers,* which makes learning even easier because it has simple line-drawn illustrations that delineate the key happenings of the whole Bible.
- Choose a Bible that includes clear, concise overviews of every book, study helps, time lines, maps, historical background, and so on. There are many excellent versions available at any Christian bookstore.
- If you're not familiar with book names, refer to the Bible's table of contents.
- In Scripture citations, the chapter number comes before the colon, and verse numbers come after, for example: Psalm 119:10 refers to Psalms chapter 119, verse 10.

- Get help from those who are trained and dedicated to teaching God's Word: ministers at a Bible-believing church, reputable Bible study organizations like Kay Arthur's Precept Ministries, Promise Keepers, Walk Thru the Bible, Bible Study Fellowship, Community Bible Study, or other church and parachurch Bible study ministries. Start with people you know and trust at your local church, including your children's pastor.

Now, what to read? I recommend all parents be familiar with these passages of Scripture.

- The Ten Commandments (Exodus 20 or Deuteronomy 5)
- Sermon on the Mount (Matthew 5–7)
- The Shepherd's Psalm (Psalm 23)
- The Lord's Prayer (Matthew 6:9-13 or Luke 11:2-4). We should also teach our children to pray this and practice praying it with them.
- The gospel according to John (fourth book of the New Testament)
- The gospels according to Matthew, Mark, Luke (first three books in New Testament), followed by the Acts of the Apostles
- Wisdom literature: Psalms and Proverbs (middle of the Old Testament)
- Romans (basic Christian doctrine)
- Hebrews (explaining the connection between Old and New Testaments)

The things God called people to remember and not forget can be found in:

- Genesis
- Exodus
- Deuteronomy
- Isaiah

Make a list of what you want to be sure your children learn from the Bible before they leave your home. Periodically "check in" to see how much each of your children knows of the basics. Each child will grow up in your family at different seasons of your life. It's easy to assume your kids have heard certain Bible stories because you remember reading them over and over. I remember one time when our family was talking about the Bible and someone mentioned Judas. Our youngest daughter, Haley, was five or six at the time. She asked, "Who's Judas?" *Who's Judas?* Oops! Something slipped by. Casey, our first child, was born in a season of our lives when we were actively engaged in youth ministry. We regaled her with Bible stories from infancy. Haley, born six years later, came into our family during a very difficult season of crisis, when we were no longer in ministry. I hadn't noticed that all those stories I read over and over were read mostly to Casey and Taylor. So be careful to think of each child individually in your Bible training.

Communicating God's Word to your kids over the course of everyday life is critical. God doesn't say to sit our kids down daily and give them a thirty-minute Bible lecture, nor to read the whole Bible to kids (some parts obviously require more maturity). And we're certainly not to just hand them a Bible (no matter how colorful the cover) and tell *them* to read or study the Bible alone. God says to teach them when we get up, when we go through the day, and as we prepare for bedtime. We are to read/hear God's Word and look for opportunities to teach it to our children. This is good for obvious reasons: You know each of your children. You know each one's level of understanding, sensitivities, questioning looks. God entrusts the communication to you as one who knows and loves your particular children. If you don't spend time with your children, you won't be available when opportunities arise to pass on God's Word. That's an important reason for us to establish a lifestyle that allows at least one parent to spend substantial time with our children rather than to delegate child care to others. I know how challenging it is to manage a lifestyle that allows for this, especially when it seems two incomes are required just to cover the necessities. If you will make this a priority, God will help you find a way to be with your children to fulfill his command while they're growing up.

Bottom line: God commands parents (and grandparents) to pass his Word on to our children (and grandchildren).

Once you accept this as your responsibility, you will see opportunities to share God's Word with your kids. It's just like any other responsibility: When you accept that it is yours, you will notice when it needs to be done and find times to do so during everyday life. Will you commit yourself to hear this part of God's Word and obey it?

FIVE

FIRST AND LASTING
IMPRESSIONS

Shortly after the public reading of the Book of the Law, King Josiah responded
to the Word of the Lord by zealously purging Judah of all that violated God's
commands, destroying forbidden forms of worship, even household gods and
idols (see 2 Kings 23:24). Afterward, he reinstated traditions and rituals God
had commanded them to keep, specifically the Feast of Unleavened Bread and
Passover.

King Josiah commanded all the people to observe these feasts commemo-
rating their deliverance from slavery. Moses had taught them,

> For seven days eat bread made without yeast and on the seventh day
> hold a festival to the LORD. Eat unleavened bread during those seven
> days; nothing with yeast in it is to be seen among you, nor shall any
> yeast be seen anywhere within your borders. On that day tell your son,
> "I do this because of what the LORD did for me when I came out of
> Egypt." This observance will be for you like a sign on your hand and a
> reminder on your forehead that the law of the LORD is to be on your
> lips. For the LORD brought you out of Egypt with his mighty hand.
> You must keep this ordinance at the appointed time year after year.
> (Exodus 13:6-10)

> The dough was without yeast because they had been driven out of Egypt
> and did not have time to prepare food for themselves. (Exodus 12:39)

Every Jewish household was to cleanse its home of any speck of yeast. Each household was to bring an unblemished one-year-old lamb inside to live with the family for four days. Then they were to sacrifice it and eat it in a commemorative meal recounting the Exodus story. The feast was called Passover because God declared,

> On that same night I will pass through Egypt and strike down every firstborn—both men and animals—and I will bring judgment on all the gods of Egypt. I am the LORD. The blood will be a sign for you on the houses where you are; and when I see the blood, I will *pass over* you. No destructive plague will touch you when I strike Egypt. (Exodus 12:12-13)

Israel had not celebrated Passover for generations before King Josiah reinstituted it (see 2 Kings 23:21-23; 2 Chronicles 35:1-5), put everyone in their places, encouraged them in the service of the Lord, gave them animals to sacrifice, and paid for it all!

Everyone performed the rituals as commanded, but in the end not all were saved from punishment for years of disregarding God's Word. Scripture says Josiah was spared because his heart was responsive to God (see 2 Chronicles 34:27). Those not spared "followed the stubbornness of their evil hearts" (see Jeremiah 3:17; 9:14; 11:8; 13:10; and 23:17), even though they went through the motions of obeying Josiah's commands. The state of their hearts, not just the observance of religious rituals, made the difference.

IT STARTS WITH THE HEART

We have to get first things first. Most of us want to impress on our children the importance of being obedient to God, because we know that will be best for them. Consider the progression God lays out in his first great commandment:

> Hear, O Israel: The LORD our God, the LORD is one. Love the LORD your God with all your heart and with all your soul and with all your

strength. These commandments that I give you today are to be upon your hearts. Impress them on your children. (Deuteronomy 6:4-7)

First we are to know the Lord *our God,* then we are to love God with *all our hearts.* Then, God says, impress this on your children. Jesus concurs:

"Love the Lord your God with all your heart and with all your soul and with all your mind." This is the first and greatest commandment. And the second is like it: "Love your neighbor as yourself." All the Law and the Prophets hang on these two commandments. (Matthew 22:37-40)

When I speak publicly on this issue, I use an object lesson to illustrate this progression. I have a heart-shaped box with a lid. On the lid, I have glued raised wooden letters that spell out, "Love the Lord with all your heart." Inside the heart box, I keep three balls of Play-Doh: yellow, blue, and purple. Each ball of Play-Doh represents one of my three children. Each unique, thus the different colors. I take out one of the balls and begin to knead and press it, representing our job as parents to mold our children. (Some require more pressure than others!) We have to work with each one to make sure the job is done right. I flatten one lump of Play-Doh until it is wide enough to cover the raised wooden letters on my heart. I press the dough against the letters, which leave an impression. This represents how the Word is on *my* heart and I *impress it* on each of my children. The Play-Doh will only pick up the impression of what is present on my heart; I cannot impress anything on my child that is not there. Likewise, anything there that rivals my heart's affections for God will also make an impression on my children.

When I peel the Play-Doh off the box, the impression of the letters is there, but the impression is a mirror image of the letters. This represents how we can impress our children, but we cannot force them to adopt our faith as their own. If we first live to "love the Lord with all our hearts" while they are growing up, they will have a true mold that is waiting for them to fill with faith of their own.

What If the Impression So Far Isn't the Best?

What if the first impressions we've made on our kids aren't in keeping with the first great commandment? Kids are not impressed by, "Do as I say, not as I do!" Even so, hypocrisy makes an impression. If our hearts are cluttered with an accumulation of "household gods," the negative effects will reach third and fourth generations (see Exodus 20:5; 34:7; Numbers 14:18; and Deuteronomy 5:9). Second Kings 17:41 tells us:

> Even while these people were worshiping the LORD, they were [also] serving their idols. To this day their children and grandchildren continue to do as their fathers did.

Concern for our children may prompt us to get our own hearts right. God commands single-hearted devotion, jealously yearning for us to be as devoted to him as a husband and wife are to each other. When our worldly loves compete with our love for God, it's time to tear down some "household idols" in our hearts. Doing so will make a good impression on our children, even if we've made a bad impression in the past.

James wrote to Christians,

> You adulterous people, don't you know that friendship with the world is hatred toward God? Anyone who chooses to be a friend of the world becomes an enemy of God. Or do you think Scripture says without reason that the spirit he caused to live in us envies intensely? But he gives us more grace. That is why Scripture says: "God opposes the proud but gives grace to the humble." Submit yourselves, then, to God. Resist the devil, and he will flee from you. Come near to God and he will come near to you. Wash your hands, you sinners, and *purify your hearts,* you *double-minded.* Grieve, mourn and wail. Change your laughter to mourning and your joy to gloom. Humble yourselves before the Lord, and he will lift you up. (James 4:4-10)

The repentance James described is similar to Josiah's right heart response to God. There's hope! We can return to God. Our return doesn't guarantee our children automatically *will* love God with all their hearts, but they won't have to overcome the bad impressions that would otherwise follow them into adulthood. If keeping the first great commandment becomes our primary aim, we can practice cleansing our hearts of sin and, in so doing, make a good impression as we demonstrate responding to God's grace with love-inspired obedience.

ROOTED AND GROUNDED IN LOVE

We've established that kids won't live godly lives just because they've been commanded to. Even someone as godly as Josiah couldn't pull that off. God's first great commandment needed to come first for them as well. Jesus said, "*If you love me,* you will obey what I command" (John 14:15). In other words, loving God motivates obedience. How do we help our children grow to love the Lord with all their hearts? The Bible says, "We love *because he first loved us*" (1 John 4:19). So cultivating obedience begins in the soil of *God's love for us.*

From the time your children are babies, use every means you can think of to emphasize God's love for them: Tell it, sing it, celebrate it, emphasize it in every possible way. With older children, as you are reading a passage of Scripture, help them look for and highlight God's love for us first, as I have done by italicizing portions of these verses:

> For you are a people holy to the LORD your God. The LORD your *God has chosen you* out of all the peoples on the face of the earth to be his people, *his treasured possession.*
>
> The LORD did not *set his affection on you and choose you* because you were more numerous than other peoples, for you were the fewest of all peoples. But it was *because the LORD loved you* and kept the oath he swore to your forefathers that he brought you out with a mighty hand and *redeemed you* from the land of slavery, from the power of Pharaoh king of Egypt. Know therefore that the LORD your God is God; he is

the faithful God, keeping his covenant of love to a thousand generations of *those who love him* and keep his commands. But those who hate him he will repay to their face by destruction; he will not be slow to repay to their face those who hate him.

Therefore, take care to follow the commands, decrees and laws I give you today. (Deuteronomy 7:6-11)

Since little children are unable to deal with abstract concepts, make the love of God personal: "God loves you! Jesus loves you!" This personal connection sparks a heartfelt desire—even in little children—to please God by obeying. When our children were little, we taught them to sing, *Yes! Jesus loves me!* We took them to church, where they could associate loving people with God's love for them. They got to know Jesus through picture books, coloring books, videos, music—through any way we could communicate it.

One bright morning when Casey was about two, she and I visited a church to attend Bible Study Fellowship. Being unfamiliar with their facilities, I happened to go into the sanctuary while looking for the child-care room. I was holding Casey's hand, and we were both struck by the unexpected beauty. A long marble aisle gleamed as sunlight came streaming through the stained-glass window at the front of the sanctuary. Our eyes were drawn upward to the brilliant image of Jesus, several stories tall, shining before us, arms outstretched as if to welcome us to himself. Casey's chubby little hand dropped from mine. Her wide eyes widened even more. She whispered, "Oh, Mommy, who is he?"

"That's Jesus, honey."

"I thought so. Can I go closer?"

I nodded in wonder as I watched my little girl, astounded by such a beautiful portrayal of Jesus, walk up that long aisle, then—step by step, never taking her eyes off Jesus—ascend the stairs, ever gazing up at him while getting as close as she could. When I joined her, she still spoke in hushed tones.

"Oh, Mommy! He's beautiful!"

She was already developing a heart of awestruck love for Jesus. Young children may not yet be able to conceive of God, or understand the major plot points to the Exodus story, or have any inkling about the precious blood of the lamb given as a sacrifice so they could escape the judgment of death for their sins. But even little children can cuddle up to Jesus, who loves all children and welcomes them to himself. As we immerse our young children in God's love for them, specifically God's love for them in Jesus, they will believe that he wants what's best for them, and they will never want to hurt him. A heartfelt desire to obey will grow out of their knowledge of love.

At age three, Casey enjoyed the animated series SuperBook, in which cartoon kids went back in time to witness Bible events. One day she watched the SuperBook Easter video upstairs while I went about my work. From downstairs, I heard Casey sobbing and running down the stairs. I raced to her, "What's wrong?"

"Mommy, they're hurting Jesus. They are hurting Jesus!"

She led me back upstairs, where the animation was showing a silhouette of three crosses against a bright flashing background. The illustrations were not graphic, but her little-girl mind understood that "bad men are hurting Jesus." She begged me to turn it off. Thereafter, she still wanted to see that video, but when the time approached for the crosses, she would jump up and run downstairs. She couldn't bear to watch anyone hurt Jesus.

We and our children are to be "rooted and grounded" in love. Consider Paul's prayer for his "children" in the faith:

> I pray that out of his glorious riches he may strengthen you with power
> through his Spirit in your inner being, so that Christ may dwell in your
> hearts through faith. And I pray that you, being rooted and established
> in love, may have power, together with all the saints, to *grasp how wide
> and long and high and deep is the love of Christ, and to know this love
> that surpasses knowledge—that you may be filled to the measure of all the
> fullness of God.* (Ephesians 3:16-19)

We can pray this prayer for our children, but learn from it too. This prayer comes at the heart of Paul's letter to the Ephesians: It falls toward the end of the first three chapters, which overflow with teachings about God's gracious love, and before the last three chapters, which read like a detailed to-do list of godly living. Paul didn't start with a "be-good" list. The godliness of Ephesians 4–6 can only grow out of grasping God's amazing grace and unshakable love for us delineated in Ephesians 1–3. Obedience arising from any source other than love will be more likely to be uprooted or wither when life gets tough.

HOW TO CULTIVATE THE SOIL

Cultivating the soil of a child's heart can begin with this simple statement: God loves you! Love him back! Moral instruction is important; just make sure to first and simultaneously cultivate the soil of each child's heart with God's love. This love is relayed on the most basic level through the love you demonstrate. We also teach children about God's love by starting their Bible training with stories that show God's love, particularly stories about Jesus, who is God's love personified. Read young children the story where Jesus invites the little children to come to him so he can bless them. Afterward, invite each child to pray and tell Jesus he or she wants to come close to him. Then you can read them stories about people who loved God back.

Even if children have not grown up knowing and loving Jesus, it's never too late to start. Every heart longs to know the love of God. Don't get discouraged if some of your children are already teens and you're just starting. I did not grasp the love of God in Jesus Christ until I was almost fifteen. That was not too late to be drawn to God's love and spend the rest of my life seeking to be godly and wise. For teens, I recommend The Visual Bible's *Gospel According to Matthew*. This four-video series is a word-for-word reenactment of the Bible book of Matthew. It makes Jesus' love come alive in a very appealing way, even for teens who aren't into reading the Bible.

Another way to reinforce God's love for us is to recount all the wonderful things God does and has done for us. Psalm 136 says over and over of God, "His love endures forever." The phrase alternates with statements about God's nature and God's mighty deeds from Israel's history. Families can make a game of this. Have family members make mental lists of things God has done in the world or for them personally that demonstrate his love. Sit in a circle. The first player names one thing from his or her mental list, then everyone says, "His steadfast love endures forever," before the next person names something else. If you can't think of some evidence of God's love in a given amount of time, or if you repeat something another has said, you're out. This is a fun way to remind one another of God's everlasting love. Similar games can be done with Psalm 103, which recounts the benefits of God's love, and Psalm 104, which shows God's power in nature.

One of the best ways for kids to truly understand God's love for them is to see God answer prayers of personal importance to them. We need to explain that God is not a heavenly vending machine, where they plunk in a prayer and watch God come through with a miraculous result. On the other hand, we can pray with them for things that are dear to their hearts, trusting that God may in his grace grant that prayer. When God does so miraculously, his act says more to a child than numerous sermons or devotional times.

When my son's thirteenth birthday was fast approaching, our finances were lacking. Taylor graciously told us that he didn't need the kind of big birthday celebration our kids have come to expect. I still hoped that we could do something special for his transition to being a teen. The Lord had helped me out in such situations before, so I lifted this need up in prayer. Later we learned that a few tickets to the Sacramento King's playoff game against the Dallas Mavericks would be sold at an affordable price that Friday morning at Arco Arena. When I dropped Taylor off for school that morning, we prayed together and asked the Lord to please bless us with tickets as Taylor's special birthday gift.

We've taught our kids that we can ask God for anything, and should openly share the desires of our hearts with him, but that God is not obligated to satisfy our whims. This was what we call a "hit or miss" prayer (James 4:3 says, "You ask and do not receive, because you ask amiss, that you may spend it on your pleasures" [NKJV]), but we trusted that God could sort that out. We thanked God for the opportunity to *try* to get tickets, made our request, and said, "Amen!"

The line at Arco was over six hundred people long, with some who had spent the night, some who had found a way to cheat to better their odds, and some who resorted to the use of amulets in hopes of increasing their chances. Each of us was given a number in order of our place in line. Only one number would be drawn. The person holding the corresponding number would go to the front of the line, along with everyone who had been waiting in line behind him. Tickets would be sold in that order until they ran out.

Three local television news channels and a major news/talk radio station were poised to pounce on the chosen few for sound bites. My number was 397; the number called was 386. The media circled around us as we headed to the front of the line. As microphones were pressed into our cheering throng, chants of "Go Kings!" rang out, along with one unusual declaration: "Prayer works!"

Kammie Lloyd of KFBK picked up on it immediately and zoomed in, "You prayed?" she asked eagerly, pushing the microphone my way.

"Yes, my son's thirteenth birthday is coming up. The tickets are for him and his dad. So, thank you, Jesus! Happy birthday, Taylor!"

That afternoon, every hour on the hour, that sound clip was played with this lead, "How *do* you get Kings playoff tickets? One woman believes she had divine intervention."

How's that for a sound bite to build a child's faith? The television networks were equally interested. That night I appeared on all three networks, giving glory to God who hears us when we pray, who cares about a boy's birthday, and who is well able to arrange for us to get tickets we could not otherwise afford. It's all about connections—and teaching our kids that God really loves them—and grace.

Taylor had a birthday he will never forget. His sister Haley gave him what every true Kings fan needs—an authentic cow bell. The last thing Taylor said as they were leaving to go to the game was, "Mom, pray the Kings win." He and Pat had a special time together, even though that was the only game in the second round that the Kings did not win. Actually, I'm a bit relieved, or Taylor may have thought I could fix the games, and I would have had more prayer requests than I could handle! Besides, the loss provided a great opening to teach a teenage boy about the sovereignty of God. I didn't need to say any more about the love of God; he had demonstrated his love in a way that spoke directly to Taylor's heart. Go King of kings!

PLANT THE REDEMPTION STORY IN THE SOIL OF GOD'S LOVE

Once the soil of our children's hearts is cultivated so that they can be rooted and grounded in love, concentrate on planting the seeds of God's Word. The Bible offers wisdom, promises, prophecy, and encouragement to help us raise our children in the nurture and admonition of the Lord in all areas of life: moral training, character development, family-life roles, modes of worship, spiritual disciplines, historical knowledge, and so on. As with a garden, these grow row upon row in the soil of our child's heart, simultaneously, some getting more attention at particular seasons of a child's life. We need to nurture the redemption story in every child's garden in every season, as we see it working in various ways throughout Scripture and life. Since Christmas and Easter are both celebrations of God's redemptive love, we should use them, and all other "holy days," to make that point.

The redemption story has these basic elements:

- People have sinned and are in danger of eternal death.
- God requires justice but loves people so much he provides a way of escape (typically involving a blood sacrifice).
- Those who obey God and take refuge in his way of escape will follow him out of danger and receive the protection and blessing God desires for all his children.
- God chooses people to receive his grace while giving us free will; those who refuse God's way of escape will perish.

This story line runs through the stories of Adam and Eve, Cain and Abel, Noah, Abraham and Isaac, Joseph and his brothers, the Exodus/Passover, Daniel and exiles of Judah, and many others, culminating in the gospel of Jesus Christ. Indeed, most Old Testament redemption stories can be used as examples of Christ's sacrifice on the cross and resurrection to a new and eternal life.

Here's an example of how you can use the Passover story to emphasize redemption in your child's heart:

1. Tell the Bible Story in an Engaging Way

An exciting story with grand characters and themes teaches children by captivating them. These days, we don't even have to worry about being good storytellers. We can play animated videos (like *The Prince of Egypt*), read beautifully illustrated books, or have animated vegetables help out! I strongly recommend also going back to a real translation of Scripture (not an abridged storybook or paraphrase) to read the original story from God's holy Word.

In the Passover story, the Hebrews were slaves in Egypt. God had chosen them to be his people long before and loved them. God heard their cries and sent Moses to deliver them from slavery. God sent judgment on the whole land. Because God's judgment of Egypt put the Israelites in danger of death, he told them how to protect their households by sprinkling their doorframes with the blood of a lamb. With mighty miracles, God helped them escape Egypt and led them to the Promised Land.

2. Connect Old Testament Redemption Stories to the New Testament Redemption Story

The blood of the lamb was essential to the Passover story. Each family had to take a lamb, a perfect one-year-old male, and bring it into their houses to live with them. The children would cuddle up to the little lamb and form an emotional attachment. Then when they slaughtered the lamb to spill the blood that would protect them from the judgment of death, that blood was *precious to them*.

There is a profound connection between this Old Testament story of redemption and the story of Christ as our redeemer in the New Testament. John the Baptist introduced Jesus to the crowds, saying, "Look, the Lamb of God, who takes away the sin of the world!" (John 1:29). Like the Passover lamb, Jesus was perfect. He came to be close to us before he died to satisfy God's judgment and penalty of death. He died at Passover time. The Last Supper was a Passover meal where Jesus made the clear connection between his mission and the fulfillment of the meaning of Passover.

> And he [Jesus] took bread, gave thanks and broke it, and gave it to them, saying, "This is my body given for you; do this in remembrance of me."
>
> In the same way, after the supper he took the cup, saying, "This cup is the new covenant in my blood, which is poured out for you." (Luke 22:19-20)

3. Tie the Redemption Story to Your Personal Story, Bringing It into Real Life

The kids of this generation base their beliefs mostly on experience. Therefore, sharing your experience is a powerful influence. This generation is also attuned to anything that doesn't ring true. Telling them stories we believe, because we have experienced God's touch in our lives, similarly brings the Bible alive for our kids. Using your own stories makes redemption real. You can use the Exodus as a model for your personal testimony.

If you're a Christian, you were in some kind of slavery before you came to Christ. Jesus said, "I tell you the truth, everyone who sins is a slave to sin" (John 8:34). Someone told you that the blood of Jesus would cover your sins if you would take refuge in him. Then God led you out of your old life. Jesus declared, "So if the Son sets you free, you will be free indeed" (John 8:36). Baptism is like our Red Sea, where our old life became dead to us, as it says, "We were therefore buried with him through baptism into death in order that, just as Christ was raised from the dead through the glory of the Father, we too may live a new life" (Romans 6:4). So, in essence Jesus rescued us from *slavery*, brought us *out*, brought us *through miraculously*, to bring us *into a new life*. Share your personal experience along these lines. You might say:

- "Before I followed Jesus, here's what my life was like… *I was in slavery in…*"
- "Someone told me the story and *I took refuge under the blood of Jesus when…*"

- *"God brought me out 'with a mighty hand'..."* (Describe the process you went *through,* including any miracles, provision, and answers to prayer experienced in the process.)
- *"God brought me into* a new life. My life today is different and better..."

If you want to include sad tales of wandering in the wilderness, or what you learned the hard way from years of disobedience, use discretion according to your children's ages, sensitivities, and any shame such revelations might bring on your children. Some sins need to be left in the "sea of forgetfulness" (see Micah 7:19).

4. Lead Your Children to Experience Their Own Redemption Story

On the night God's Spirit passed over Egypt, all members of each Israelite family took refuge "under the blood of the lamb." Certainly, those parents were not nonchalant about whether their children came inside that night! Likewise, every parent should personally direct and urge their children to take refuge in Jesus. We can't force children to receive Jesus as their Savior, but in many accounts in the book of Acts when someone is saved, his family is too. Get whatever help needed from your church, but personally make sure the way of salvation has been presented to each of your children. For young children I recommend *Steps to Jesus* by Linda Sattgast as a clear message of what Christ has done for us. Lead your children into a personal relationship with Jesus, and have them baptized according to the Scripture.

REINSTATING BIBLE-BASED RITUALS AND TRADITIONS

We began this chapter by looking at how King Josiah's right heart of love for God was expressed in reinstating the Feast of Unleavened Bread and Passover. Once we give our attention to the first great commandment, then root and establish our children in the love of God, we are ready to look at the beauty and importance of rituals and traditions. Scripture establishes and affirms these; therefore, so should we in our families. While rituals, liturgy, and tradition are no substitute for a love relationship with God, they can form deep impressions and "God-shaped" yearnings that may draw our children back to God later in their lives.

Just recently I had the joy of reconnecting with a young woman whom I had discipled when she was a teen. She is now a mother of four, devoted to the Lord and her family, serving God in her church community, and raising her children to know and love the Lord. She shared how she had gone through several years of not following the Lord but was eventually drawn back to him. As we discussed how she could help ensure that her children don't repeat her years of wandering, she told me that her deep hunger for the beautiful rituals and religious traditions she had experienced as a young child played a significant role in drawing her back to God. She said that her father, who had introduced her to these rituals, had lacked a deep faith, but the rituals themselves left her with a sense of God's grandeur. How much better when we can infuse such traditions with faith and meaning throughout the years when our children are growing up, on into the years when we celebrate these with our children's children.

Biblical rituals and traditions tend to have the following elements. I'll illustrate what I mean with examples of how most of us already incorporate these elements in Christian celebrations. You can think through how you could enhance all your holiday celebrations and biblical rituals/traditions by making sure to include or enhance these elements:

- *Experiences related to Scripture.* For example, during Christmas we read the story from Luke 2 or go to functions where verses such as Isaiah 9:6 are quoted. These verses of Scripture are read, sung, found on Christmas cards, and so on.
- *People coming together with a place to belong and a part to play.* For example, some families celebrate Advent in preparation for Christmas. Their celebrations may include each family member's having a part to play such as the older children lighting the Advent candles and younger ones blowing them out. Christmas festivities usually include gathering together around a Christmas tree, dinner table,

or gathering together at parties where everyone is made to feel a sense of belonging.

- *Emotion-laden celebrations of God's goodness or commemoration of monumental events.* Christmas is all about God's goodness and commemorates the most monumental event in history. This is *felt* at Christmastime more than just told. We get in the "Christmas spirit" through elements that touch our emotions such as giving to others, lights, decorations, singing, and music. Look at the emotion of "*Joy to the world...*" tied to a monumental event—"the Lord has come."

- *Connections to those who have gone before us, making us participants in God's ongoing story throughout history. Repetition, ritual, and tradition connect us in turn to the assurance that God's eternal story is being played out on the stage of time, and we have important parts to play.* For example, families carry on their own traditions by repeating activities or menu items from years or generations before. Christians pass on hymns written and sung for generations. We recall God's promises made through Old Testament prophets who lived long before Jesus came. Traditions connect us and our children with those who have gone before.

- *Symbols that make life meaningful. When connected to God's Word, these are powerful teaching tools children enjoy and remember.* For example, we can make Christmas celebrations more meaningful by explaining symbols to our children. Evergreen trees mean the eternal life Jesus came to bring; an angel on the treetop signifies the angels who came to announce Jesus' birth; lights equate to Jesus as the light of the world who came into the world on a dark night; gifts represent not only God's so loving the world that he gave his only Son but also the gifts the Magi gave Jesus to worship him.

- *Sensory experiences.* These include hearing, seeing, smelling, tasting/eating/drinking, and touching. For example, at Christmas we *hear* special music like carols. We *see* the beauty of manger scenes and beautifully decorated homes and gifts. We *smell* the scent of pine, cookies, or spice cake baking, chestnuts roasting on an open fire, and so on. We *taste* Christmas dinner, candy canes, and so on. We *touch* special fabrics of holiday clothes, prickly needles of the tree, gifts we may be shaking to discover what's inside. All of these sensory experiences go together to make our rituals more memorable. Research shows that people remember 5 percent of what they only hear, but up to 95 percent of what they experience with all their senses.

As we plan our family holidays (to celebrate holy days set apart for a special purpose), there is great value in carefully planning how to incorporate each of the above elements into our rituals and traditions. As you will discover in the study guide at the back of this book, God gave us a good example to follow in the rituals he commanded the Jews to incorporate into the Passover celebration.

We are not required to go to God's temple three times a year to celebrate prescribed feasts, as every Jewish man was commanded to do in the Old Testament. Indeed, no Jewish temple now stands in Jerusalem (although Daniel prophesied that it will be rebuilt). Allowing for our freedom in Christ, let me suggest some categories to get you started in enriching your children's spiritual lives through biblical rituals and traditions. Jesus celebrated some of these with his family while he was growing up. There are still grand themes we can learn from and share with our children.

- Celebrate the observances celebrated by the Lord in the New Testament: communion (the Lord's Supper), Resurrection Sunday or Easter, a Passover Seder, Feast of Dedication (Hanukkah). For help with understanding the Christian meaning that can be derived from Old Testament feasts, I recommend the book *Celebrate the Feasts* by Martha Zimmerman. It is an excellent, simple guide to celebrating Old Testament feasts in your own home or church, along with a basic Christian understanding of our Old Testament roots.
- Celebrate significant events in the church calendar. Check with your church leaders for helpful instruction or resources to guide you. Read books to help you explore rituals that can enrich your appreci-

ation of your family's spiritual heritage. There are also beautifully illustrated children's books such as *Come Worship with Me* by Ruth L. Boling (Geneva Press) that take children through the church year and explain the meaning of traditions related to the church calendar.

- Reinstate some celebrations from your family heritage or faith tradition. Ask parents, grandparents, or your church leaders about their favorite spiritual or scripturally based traditions that are no longer practiced in your family. Rediscover some of these with your children.

- Try some fresh resources to begin new traditions that add scriptural meaning to holiday traditions you already celebrate: An excellent example of this is Adorenaments from FamilyLife resources. This product has twelve Christmas tree ornaments, each bearing a symbol that represents some aspect of Christ's nature. These come with a book that explains the meaning of each symbol. Year after year as children put each Adorenament on the branches, they will be reminded of the true meaning of Christmas. As you find new resources that help your family create and celebrate biblical rituals and traditions, incorporate these to make your holidays truly holy days.

The combined effect of getting the first great commandment first in our own hearts, then rooting our children in God's boundless love, planting the redemption story in their hearts, and reinstating biblical traditions will make a lasting impression that will contribute significantly to their growth in godliness and wisdom.

SIX

RAISING SONS AND DAUGHTERS DETERMINED NOT TO DEFILE THEMSELVES

Daniel's parents raised their son in the shifting shadows of fearful possibilities, never losing sight of the flickering light of their hope in God's promises. They believed Jeremiah's prophecies that God was judging their wayward nation, but they also believed it when God said he would bless those who walked in his ways and taught his laws to their children.

Given the outcome of Daniel's remarkable life, we can reasonably deduce that someone was diligent about his spiritual training. We have no reason to believe that was not his parents, although they were never identified by name. They raised him to know the Lord their God and to know there is no other God. They taught him the curses of disobedience and the blessings of obedience laid out clearly in the Book of the Law, and they no doubt urged him at all times to choose life (see Deuteronomy 30:19). Their family carefully followed God's dietary laws, prayed regularly, and encouraged Daniel to make friends with peers who were also faithful to the Lord. He was raised to expect that a time would come—God only knew when, but sometime after King Josiah's life was over—when their people would be taken captive to Babylon by their enemies. Jeremiah's prophecies repeatedly made this clear. No doubt they hoped and prayed that their fellow citizens of Judah would repent, and that God would refrain from sending the prophesied judgment. As Daniel approached the age of accountability—when Jewish youths accept their responsibility to take God's Word on their own shoulders—surely his parents prepared him to face the moral choices he would have to make. They must have discussed the grand blessings promised to those who walk in the Lord's ways as well as the dreadful consequences predicted for those who disobey.

Shortly after Daniel reached the age of accountability, King Josiah was killed in battle against Pharaoh Neco. He wasn't even forty. Suddenly, all the training and moral preparation Daniel had received from his parents called for urgent review. God's judgment could come swiftly.

The entire nation mourned their honored king and protector. Pharaoh Neco appointed Josiah's son Jehoahaz as a vassal king, but he did evil in the eyes of the Lord. In only three months he rebelled and was taken captive to Egypt, where he later died. Pharaoh then appointed Josiah's son Eliakim as king, naming him Jehoiakim. He, too, did evil in the sight of the Lord. Pharaoh exacted heavy payments of silver and gold from King Jehoiakim, and the people of Judah suffered directly because the payments were exacted from them (2 Kings 23:33-37). As predicted, the world powers soon shifted, with Babylon replacing Assyria as the predominant governing force. Within a few years Nebuchadnezzar, king of Babylon, defeated Egypt, seizing the best of the land of Judah as part of the spoils of war. Daniel and his friends Azariah, Mishael, and Hananiah were among the best Judah had to offer.

In the third year of the reign of Jehoiakim king of Judah, Nebuchadnezzar king of Babylon came to Jerusalem and besieged it. And the Lord delivered Jehoiakim king of Judah into his hand, along with some of the articles from the temple of God. These he carried off to the temple of his god in Babylonia and put in the treasure house of his god.

Then the king ordered Ashpenaz, chief of his court officials, to bring in some of the Israelites from the royal family and the nobility— young men without any physical defect, handsome, showing aptitude for every kind of learning, well informed, quick to understand, and qualified to serve in the king's palace. He was to teach them the language and literature of the Babylonians. The king assigned them a daily

amount of food and wine from the king's table. They were to be trained
for three years, and after that they were to enter the king's service.

Among these were some from Judah: Daniel, Hananiah, Mishael
and Azariah. The chief official gave them new names: to Daniel, the
name Belteshazzar; to Hananiah, Shadrach; to Mishael, Meshach; and
to Azariah, Abednego.

But Daniel resolved not to defile himself with the royal food and
wine, and he asked the chief official for permission not to defile himself
this way. (Daniel 1:1-8)

POINTING YOUR CHILDREN TO GOD'S GOOD PLANS FOR THEM

By the time they reach the teen years, children need to be prepared to determine in their own minds that they will not defile themselves. To defile means
to profane, pollute, or make something unclean. In Old Testament times,
God's people were careful not to defile themselves physically (by eating food
God had forbidden in their dietary laws), sexually, ethically, or ceremonially
(by touching something God said not to touch, like a dead body). The kind
of defilement we want our children to avoid includes sinful thoughts, patterns
of life, or behaviors that would make them "unclean" by God's standards. Jesus
defined this kind of defilement in Mark 7:20-23:

> He went on: "What comes out of a man is what makes him 'unclean.'
> For from within, out of men's hearts, come evil thoughts, sexual im-
> morality, theft, murder, adultery, greed, malice, deceit, lewdness, envy,
> slander, arrogance and folly. All these evils come from inside and make
> a man 'unclean.'"

Teaching and inspiring our children to care about remaining true to God
and clean spiritually are lifelong endeavors. Our goal is to help them become
self-governing by the time they leave our homes. We can do many things from
our children's earliest years to prepare them. These preparations will take on

more urgency as they reach the "tween" years—especially if we didn't take advantage of an early start.

Parents can begin to use the following ideas while their children are still young, aiming to have the principles solidified in their children's lives before their early to mid teens. After that, our kids may not be off to Babylon, but they will be in a position of having to make their own moral decisions— ready or not. So let's get them ready. If your kids have already reached the tween or teen years without this kind of motivation being developed by parental training, it doesn't mean it cannot happen. In my own life, God did a miraculous work suddenly while I was a teenager. So, if that's your situation, begin to pray earnestly that God will make up for whatever time you have missed.

As in other areas of parenting, our goal in teaching purity is to wean our children from parental control to self-control. If we attempt to keep our children as children, we may miss prime opportunities during the years when they are quite receptive to instruction. If we don't progressively help them practice personal purity while it is time for them to grow up in every way—including spiritually—they may not be prepared when they face personal choices over which we will not have direct control.

On the other hand, if we accept the realization that our children will be faced with a natural progression of personal choices during the teen years, we can help them make that transition confident in what they have learned. I have eagerly looked forward to my kids' tween and teen years, and I have found this season of parenthood to be tremendously positive and rewarding. God wants our kids to grow up well, and he will help them do so. Resist the fear the world would put in us that kids will morph into monsters when puberty hits. Wise preparation on your part can make your kids' teen years a transition into the excellent future God has planned for them.

I draw the following advice from the model we see with Daniel and his friends, from a decade of helping parents work through this transition when I was a youth pastor, and from applying these strategies to the lives of our own children. I hope what I learned while working with other people's children, taught according to the Word of God, and practiced (successfully so far) with our own children, will help you now.

1. Help Them Establish Their Personal Relationship with the True and Living God

We must make sure our kids know *who* God is as he is revealed in the Bible. There is much confusion in the world as to what one means by "God"—as if whoever or whatever someone calls God is real. We must teach these basic truths about the Lord our God: He is the *only* God, the living God, all-seeing and all-knowing, a loving and merciful God. Most importantly, our children must understand that while we love people of other faiths with the love of Christ, there is *no other God* than God, and *besides him there is no Savior*.

> I am the LORD, and there is no other;
>> apart from me there is no God....
> from the rising of the sun
>> to the place of its setting
> men may know there is none besides me.
>> I am the LORD, and there is no other....
>
>> There is no God apart from me,
> a righteous God and a Savior;
>> there is none but me.
>
> Turn to me and be saved,
>> all you ends of the earth;
>> for I am God, and there is no other.
>>> (Isaiah 45:5-6,21-22)

Our children must believe that God has their best interests at heart. God loves them and wants them to have an "abundant life" (see John 10:10). They must be persuaded that God's rules and laws are for their protection and long-term happiness.

They must also possess a sense that they belong to God. Daniel and Friends would likely have committed Isaiah 43:1 to memory:

> But now, this is what the LORD says—
>> he who created you, O Jacob,
>> he who formed you, O Israel:
> "Fear not, for I have redeemed you;
>> I have summoned you by name; you are mine."

Likewise, our children must know God created them (that is, they did not evolve from some other animal). Teach them the wonders of Psalm 139, which tells how much God loves them personally. They must know that God redeemed them with the precious blood of his only Son, Jesus. They must know that God has called each of them by name and that they belong to him. Teach them Malachi 3:17-18, which confirms that they are God's treasured possession. Delve into the rich blessings of belonging found in Ephesians 1 until your children are assured that they *belong* to God, and nothing can separate them from the love of God in Christ Jesus (see Romans 8:38-39). Lead them to Jesus, as his sheep, then continually reassure them that they belong to him and he will never let them go (John 10:27-28). Make sure they understand that their salvation is based on the grace of God in Christ Jesus, not on their performance to earn God's favor. They will receive the desire and power to obey God because they do belong to him. Reassure them that they belong to God long before they hit their teen years, and that God will never leave them or forsake them.

When they enter puberty and begin wrestling with their emerging sexuality, along with experiencing a measure of individual freedom, they will discover that they are not entirely the "good little boy or girl" they may have thought themselves to be. This is a crucial turning point in adolescence. If kids do not understand that everyone has a sin nature, everyone has to wrestle with temptations and desires that are not godly, they may wrongly conclude this means they do not belong to God. Therefore, they may give up seeking to follow the Lord and stop resisting the natural inclinations of their human (sin) nature.

Prepare them to understand that they will discover their own unique weaknesses and temptations, but that does not mean that they do not belong to God. It does mean they may need to draw closer to God and to friends who will encourage them to stay away from temptations they are not prepared to handle.

2. Teach Them That They Have a Unique Destiny to Fulfill in Keeping with God's Dreams for Their Life

This is huge! Kids need to understand that God designed them as a unique masterpiece of his creation. According to Ephesians 2:10,

> For we are God's workmanship, created in Christ Jesus to do good
> works, which God prepared in advance for us to do.

"God's workmanship" is a phrase that describes a unique work of art or poetry by a master artist or poet. Our children need to know that God didn't just create them; he created them unique, the same way a master artist would create a fine, priceless work of art. That's why I love the picture of the frame around the girl on the cover of this book; it reminds us that our kids should think of themselves as God's priceless work of art meant to be displayed beautifully to the world. Everything about their personalities, physical forms, abilities—or so-called disabilities included—learning styles, talents, interests… Everything that makes them uniquely who they are is part of the masterpiece God made when he made them.

In the best-case scenario, we will recognize and affirm our child's uniqueness from her earliest days. Some parents may have to backtrack to undo a lack of affirmation, or even disparaging remarks. Yet it is never too late to begin to notice and affirm each child's unique design, with the understanding that God has designed each one "to do good works, which God prepared in advance" for him or her to do. This phrase can awaken our children's imagination to all the wonderful possibilities for their gifts, talents, even handicaps. It affirms that God made us as we are *for a reason.* God intends to one day use our design for some good purpose, which means God has a purpose for our lives and has made us as we are in anticipation of seeing us fulfill that purpose.

This knowledge has a powerful impact on a child's self-concept and personal motivation in life. It also has a powerful impact on our approach to parenting, as God's design is seen in the context of an often misunderstood verse regarding child-rearing. Proverbs 22:6 says, "Train a child in the way he should go, and when he is old he will not turn from it."

Let me quote pastor Charles Swindoll's comments on this verse from his excellent book *You and Your Child.*

As you read those words, perhaps you might assume, "I know in my mind the right way for that child to go. I'm the parent and therefore I know what he is to be. So I will set out to train him accordingly, so his life will fit what I know is right. I will apply the same kind of training to each of my children in the same way because they are all to go in the same way."

At first glance, Prov. 22:6 would seem to deny the idea of individuality. But I want you to know it is just the opposite. Here's why.

"Train up a child *in....*" The term *in* means "in keeping with," "in cooperation with," "in accordance to" the way he should go..., "according to his way." That's altogether different from *your* way. God is not saying, "Bring up a child as *you* see him." Instead, He says, "If you want your training to be godly and wise, observe your child, be sensitive and alert so as to discover *his* way, and adapt your training accordingly."[1]

I discovered the wonder of this truth with our second child, Taylor. One child is amazing enough. Then when the next comes along you discover how uniquely God has created each one. Our first, Casey, loved colors and books. From her crib, she would call out, "More colors! More books!" If I wanted any sleep, I would comply by giving her more color crayons and coloring books, or more picture books. When I took her on the carousel, she would marvel at the beautiful colors of the various wooden horses, carefully selecting the prettiest one.

Then along came Taylor. He wasn't interested in color, but construction.

My first clue was when he dismantled his baby swing by hand before the age of two. When I took him on the carousel, he didn't care which horse we chose. His eyes were riveted to the mechanism that made the horses go up and down while the carousel went around. His little hands mimicked the mechanism as he figured out what made it work the way it did. This fascination with how things work extended to every facet of his life, even when he was a toddler. When my girls had their first experience being sick to their stomachs, they were grossed out; not Taylor. The first time he ever threw up, he looked up at me with wide-eyed wonder and exclaimed, "Hey, how'd I do that?"

So throughout their lives, I have encouraged Casey (and my other artistic daughter, Haley) in their artistic pursuits, asking, "I wonder how the Lord plans to use such artistic talent?" With Taylor I ask, "What good do you suppose the Lord has in mind for you to use your talent for building?" Somehow I don't think it culminates with building his cat-trap-tions (various ways to catch our cat), or his elaborate Daddy-traps (where he rigs trip lines and stuffed animals to spring up or drop down on his unsuspecting father), or even his amateur BattleBots. But I do see these as evidence of emerging talents and interests God has built into him for some *good* purpose. Therefore, we encourage and direct this interest—to the chagrin of the cat.

When you discover, notice, and affirm each child's unique gifting or bent, make a connection between it and the truth that God has created him to fulfill a special purpose only he can fulfill. Teach children to be good stewards of their talents and begin looking for ways the Lord can use the gifts he gave them. This awareness will do several positive things for your children. It will create a positive anticipation of something wonderful the Lord has waiting for them; what better motivation for self-discipline and personal development! It will also create a desire not to miss the good works God prepared in advance for them to do.

If we teach our children that their talents are God's gifts to them, and what they do with those talents are their gifts back to God, they will be highly motivated to learn and grow in positive ways. They will also be less likely to get bogged down with the kind of self-hatred that can derail kids during adolescence if they don't have a sense of their own talents. Outlets in keeping with their developing talents help compensate for some of the self-doubt that comes during the teen years. Look for opportunities that match your child's gifts from an early age. Casey's longing for "More colors! More books!" translated into a job illustrating a girl's journal for Young Women of Faith when she was fifteen. Haley's analytical mind and good sense about how people are feeling were put to good use designing what went into the content of that same journal. So from an early age, they are *looking forward* to the good things God has planned for them to accomplish. A personal calling from God goes a long way in developing motivation not to mess up their lives or their chances of fulfilling God's dreams for them.

3. Teach Them That They Have a Path to Choose as They Venture Out into Life

Kids who feel their parents are trying to hold them back tend to rebel. Instead, if we begin to teach our children that soon they will be venturing out into life in ways of their own choosing, this gives them a sense of independence they long to have.

Teach them the promise from 2 Chronicles 16:9:

For the eyes of the LORD range throughout the earth to strengthen
those whose hearts are fully committed to him.

Assure them that as they venture out with their lives fully committed to God, he will watch over them and give them the strength and help they need along life's way. Just make it clear that they must choose their way carefully. Give them some tips for the road. Contrast for them the Bible's description of the "narrow way"—that is, the right way God says to go, which is more difficult but leads to a good life, indeed eternal life—with the "broad way" that most people will follow, which leads to dangers in this life (see Matthew 7:13). For those who never choose God's way, their path will take them to eternal destruction. Show them verses like Isaiah 35:8-10, NASB, which describe the

"Highway of Holiness," and Proverbs 16:17, which says "he who guards his way guards his life." Those who determine to go God's way all the way will have supernatural protection. Then reinforce that you recognize they will choose their path, and pray they will choose the godly one, because it leads to eventual—but certain—blessing.

4. Teach Them That They Have an Enemy to Conquer

Point out that ferocious beasts don't roam freely on the "Highway of Holiness," but those who leave God's way will be sure to find that they have to face the enemy, of whom God says,

> Your enemy the devil prowls around like a roaring lion looking
> for someone to devour. Resist him, standing firm in the faith.
> (1 Peter 5:8-9)

Our children need to know we have a real spiritual enemy, an evil foe who would delight in destroying them and keeping them from fulfilling the good purpose God has for their lives. Teach them what Satan is like: His nature is deceptive; he will promise them everything they want while aiming to kill, steal, and destroy their lives. The spiritual war we must all engage in is personal: There is a personal God who loves them versus a personal evil spiritual being who wants to harm them. As your children grow up, remind them that every time they say yes to God's will and what the Bible says is right, they are helping to overthrow the forces of evil in the world. Even young children love to be on the winning side in the battle between good and evil. As they get older, teach them more details about how to fight the good fight spiritually.[2]

Teach them that their temptations will not only come from the devil but also from the natural desires of their own human (that is, sinful) nature and the world around them. Discuss specific temptations they can expect to encounter: drugs, alcohol, sexual temptations, and their own natural desires that overtake God's desires. If you prepare them to anticipate such temptations, and to counter them, they will be better able to do so when they arise.

Tips to Help Kids (and Grownups) Tackle Temptation

Entire books have been written on how to handle temptation; however, here are a few of the most important tips for kids to bear in mind in preparation for overcoming temptations.

- The best way to beat temptation is to avoid it. Jesus taught his disciples to pray, "Lead us not into temptation, and deliver us from the evil one." Teach your children to sincerely practice praying that God help them avoid temptations whenever possible.
- God never tempts us to do evil. James wrote:

> Blessed is the man who perseveres under trial, because when he has stood the test, he will receive the crown of life that God has promised to those who love him.
> When tempted, no one should say, "God is tempting me." For God cannot be tempted by evil, nor does he tempt anyone. (James 1:12-13)

Even though God does not tempt us, every temptation can be considered a test God wants us to pass. At times God's Spirit will actually lead us into situations where we will be tempted, as the Spirit led Jesus into the wilderness to be tempted by the devil. We resist temptation the way Jesus did, by the power of the Holy Spirit and relying on the Word of God. Every time Jesus was tempted he responded with the Word of God, which he knew in relation to that particular temptation. Therefore, we can help our kids by teaching them specific Scripture passages, commands, and promises related to specific temptations. For example: In anticipation of temptations related to drugs and alcohol, teach them, "Do not get drunk on wine, which leads to debauchery. Instead, be filled with the Spirit" (Ephesians 5:18).

- Remind them that staying pure isn't just about what not to do; it's about the positive alternative of relying on God's Spirit for the power needed to resist temptation. They must pray whenever they find themselves being tempted, admit their potentially sinful desires, and ask God to cleanse their hearts and minds (the sources where their temptations are experienced).

- Teach them the progressive nature of temptation:

> But each one is tempted when, by his own evil desire, he is dragged away and enticed. Then, after desire has conceived, it gives birth to sin; and sin, when it is full-grown, gives birth to death. (James 1:14-15)

Kids need to know that temptations start with something they want. It can even be a desire that is not wrong in itself. It may grow to be wrong if they have to do something wrong to get what they want or try to get it in a wrong way (stealing) or at the wrong time (having sex before marriage). It can be a good desire that becomes an over-desire (eating too much candy) or desiring something that is always wrong (using foul language to impress their friends or getting drunk).

The progression goes like this: You conceive a desire…that desire can grow into a sin (doing something wrong or disobedient to your parents, which automatically makes it wrong, since God commands children to obey their parents)…that sin will grow (think of how a lie grows the more you try to cover it up)…eventually something deadly results. That can be the death of trust or actual death from the dangers associated with wrong behavior.

- The way of escape God promises comes early in the temptation process. God promises:

> No temptation has seized you except what is common to man. And God is faithful; he will not let you be tempted beyond what you can bear. But when you are tempted, he will also provide a way out so that you can stand up under it. (1 Corinthians 10:13)

- Flee first: There are some occasions when they will have to stand firm to resist temptation. The first and most reliable response is to *get out of the situation.* Kids need to be taught to "flee youthful lusts" as soon as they can see that a situation *might* lead to a temptation to do wrong. Otherwise, if they wait too long they won't have the power to resist, and the exit God offered will have been missed.

There are good Christian resources to deal with each of these areas of temptation. It's best to prepare and use such resources before they become needful. Some resources I recommend include anything written by Jim Burns (of YouthBuilders), *Every Young Man's Battle* by Stephen Arterburn and Fred Stoeker (dealing with sexual temptation), and resources recommended by Focus on the Family and FamilyLife.

5. As They Enter Their Teen Years, Transfer Personal Accountability to Them, Even Though You'll Continue to Be God's Agents of Discipline and Some Consequences

Whether parents like it or not, our teens will be making personal choices that will have lifelong consequences for good or bad. Instead of resisting this reality, empower your young teens to resolve in their own minds not to defile themselves. Daniel's parents surely laid out the curses and blessings listed in Deuteronomy 28 for him, and they urged him to "choose life" as it says in Deuteronomy 30:19. We should do something similar.

Teach them that they are free to choose, but once they have made a choice, they cannot choose the consequences. Think of several people you know who made right or wrong choices in their early teen years (or later). Talk about the choices they made freely and the consequences they could not escape. Point out examples of people who made wise choices that were difficult at the time but that brought about good consequences. Point out to them that the right choice is usually the more difficult choice, and that crowds usually go the wrong way. Instead of threatening to chain them to the bedpost before you ever let them be in a situation where they have the slightest opportunity to make a wrong choice, let them know that they are accountable to God and that they will live with the consequences of whatever choices they make.

For example, when talking about choosing to resist sexual temptation, discuss the predictable ramifications of sexual sin (including the use of pornography) and the varying degrees of risk: shame; dishonoring your body, which is the temple of the Holy Spirit; disappointing the Lord; guilt and disturbing your sense of closeness to God; risk of contracting sexually transmitted diseases or pests (such as genital crabs or body lice); pregnancy (for girls); possibility that any unborn child of yours could be aborted against your will (for boys); lifelong consequences to a child conceived; damage to trust and family relationships; dramatic change in future plans and dreams. Talk about the rewards of waiting until marriage to enjoy sex as God intended. In addition to talking about it, give them good books such as those in the True Love Waits series.

Once you have acknowledged their free will and that they could disobey God and you, as their parents, you hope and pray that they will seriously weigh all the ramifications and choose the path of obedience. Then common sense and our role as parents dictate that we limit their opportunities to be in tempting situations where it would be reasonable to expect sin could occur. In this case, that would mean not leaving a teen home alone with someone of the opposite sex.

It may help to explain that God's laws are like the law of gravity. You don't really break God's laws of how life works, but if you decide to disobey them, they may break you! Let's say someone decides he doesn't like the law of gravity. Perhaps it doesn't seem fair that things fall down to earth. Perhaps it looks like fun to jump off tall buildings. People are free to choose to rebel against the law of gravity by jumping off a building. However, that act of rebellion will not change the reality described by the law of gravity. The only thing that may be broken is their body. Likewise, God's laws and rules of life convey God's true knowledge of how life works. When God declares, "Do not be deceived: God cannot be mocked. A man reaps what he sows" (Galatians 6:7), that law is not really broken by someone committing a sin and seemingly getting away with it. In time, here or hereafter, that person will bear the consequences. If we help kids see God's revelation of his Law, which is an immutable law of the universe, they will be more inclined to learn to live with that reality in a way that is safe and good for them. By acknowledging that God has given them the freedom to choose—even to disobey—but that they will bear the consequences, we build in a healthy fear of God without inciting their sinful nature to rebellion.

The transfer of accountability can be combined with a positive look forward to God's best for them at a significant milestone in their lives. For example, on Casey's thirteenth birthday, Patrick and I took her out to a fancy restaurant and told her how proud we were of the young woman she was growing to be. We told her how from her youngest days we have been praying that the Lord would one day bless her with a husband who will love her as God would have her loved, and that she will be spared the pain of broken relationships many people suffer. Then we gave her a ring with a diamond chip inside a little heart. We told her that we treasure her in our hearts and pray she will keep herself set apart for the Lord until she is married. We gave her the ring and asked her to wear it as a reminder that her body belongs to the Lord as holy, and to wear the ring on her wedding finger until she actually devotes herself to the man she will one day marry. We also acknowledged that there would be times before that day when she might be in a situation to compromise her chastity, and that our prayer was that she would determine in her own heart (thus the heart on the ring) not to do that. Combined with our casual conversations about others whose lives had gotten off track by sexual sin and sexually transmitted diseases, this kind of approach makes for a powerful positive influence. It also acknowledges the truth that these kinds of moral choices will be made in the privacy of their own hearts, when we are not with them.

This kind of consequential training can begin when children are very young and continue throughout their upbringing. There are two categories of consequential learning we can employ. There are consequences we impose, such as telling a child to take out the trash before dinner or they will not get to watch television after dinner; then we follow through with the consequences if the task is not done. There are also times when we can let reality teach our children that they need to learn to trust and obey us as their parents, who know more about how life works than they do, especially if we are teaching them to obey God. One of these opportunities came when Haley was a toddler learning to drink from a cup without a sipper lid. I taught her to lift the cup to drink. One day she wanted to drink from her cup without the lid but with a straw.

So I told her, "Okay, put the straw in, leave the cup on the table, and sip through the straw."

She put the straw in, put the straw in her mouth, and began to lift the cup up. I stopped her and said, "No, if you do that your juice will spill on your face. Leave the cup on the table, and sip through the straw."

She looked at me with defiance, picked up the cup with the straw in it, put the straw in her mouth, and tipped the cup up. I let her spill her juice all over her face. Then I said, "See, that happened just like Mommy told you it would."

Then I repeated my instructions. This little tug of war repeated itself several times until finally she realized that her way was not going to work as she thought it would. This lesson in real consequences did not hurt her (or I would not have let her go that far). However, it did help her learn that the things I tell her to obey are for her good.

6. Do All You Can to Encourage and Facilitate Relationships with Faith-Full Friends Who Can Be Allies As They Venture Out into Life

One key to Daniel's success was his close relationship with faith-full friends who stood with him, stayed with him, resisted temptation with him, and prayed with him when they ventured out into Babylon without their parents. It is never too early to start praying for God to send our children faith-full friends with whom they can bond and develop deep relationships. First Corinthians 15:33 says, "Do not be misled: 'Bad company corrupts good character.'"

Don't just keep your kids away from bad company; go on the offensive by praying for and doing all you can to help them stay in good company. When we made this one of our highest priorities, God worked with us in response to our prayers. He will do the same for you.

When Casey was in sixth grade, she asked to go to Christian school. We transferred her, and unfortunately the small class she transferred into had about six girls who had been together since kindergarten. They were not interested in including a new girl in their group. Casey cried a lot in sixth grade; she still says it was the worst year of her life. That was not what we hoped for! Knowing how vital it is to have strong Christian friends going into junior high, and seeing how broken-hearted she was, we told Casey that God cared deeply about whether she had close friends. We assured her that God had just the friend for her out there somewhere.

So we took this need to the Lord in prayer. We decided to homeschool Casey for her seventh-grade year because she was still emotionally troubled by the rejection she experienced from her peers. Our only hesitation was that she would not have a way to find that friend we were praying God would send. But we trusted that God could figure that out. My husband, Pat, home-schooled her that year while I worked writing and speaking.

We listened to what was on Casey's heart and considered what we thought a girl like Casey needed in a friend. Then we prayed with Casey, quite specifically. We asked God for (1) a friend who was a Christian or would become a Christian, (2) someone who lived close to our house, (3) someone Casey could laugh with, since she'd been so sad, and (4) someone intelligent but fun. A few weeks later, we met Darcy at a yard sale a few blocks from our house. She and Casey had gone to the same elementary school but were on different tracks and didn't know each other. Oh, how God has answered our prayer, exceedingly and abundantly more than we could have imagined.

Darcy and Casey can hardly be together *without* laughing. On some nights during Casey's high-school years, Pat and I would just look at each other as we heard giggles and guffaws coming from Casey's room in the middle of the night. We'd say, "We prayed for that." Darcy came from a Christian family and later joined our Bible study and girls' small group. She has grown into one of the finest Christian young women I know.

She and Casey share common interests (God, art, and Disney animated movies). She and Casey both graduated at the top of their respective classes (attending different high schools), challenged each other in academics, and prayed together that God would make a way for them to go to Westmont Christian College. God answered all these prayers! Casey and Darcy are rooming together at Westmont, growing in the Lord, encouraging each other in their faith, prodding each other to do their best in academics and artwork, and giggling and laughing heartily!

If your children are already in their tweens or teens, and you didn't get an early start instilling the desire in them to determine in their own heart not to defile themselves, there is still hope that you can help them do so. Don't disregard this chapter just because it is more challenging to start when they are older. Instead, I suggest you get a few close friends to join you in strategic prayer for God to give you wisdom for your particular situation, and for the Holy Spirit to begin a fresh work in the hearts of your tween- and teen-aged children. God can show you ways to best begin applying these teachings even later in the process, and he can change your child's heart in response to your prayers.

As we help our children navigate both the practical and spiritual aspects of life in obedience to God's commands and in hopes of fulfilling God's purpose for their lives, we are helping them determine not to defile themselves.

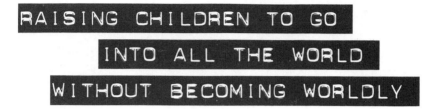

SEVEN

RAISING CHILDREN TO GO INTO ALL THE WORLD WITHOUT BECOMING WORLDLY

God had a greater purpose in sending Daniel and his friends into Babylon, but that only became evident as their roles were established there. Because these youths knew the Word of God, loved the Lord their God with all their heart, soul, mind, and strength, because they determined not to defile themselves, and because they chose to engage their culture while loving the pagans, God was able to use them to achieve a greater purpose. They became lights of the world. They helped preserve the Word of God, but they also helped proclaim it. As God blessed their obedience in all they were called to do, twice King Nebuchadnezzar made formal proclamations about their God to the people. First, after Daniel revealed the king's dream (which we'll examine in chapter 8),

> The king said to Daniel, "Surely your God is the God of gods and the
> Lord of kings and a revealer of mysteries, for you were able to reveal
> this mystery." (Daniel 2:47)

And later, after God miraculously delivered Daniel's three friends from the fiery furnace (which we'll examine in chapter 9),

> Then Nebuchadnezzar said, "Praise be to the God of Shadrach,
> Meshach and Abednego.... Therefore I decree that the people of

any nation or language who say anything against the God of Shadrach, Meshach and Abednego be cut into pieces and their houses be turned into piles of rubble, for no other god can save in this way." (Daniel 3:28-29)

Even when new administrations arose, Daniel's faith continued as a light to the Gentiles:

Then King Darius wrote to all the peoples, nations and men of every language throughout the land:

"May you prosper greatly!

"I issue a decree that in every part of my kingdom people must fear and reverence the God of Daniel.

"For he is the living God
    and he endures forever;
his kingdom will not be destroyed,
    his dominion will never end.
He rescues and he saves;
    he performs signs and wonders
    in the heavens and on the earth.
He has rescued Daniel
    from the power of the lions." (Daniel 6:25-27)

Daniel and his friends needed courage to live in that dangerous world, but the God who sent them *into* it stayed with them and protected them. Daniel's parents had to have been deeply concerned about the world their son went into; yet we see that God protected Daniel as well as his friends to achieve the greater purpose of using them as lights in that pagan, lost, and dark world.

Courage to One Day Send Our Grown Children into All the World

It is natural for us to want our children to be safe. However, there are times God calls us to die to self for the sake of his kingdom. Of course we should not let our children encounter dangers unprotected, but God asks us to be willing to let them fulfill his will for them, trusting him to protect them as they follow his ways. When our children are under our care, we need to protect them and teach them to take refuge in God. We must not forget that if we want our children to be godly, that means they will follow God's commands, including the command that—as disciples of Jesus—they will one day need to *go into all the world.*

Jesus' command was hazardous when he gave it to his first-century disciples. I suppose they, too, had parents who worried about the physical dangers of obeying the Great Commission. Wouldn't it be terribly risky? Indeed it would. Jesus warned them that the world would hate them and treat them as it had treated him. Jesus never suggested Christians find a safe place to hide until he came back. Like Daniel and his friends, all disciples of Jesus will anticipate some level of participation *in the world,* trusting God's promises that he will be with them wherever they go.

What better model could we have than Jesus, when it comes to providing peace, joy, and protection for our children? Jesus states his desire for his disciples to experience all of these, but it's not by keeping them out of the world. Look carefully at the prayer of Jesus for his disciples, then and now, to see God's plan to provide peace, joy, and protection in the midst of a perilous world:

"I have told you these things, so that *in me* you may have peace. *In this world* you will have trouble. But take heart! I have overcome the world."

After Jesus said this, he looked toward heaven and prayed: "Father, the time has come. Glorify your Son, that your Son may glorify you.

For you granted him authority over all people that he might give eternal life to all those you have given him. Now this is eternal life: that they may know you, the only true God, and Jesus Christ, whom you have sent. I have brought you glory on earth by completing the work you gave me to do. And now, Father, glorify me in your presence with the glory I had with you before the world began.

"I have revealed you to those whom you gave me out of the world. They were yours; you gave them to me and they have obeyed your word. Now they know that everything you have given me comes from you. For I gave them the words you gave me and they accepted them. They knew with certainty that I came from you, and they believed that you sent me. I pray for them. I am not praying for the world, but for those you have given me, for they are yours. All I have is yours, and all you have is mine. And glory has come to me through them. I will remain in the world no longer, but *they are still in the world,* and I am coming to you. *Holy Father, protect them* by the power of your name—the name you gave me—so that they may be one as we are one. While I was with them, I protected them and kept them safe by that name you gave me. None has been lost except the one doomed to destruction so that Scripture would be fulfilled.

"I am coming to you now, but I say these things while I am still in the world, so that they may have the full measure of my joy within them. I have given them your word and *the world has hated them,* for they are *not of the world* any more than I am of the world. *My prayer is not that you take them out of the world but that you protect them from the evil one.* They are not *of* the world, even as I am not of it. Sanctify them by the truth; your word is truth. As you sent me *into the world,* I have sent them *into the world.* For them I sanctify myself, that they too may be truly sanctified.

"My prayer is not for them alone. I pray also *for those who will believe in me through their message,* that all of them may be one, Father, just as you are in me and I am in you. May they also be in us *so that the world may believe* that you have sent me. I have given them the glory that you gave me, that they may be one as we are one: I in them and you in me. May they be brought to complete unity to let the world know that you sent me and have loved them even as you have loved me.

"Father, I want those you have given me to be with me where I am, and to see my glory, the glory you have given me because you loved me before the creation of the world.

"Righteous Father, though the world does not know you, I know you, and they know that you have sent me. I have made you known to them, and will continue to make you known in order that the love you have for me may be in them and that I myself may be in them." (John 16:33; 17:1-26)

In his excellent book, *Fearless Faith,* John Fischer gives an analysis of the implications of Jesus' prayer in John 17. I agree with his view:

He [Jesus] doesn't intend for us to be removed from the world, but to be protected in the middle of it. He doesn't want us removed from danger, he wants us surrounded by danger on every hand—but safe from the evil one.

It is important to realize… If Jesus prays for our protection, then it is because he knows God fully intends to protect us. And if he prays for us not to be removed from the world, it is because he has no intention of rescuing us out of the world. This is not a well intentioned wish on the part of Jesus. It is the will of God to leave us in the world and meet us with all the provisions and protection we need to be here and be involved in the world. Anything short of this is less than what God intends for us.

Two things are clear about these petitions from the last request of a dying man who also happens to be the Son of God. The first is that he expects us to be in the world, and the second is that in doing so we will

be in danger.... Notice also that there are no qualifiers to this statement—as in "keep the world from getting too bad so it isn't so hard on
them." No matter how bad the world gets, he still wants us in it.[1]

Let's assume we aim to obey God's commands and want to prepare our
children to go out. They cannot spend all their years under our direct supervision avoiding the world; if they do, how and when will they prepare to go
into it? So we have to start preparing them early enough so that the job is done
before they leave our homes. Yes, these are perilous times. But God knew that
when he chose us and our children to be living in these times. We can trust
God to protect us and our children as lights in this world.

> You, dear children, are from God and have overcome them, because
> the one who is in you is greater than the one who is in the world.
> (1 John 4:4)

God has not given us a spirit of fear, but of power and of love and of a
sound mind (see 2 Timothy 1:7, NKJV)! Our desire to keep our children sheltered *from* the world as long as we can is understandable but can be detri-
mental to their development. It is going to take courage on our part to
diligently prepare them and actually look forward to the day they will *go out
into* all the world as lights in the darkness. That doesn't have to be a scary
thing; it can be an exciting hope for the future our children will treasure as an
adventure.

ARE WE RAISING OR RESTRICTING THE LIGHT OF THE WORLD?

Jesus said people stay in the darkness because their deeds are evil. Therefore,
it's understandable that parents are reluctant to have their kids exposed to the
darkness that overwhelms the world. In the same verse Jesus said that God
didn't send his Son to condemn the world. We have to find some way to share
the light of God with a dark world. That will not be accomplished by staying

away from the world or by just condemning the culture of the world and the darkness evident in the world. God's answer was to send his Son *into* the world, and his Son sent his followers into the world after him.

> For God so loved the world that he gave his one and only Son, that whoever believes in him shall not perish but have eternal life. For God did not send his Son *into the world* to condemn the world, but to save the world through him. Whoever believes in him is not condemned, but whoever does not believe stands condemned already because he has not believed in the name of God's one and only Son. This is the verdict: *Light has come into the world,* but men loved darkness instead of light because their deeds were evil. (John 3:16-19)

Jesus also said,

> While I am in the world, I am the light of the world. (John 9:5)

However, he directed his followers to carry the light to shine in the world, saying,

> *You are the light of the world.* A city on a hill cannot be hidden. Neither do people light a lamp and put it under a bowl. Instead they put it on its stand, and it gives light to everyone in the house. In the same way, let your light shine before men, that they may see your good deeds and praise your Father in heaven. (Matthew 5:14-16)

Our lives and the lives of our children are to become shining examples before a dark but watching world. We don't thrust our young children into the dark of the world any more than we make them sleep without a night-light when they are toddlers. We are to train them up for the purpose of being the light of the world, not hiding from the darkness cowering in fear. How can our children be "the light of the world" if they are not out in the midst of the world on some visible level? Sometimes, even church culture or other parents can reinforce our inclination to perpetually keep our children away from "the world" and safely undercover.

The key to being at peace with having our children in the world is knowing that their hearts are not *of the world* and they are "keeping a clear conscience, so that those who speak maliciously against [their] good behavior in Christ may be ashamed of their slander" (1 Peter 3:16).

I recently had a conversation with a Christian mother whose twenty-year-old son, James, has become a light to the world in an unusual way. He and some of his Christian friends attend secular concerts and hang out at the mall with others their age whose appearance might draw a second look from some church folk. James is a solid Christian with a girlfriend who is also committed to Christ. While among non-Christians, he noticed that he often heard people asking if anyone had a light for whatever they might be smoking. James decided to carry a lighter to make contact with these people. At a recent concert, a guy asked if anyone had a light. James was the first with the flame, which was followed by a conversation that went something like this:

"Thanks. You're not smoking?"

"No, I don't smoke," said James. He and his girlfriend both smiled.

"Why?"

"We're Christians."

"Hey," the now-smoking guy said, "can I ask you a personal question?"

"Yeah."

"Are you guys virgins?"

What seemed like an odd and indeed personal question was a chance for James and his girlfriend to share their commitment to the Lord, which is demonstrated by their commitment to remain celibate until marriage. "Yes, we are, and we intend to stay that way until marriage."

The guy replied, with a nod, "That's good. I know some people who say they are Christians, but they're not virgins. That seems lame to me, like they're not living what they're supposed to believe."

James and his girlfriend were shining lights in the world. This young man saw testimony of their good deeds, as they brought glory to God without condemning him.

Another time James and his friends were at the mall having a Bible study, although they don't look like your stereotypical Bible study group. A middle-aged woman approached and asked if anyone had a light. Again, James was the first with the flame. Then she noticed their open Bibles.

"What are you doing?" she asked.

"We're having a Bible study."

"Wow, you young people are studying the Bible. That's nice."

It's not too surprising that when James' mother shared this story with women at a women's ministry leadership group, some of her peers were reserved in their enthusiasm. However, Lisa isn't worried. She knows her son is following the Lord and has found an unusual way of being the light of the world. Figuratively and realistically he understands that if he keeps his flame undercover, it will go out. Then who would be there in the darkness to offer a real light to those who need it?

PERHAPS WE NEED TO RETHINK OUR RELATIONSHIP WITH CULTURE

If our children are going to grow up to be such a light, neither snuffed out by going undercover in a Christianized subculture nor giving in to the darkness, they must be raised to think critically and creatively. This interview with Chris Seay from the *Dick Staub Show* (www.dickstaub.com) sheds light on this. Chris Seay was the founding pastor of University Baptist Church in Waco, Texas, and now pastors Ecclesia of Houston. He's also the author of *The Gospel According to Tony Soprano*.

> Seay: We believe that artists are our current day preachers and storytellers, so we do things through visual art and film and literature that we couldn't do otherwise. We believe that's the best way to tell the story of God.
>
> Staub: When you grew up, Christianity was also a subculture cocooned from the broader culture.

Seay: I still think one of the great fallacies of Christian thinking is this kind of garbage in/garbage out mentality. You know, I remember being 16 years old and being taught that kind of thing, "Stay away from culture because what you think you will absorb. See, your brain is a sponge, you'll absorb whatever you hear and see."

And I began to study Scripture and read passages like that in Daniel, where Daniel was educated by sorcerers, magicians, pagan priests, and astrologers. It says at the end of chapter one that he became ten times wiser in those things than the people that taught him. And yet, clearly, he wasn't a pagan priest or a sorcerer. Scripture was his guide through all of the mess of his own pagan culture, which I find to be very similar to our own culture.

Staub: What did you come to understand culture is about?

Seay: I've found it is a place where people are longing and asking spiritual questions. In music and movies, you see all of these deep spiritual questions. And the people who are supposed to engage those questions have removed themselves. We pull away from culture to the point where we can no longer affect it. Somewhere right in the middle is a really healthy place, but it's a difficult one to find.

Staub: How does one identify beliefs and provocative issues out of any cultural artifact?

Seay: Think critically. Do I agree with that? Do I not agree with that? Is this something that is explicit Christian truth?[2]

Last year I appeared on *FamilyLife Radio* to take part in a discussion called "Wizards, Hobbits, and Harry Potter." Our talk addressed similar questions as we considered the use of fantasy literature, movies, and storytelling as classic ways to reach hearts, minds, and emotions with tremendous impact.[3] Off air, the host, Dennis Rainey, posed an important question: "If this is a powerful way to communicate with the world, where are the young people who are being raised to become storytellers, authors, artists, and moviemakers who will keep Christ in the imaginative conversation of our times?"

I hope and pray that we are raising our children to be among them. Many Christian families boycott Disney. Our family respects that conviction, but we've taken a different approach. We have used Disney classic movies to teach our kids to think critically and identify glimmers of the gospel they could share with their friends through those stories familiar to most everyone (more on this in the next chapter). Our daughter Casey was once required to do a report on one of the most influential artists in the world today. She chose two Disney directors whose work she admires. She made a convincing case for the vast influence they have culturally and globally. She wants to have influence like that, too, as an artist, storyteller, songwriter—and as a Christian. Therefore, she wants to influence her world by one day working *for* Disney Animated Features (God willing).

When I recently visited her dorm, she excitedly showed me a film clip featuring Glen Keane, from the DVD of Disney's *Beauty and the Beast*. Mr. Keane, a senior animator for Disney, is a Christian. In this clip, he shared how one of the pinnacles of his career was being able to animate the moment when Beast was transformed into the prince. To him, this was a powerful depiction of the work of Christ in a human soul. Casey's face lit up as she said, "Mom, this inspires me to keep going!" I'm grateful that there are Christian role models like Glen Keane who are in the world, but not of the world. Thank God for such a man who is using his gifts and skills so well, shining a glimmer of the gospel to the world. I'm pleased that Casey aspires to do likewise, not just with her artistic contribution, but with the transformation of her own life that will shine in the darkness of this world.

In high school, for her senior project, Casey adapted Disney's animated feature *Atlantis—the Lost Empire* into a stage musical. She practiced her animation/artistic skills in costume design and wrote several original songs (since *Atlantis* didn't have any). Some Christians might object because a major plot point involves a crystal with mystical powers. Casey understands; she is familiar with New Age beliefs and does not share them. However, when queried, she pointed out that—according to the movie—"Atlantis sank under the ocean over 8,500 years ago. So, historically, they probably would have had pagan beliefs, as did Abraham before he left the land of Ur. Besides, 8,500 years ago Christ hadn't been born yet." She was thinking critically.

Her premise for the stage play adaptation was this: *The passing on of wisdom and knowledge brings renewed hope for the future.* She tied in—in her own thinking—the Shepherd's Journal, a book of knowledge that held the key to saving the civilization and people of Atlantis. She thought of this Journal in terms of how the Bible holds the key to saving us, and how the passing on of that wisdom and knowledge brings renewed hope for the future. It's all a matter of how you think about it. My delight was that she demonstrated that she *was* thinking about it, and able to think about it biblically and articulately.

Pat and I raised Casey to believe "…to whom much is given, much is required." She is faithful to diligently develop her talents: in academics, art, music, and drama. She wants to use these to the glory of God. Sometimes she expresses her art for the sake of art—and for whoever is blessed by the beauty of it. Sometimes she uses it for God's service, like when she illustrated a Young Women of Faith girls' journal titled *Hey! This Is Me!* Sometimes the development of her skills takes her into a very worldly environment, but we know her aim and her personal commitment to be in that world by the grace of God and for his purposes. When she was given the honor of being selected as a California Arts Scholar and invited to attend the animation program at Cal Arts Summer School for the Arts, we realized she would be spending a month among mostly non-Christian young people who were also talented in all forms of the arts. She eagerly accepted the opportunity to learn among them. Yes, she was keenly aware of their different worldview and worldliness. She was not attracted to it, but was instead driven to prayer for them while still developing her skills in hopes of being better prepared as an artist to communicate powerfully with her world.

THE JOY OF SENDING ONE INTO ALL THE WORLD

Casey graduated from high school this past June at age seventeen. The morning after graduation, I took her to the airport at 5:30 A.M. to catch her flight for a tour of Ireland, Scotland, and England with a group from her school. She had saved her own money to pay for the trip. Given terrorist threats against Americans, several people asked, "Aren't you afraid to let her fly overseas at a time like this?" We had considered the dangers and prayed for God's guidance. Pat, Casey, and I all had God's peace about the decision, understanding that God could keep her as safe in the air as on the ground and protect her just as well in Europe as in America. Therefore, we were able to share Casey's thorough excitement at her setting off for the adventure of a lifetime.

Besides, we trust that the Lord is sovereign over all the earth. He was going with her. When Casey and I found her group at the airport terminal, one of Casey's English teachers who had not originally planned to accompany the students was there. This teacher had prompted several good conversations at home, since she ardently holds spiritual views far different from ours. She set up her classroom according to the principles of feng shui. She believes in reincarnation and once told Casey she was "an old soul"—suggesting Casey'd lived several incarnations. To which Casey quipped, "No," then under her breath, "I just have wisdom from the Lord." Was I worried about Casey spending ten days with this teacher and perhaps being swayed by her views? Not a bit.

You see, in the years while Casey was in this teacher's class, we used their interactions to examine how our beliefs contrasted with hers (more on this in the next chapter). We discussed her teacher's beliefs (which are common in our culture) in light of the Bible. We prayed together with Casey for opportunities for these contrasts and Bible truths to be revealed in classroom discussions. This meant that our family spent time discussing *Hamlet, Beowulf,* other poetry, and various literary themes in a biblical light (although Casey had to bring us up to speed on some of the literature). Casey always showed loving respect for her teacher, even while having far different spiritual perspectives. Because of the way she has been raised, Casey is familiar with New Age beliefs popular today, but she is neither frightened by them nor attracted to them. She *knows* the Lord personally and believes that our God is Lord of all—even though that's not what most of her classmates or even her teachers believe.

One time in class during a discussion of Blake's *The Garden of Love,* the

poem was presented so as to give the impression that God or religion con-
stricted and brought death, killing the joy of life. Casey was pleased that she
had the opportunity to present a more positive view of the Bible's message by
putting the poem in a different light for the teacher and the class. Casey was
able to share with her class how chains of legalism bring death, but God's love
given freely to us causes us to flourish.

> For the law of the Spirit of life in Christ Jesus has set you free from the
> law of sin and of death. (Romans 8:2, NASB)

It took extra time, effort, and even continuing education on our part as
parents to help Casey and our other two kids engage in this kind of critical
thinking about popular beliefs, popular literature, and culture, but we see it
paying off. Never did I realize this as clearly as when I was driving away from
the airport that morning after sending Casey off to Europe. Tears streamed
down my face, but they were not tears of regret, nor fear, nor sadness. They
were tears of joy! By the grace of God, our goal for this phase of Casey's life
had been fulfilled. She was going out into all the world, literally the day after
graduation.

When she returned from Europe, I asked what was her favorite part of the
trip. She said, "It had to be our last day in London." Her English teacher and
a few students parted from the rest of the group to choose theater over sight-
seeing.

"We saw *Les Misérables* at The Palace Theater! Can you believe Ms. P. [her
English teacher] had never seen *Les Mis?* And while we were riding the London underground, I was able to share how the story of *Les Misérables* parallels
the message of the gospel!"

Casey, Darcy, and I had once taken a Sunday-school class on "The Gospel
According to *Les Misérables*." We'd studied Victor Hugo's classic novel as a
beautiful allegory of the ongoing conflict between the demands and impris-
onment of the law (seen in Javert's character) versus the grace of God demonstrated in the life story of Jean Valjean. We see grace extended to Jean Valjean

at the beginning when the bishop, who releases him after he stole the candlesticks, says, "I have bought your soul for God." We see grace extended through Jean Valjean when he befriends Fantine, when he adopts Cosette, and when he releases Javert instead of killing him. After being taught these parallels, our class saw the musical together and discussed it in light of its gospel themes.

I was very proud of Casey but not surprised to hear that she was able to share her faith in that way. Her attitudes and actions reflect our goals in raising her, which we have worked at little by little throughout the precious years we had her in our home. She can do what she does because her thinking and view of the culture in which we live have been immersed in the Word of God and tested by it.

OUR AIM AND PRAYER

Let us, along with our children, grow strong enough in faith to raise them to confidently go into all the world without becoming worldly. Let us be in the world, but not of it ourselves; not condemning the world, but seeking its salvation. Let us love people as God so loved them, let us give them his message in ways that they can grasp so that they may not perish but have everlasting life. Let us be a blessing to those who do not know him by revealing God's glory in the light of his love. Let us also make sure that before our children go out, they have been empowered by and are continually being filled with the Holy Spirit. He is the one who gives us and our children power from on high to be God's witnesses in this dark world—and power to remain holy as we do so.

EIGHT

RAISING CHILDREN TO ENGAGE THEIR CULTURE AND LOVE THE LOST

While most of the people of Judah were trying to shield their children from the dangerous enemies outside the walls of Jerusalem, there were those who understood that God's plan included sending them and their children into Babylon. Some of the prophecies said simply that God would send the nation of Judah into exile in Babylon—those who were not killed mercilessly because they refused to surrender as God told them to do. Other specific prophecies indicated that some parents would be separated from their children:

> Your sons and daughters will be given to another nation, and you will wear out your eyes watching for them day after day, powerless to lift a hand.... You will have sons and daughters but you will not keep them, because they will go into captivity. (Deuteronomy 28:32,41)

Some parents believed that the predictions of Deuteronomy and Jeremiah's repeated warnings of judgment applied to their generation. They knew they must prepare themselves and their children for a possible future of captivity in Babylon—whether together or separated. They probably were not comfortable with this reality, but they accepted it and prepared for it. Most likely, Daniel's parents were among these.

Scripture does not tell us what Daniel and his friends felt as they prepared to go to Babylon, but it does show us that these young men went into Babylon with courageous trust in God. Those whose parents taught them the book of Deuteronomy, as God commanded them to do, would have surely emphasized the hope of the promised blessing for those who obeyed God:

> Now it shall be, if you will diligently obey the LORD your God, being careful to do all His commandments which I command you today, the LORD your God will set you high above all the nations of the earth. And all these blessings shall come upon you and overtake you, if you will obey the LORD your God. (Deuteronomy 28:1,2, NASB)

We can only imagine what it must have been like for those parents to watch their young teens—however well prepared—be the first to go, never knowing if they would see them again, wondering if they were really prepared, wondering if God would prove himself true to his promises, wondering if they had done a good enough job of teaching their children God's Word, wondering if it was enough to prepare them to successfully survive a pagan culture. God had promised to set them above all the nations of the earth. I wonder if it crossed their minds that God might set them above all the nations by sending them out to live among them.

In the midst of God's judgment against their nation, we see God's blessings applied to those few who chose obedience and walked in faith. But that's not what the parents saw as their boys were being led away in chains to go into the pagan culture of Babylon. What they saw was a hostile culture systematically planning to destroy their children's faith, and even their identities, from day one.

It took faith and courage on the part of the parents to watch their sons go. They really didn't have a choice about sending their children to Babylon. I've had people argue the point that we Christian parents today have a choice whether or not to send kids into a pagan culture. I can't accept that fully; while we can do our best to shield them from sinful influences and activities, our culture has been taken over to a large degree by non-Christian beliefs, attitudes, and almost inescapable media images that amount to our children's living in a paganized culture whether we like it or not. Perhaps, like the parents of Daniel and Friends, we have *no choice* about whether our children will be submerged in such a culture; it has already happened. The choice we *do* have is to trust in God's promises of protection and blessing in the midst of such a culture and guide our kids to be the recipients of those promises.

First off, Daniel and his friends were renamed after Babylonian deities. They would have had to hold on to their inner conviction that God who formed them had called them by name. They had to know their identities before God to engage their culture without losing their faith. As soon as they arrived in Babylon, they were selected to go to the highest pagan institution of learning, the equivalent of Babylon University.

> Then the king ordered Ashpenaz, chief of his court officials…to teach
> them the language and literature of the Babylonians. (Daniel 1:3-4)

Daniel and his friends didn't shy away from this pagan culture; neither did they disobey God by practicing the forbidden things they were learning about. Rather, they engaged their culture while applying the best of their intelligence and diligence to their studies. They gained understanding of the language and literature, which would later put them in a position to communicate truth about the true and living God to this pagan culture. These Hebrew youth even outshined their Babylonian classmates:

> To these four young men God gave knowledge and understanding
> of all kinds of literature and learning. And Daniel could understand
> visions and dreams of all kinds.
>
>   At the end of the time set by the king to bring them in, the chief
> official presented them to Nebuchadnezzar. The king talked with them,
> and he found none equal to Daniel, Hananiah, Mishael and Azariah;
> so they entered the king's service. In every matter of wisdom and un-
> derstanding about which the king questioned them, he found them
> ten times better than all the magicians and enchanters in his whole
> kingdom. (Daniel 1:17-20)

Although fully schooled in Babylonian religion, pagan literature, sciences, and all manner of learning, they embraced *nothing* that contradicted their faith in the true God or his commands. They were, in that world, respectful of others who held differing beliefs, but these young men did not become one *of them*. This became evident when a crisis arose that no one but God could resolve. The king had a troubling dream, which escaped him upon waking. He ordered his magicians to describe the dream to him and then interpret it. When they could not, he ordered the execution of all his wise men, which included Daniel and his friends (see Daniel 2:1-13).

This crisis exhausted the powers, beliefs, and the best Babylon's pagan world had to offer the king. At that moment, Daniel and his friends turned to the God they had never stopped serving or believing in while dedicating themselves to learning the language and literature of their pagan culture and classmates. They did not have to repent of any ungodly interaction with the culture; rather, we see them in a unique position to stand before God on behalf of this king and those living under the threat of death. We see them ready to enter into God's presence to request compassion for their ungodly peers and troubled pagan king, along with concern that their lives also be spared:

> Then Daniel returned to his house and explained the matter to his friends Hananiah, Mishael and Azariah. He urged them to plead for mercy from the God of heaven concerning this mystery, so that he and his friends might not be executed with the rest of the wise men of Babylon. During the night the mystery was revealed to Daniel in a vision. Then Daniel praised the God of heaven and said:
>
> "Praise be to the name of God for ever and ever;
> wisdom and power are his.
> He changes times and seasons;
> he sets up kings and deposes them.
> He gives wisdom to the wise
> and knowledge to the discerning.

He reveals deep and hidden things;
> he knows what lies in darkness,
> and light dwells with him.
I thank and praise you, O God of my fathers:
> You have given me wisdom and power,
you have made known to me what we asked of you,
> you have made known to us the dream of the king."

Then Daniel went to Arioch, whom the king had appointed to execute the wise men of Babylon, and said to him, "Do not execute the wise men of Babylon. Take me to the king, and I will interpret his dream for him."

Arioch took Daniel to the king at once and said, "I have found a man among the exiles from Judah who can tell the king what his dream means."

The king asked Daniel (also called Belteshazzar), "Are you able to tell me what I saw in my dream and interpret it?"

Daniel replied, "No wise man, enchanter, magician or diviner can explain to the king the mystery he has asked about, but there is a God in heaven who reveals mysteries. He has shown King Nebuchadnezzar what will happen in days to come. Your dream and the visions that passed through your mind as you lay on your bed are these:

"As you were lying there, O king, your mind turned to things to come, and the revealer of mysteries showed you what is going to happen. As for me, this mystery has been revealed to me, not because I have greater wisdom than other living men, but so that you, O king, may know the interpretation and that you may understand what went through your mind." (Daniel 2:17-30)

Notice how God revealed *himself* through Daniel. He did this by employing the gifts he had given Daniel (being able to understand all kinds of visions and dreams), and the position Daniel and his friends had attained within that culture. Daniel was respectful of the king and the culture; he never referred to his God as "the God of the Hebrews," but rather as the "God in heaven." In so doing he introduced the only God to this pagan king in terms that met him at his point of need. Daniel acknowledged that none of the wise men, conjurers, magicians, or diviners, could reveal the dream, but he did not condemn them. Instead, Daniel's act of revelation actually saved their lives.

After hearing the correct description of the dream and its interpretation, which revealed what God planned for all the kingdoms of mankind, the king said to Daniel,

> Surely your God is the God of gods and the Lord of kings and a revealer
> of mysteries, for you were able to reveal this mystery. (Daniel 2:47)

Then the king appointed Daniel to a high position and gave him many expensive gifts. He made him ruler over the whole province of Babylon, as well as chief over all his wise men, magicians, conjurers, and diviners. At Daniel's request, the king also appointed his three friends to be in charge of the affairs of the province of Babylon. How's that for being blessed by being the head and not the tail, above and not beneath?

AN INEVITABLE EVENT

God's Word tells us that we are here on earth for the express purpose of going *into all the world*, and once there, we are to be lights of God's love for the lost (see Mark 16:15; Matthew 5:14-16). I've always endeavored to understand and relate to our culture from a position of firmly held Christian convictions. When Pat and I became parents, I was never persuaded that keeping our kids completely sheltered from the culture would prepare them to go into the world.

Many parents seem to lean toward isolating and insulating their children from the culture to keep them from becoming worldly. This always made me wonder when kids would be taught to encounter their culture, how they were supposed to learn discernment, and who would teach them—if not parents—

before they had to face the world on their own. I never bought the view that kids exposed to contrary beliefs or differing views of life would necessarily be corrupted by them. It seemed to me that we parents should begin helping our children understand the "language and literature" of their culture from a Christian perspective as early in life as possible.

Pat and I opted to teach our children to engage their culture while aiming to remain holy and love the lost. Perhaps some of our perspective will be of help to you while making the kinds of personal decisions all parents must make. The reality facing us is that kids today cannot completely escape their culture, nor can they avoid engaging other cultures as our world grows ever smaller. Therefore, preparing them to go into all the world includes preparing them to lovingly engage other cultures as well as our own, with a heart devoted to God and a biblical understanding of life.

Now that our children are tweens and teens, these issues are far less academic than they once were. We, like most parents I know, are less self-assured and far more dependent on God. I think we all can relate to the uncertainty, even with faith in God, that Daniel's parents must have felt when they realized their child was actually going out into that pagan world—without them. There was no telling what he would face. If we have prepared our kids to engage a culture foreign to Christianity without losing their faith in God, we can rejoice in their point of departure over the hope of seeing God's will fulfilled for, and through, each of our children—even though we cannot know what the future will demand of them.

RAISING KIDS TO ENGAGE THEIR CULTURE POSITIVELY AND PROGRESSIVELY

If we believe that the Lord our God goes with us wherever we go, we can dare to engage the culture with a positive attitude. We need to be sensitive to the Holy Spirit and keep a clean conscience, which will help us make personal decisions about what our children will be allowed to see, hear, and read, and where they will go. In this way we will not engage life from a place of fear. We teach our kids *what* to think in keeping with the Bible, but we also aim to teach them *how* to think critically as well.

Before we take on the culture, which includes books, movies, videos, music, arts, theater, events, all of life within a larger community of people, we need to know what meaning it already holds for our children. Consider the little boy who came home from school and asked his dad, "What is sex?" After dad's sweaty-palmed and overly long explanation of human reproduction, his son held up a school information form and said, "Would that be *M* or *F?*"

We should allow a principle of progression to operate with regard to teaching our children to engage the culture: (1) What is your child's emotional and intellectual maturity? (2) Can he understand and process what you teach in order to discern good from evil in new ideas? (3) Are images of violence or sinful lifestyles something your child can learn from under your guidance, or do they present too high a risk (for example, will your child simply imitate what he sees)? There is great value in discussing characters who are doing things your child is taught not to do, thereby letting him learn from someone else's mistakes (think of Huck Finn). Stories that present a complex moral situation in which a character must decide whether to break lesser rules to uphold a greater principle are also valuable. Almost any story can become useful *if* parents will participate with the child and use it as a springboard back into the Bible. We should never expect any secular story or media influence to do the job God gave us to do, and our job can only be done well when we put everything into the context of biblical truth.

Given that caveat, here are some guidelines for the kind of progression involved in teaching our children to engage their culture positively:

1. First, keep them completely away from things that you have not prepared them to process, anything that would lead them to participate in or emulate something wrong. Tell them what these things are. When Casey was in sixth grade, she wanted to look at *Seventeen* magazine. We decided the material was inappropriate, said no, and turned her interest to other reading material.

2. When they are mature enough for you to help them process these things, review the item with them, pointing out anything that you find objectionable, and explaining why. Whenever your reasoning is based on a direct command from the Bible, go there. Let them read it.

3. When you watch, read, or listen to something with your children, ask them questions about what they like or don't like. Find out why. Ask if they can pick out anything in the material that represents feelings they have or questions they've thought about. Ask if it reminds them of any of their friends, or if they can see anything in it that relates to Bible teachings. Listen with an ear for whether they are learning to sort out the good from the bad.

4. All along parents should carefully supervise and exercise control over what children are allowed to take in or participate in. Children are under our protection and authority; therefore, their well-being is our responsibility before God. We parents need the guidance of the Holy Spirit to make good choices for them until they reach an age of accountability and demonstrate the ability to make good choices for themselves. We practice discernment first on their behalf by telling them specifically what they must avoid (and enforce those rules). When they demonstrate the ability to choose that which is good and of redeeming value and avoid the bad (according to your definition, which you have identified for them from a biblical worldview), it becomes reasonable to gradually shift your control and allow them the freedom to make their own choices if you can do so with a clear conscience. Let me offer this example: Power Rangers were extremely popular when Taylor was five and six. We couldn't escape being bombarded with the excitement his friends and classmates (not to mention the toy stores and media) were generating over Power Rangers. He *wanted* to watch and play Power Rangers with his friends. Each episode of the television show followed a simple formula, which I was able to present as a parable of spiritual warfare (see below), so our only remaining concern was

that the kids might imitate the martial arts moves—without the training and discipline—and someone could get hurt. So we told Taylor plainly that the only way he could watch the show was if we were with him and there was no personal combat or physical violence between him and his friends. He agreed to only use action figures to play out the battles between good and evil. As long as Taylor and his friends obeyed this restriction, they could watch and play Power Rangers at our house. Taylor was self-motivated; he helped us communicate our rules to his friends. They willingly followed the rules. Plus, their play reinforced the Bible lessons we had taught Taylor about the spiritual battle between good and evil.

5. If you are assured that they have developed necessary skills of discernment, let them view or read the items in question selectively. Anything that causes them to sin will never be okay, and discernment will simply help them understand that. You may wonder if children can exercise such discernment before we're sure they are operating under the direction of the Holy Spirit. Pat and I tend to operate on the belief that we parents are the ones who need to be guided by the Holy Spirit while our children are young; they are to be guided by obedience to their parents and submission to parental authority. As they get older (especially after they have accepted Christ and are learning personal obedience to God, are following the leading of the Holy Spirit, and have developed a biblically informed conscience), they will begin to transition into making their own wise choices about how to handle cultural influences. For example, when Casey became a high-schooler, we decided she was mature enough to sort out the good from the bad in *Seventeen*. We began by reading it together. I had her go through one issue and show me articles she planned to read, which she skipped, and those she read but disagreed with. Then we talked about the issues that her peers were talking about. I was able to help her put her culture in a biblical context and practice articulating her views, which differed from most of the articles because hers were guided by the Bible.

6. Watch carefully to see what effect the exposure is having, and make necessary adjustments. At every stage of allowing kids to venture further into cultural influences, parents must closely monitor what is going on in their children's thinking, spirits, self-concept, and emotions. If something is causing them to become sullen, angry, violent, upset, or fascinated with anything dark, rescind the privilege until you can figure out what is having that influence. With *Seventeen,* we watched Casey react to their amoral stance with indignation. She became better able to articulate her moral stance in reply, but she often seemed depressed after her new issue arrived. When I asked about this, she began to share that those scantily clad, skinny models made her feel unattractive in comparison. We talked about the value of the articles versus the emotional upset. We decided to cancel that subscription in favor of one that focused on girls' accomplishments instead of primarily on an unrealistic body image.

If you don't have time to go over something with your children, it's best to postpone it. It's okay to say, "Sorry, I can't preview that, and you can't watch it until I do, or until I can watch it with you." However, if you find that you are saying this repeatedly, maybe you'll need to rearrange your schedule. Achieving this kind of progressive growth in spiritual maturity requires time together between parent and child. That's what I think the Bible is talking about when it says we are to pass on God's teachings when we rise up, when we walk along, when we lie down. If your child is being limited from things that might be okay just because you have no time to give it serious consideration, perhaps you need to reconsider your commitments to make time for this kind of interaction.

ENGAGING CULTURE WITH OUR CHILDREN INCLUDES...

Discerning Differences in Belief Systems

Daniel learned the literature and language of the Babylonians. Much of their literature involved a complex mythology and systematic worship of many gods. There were also many stories teaching how to appease these gods or protect oneself from spirits of the gods (who were believed to be easily offended). Daniel took all of this in, even though he did not adopt faith in these so-called gods. He held on to his belief that there is only one God, who created everything. He did this while being called by a pagan name, Belteshazzar, which meant "Bel protect his life." He never believed in Bel, nor that some pagan deity was his protector. Even as he learned all the details of these elaborate stories and pagan beliefs, he was able to see the contrast between those beliefs and his own faith.

Just because kids see something, even in a story or video, doesn't mean they will automatically accept it as true. We are human beings with the capacity to think, question, reason, object, and make up our own minds. Kids' critical reasoning ability can be put to use whenever they see or hear anything—if we teach them how. Encountering something that presents a perspective that differs from the Bible gives parents an opportunity to draw contrasts and point out distinctions. This helps them clarify what we believe and how it is different from contrary beliefs. For example, parents could view the Disney video *Mulan* and turn it into a discussion of the difference between religions that practice ancestor worship and our faith, which reveres but does not worship the godly people who have gone before us. We can also teach them to be respectful of those who hold such beliefs, but not to share those beliefs.

We have freedom as Christians to enjoy various kinds of art. However, if the art employs devices that might confuse our children, it is our responsibility to help them sort it out. In storytelling, for example, we need to help them understand important distinctions between fantasy and reality, between literary motif and the underlying meaning of the story. Many stories in classic children's literature use "magic," spells, and supernatural occurrences to take kids into an experience beyond their own. Such stories may also include witches, magicians, sorcerers, ghosts, diviners, and the like as characters in a fantasy story.

Whenever literary devices or fantasy elements overlap with real-world practices that are forbidden in the Bible, we can use that story to draw out important distinctions for our children. We can take our children to parts of the Bible that teach about such practices and people playing such forbidden roles in our real world. The story itself can be enjoyed, but we will need to discuss it first to clarify the difference between what they do in the story and what God forbids us to do in real life—whether it's *Wizard of Oz* ("Glenda is pretty, but the Bible says there is no such thing as a good witch"), *Cinderella* ("Even though Fairy Godmother uses a wand and says, 'Bippity-boppity-boo,' God says we are never to use spells"), or any Harry Potter books ("In our world, all witchcraft is the same as the Dark Arts taught at Hogwarts").

Daniel and his friends were tested on their knowledge of what they learned after three years of schooling in Babylon. This included their schooling in the practices of magicians, sorcerers, astrologers, and seers. They were found ten times better than their classmates. However, knowing all about these things, knowing the stories and even the practices that God had forbidden in Deuteronomy 18, was not the same as practicing these things. Likewise, we believe that parents can use popular culture as a means to discuss and teach children the differences between what we do as Christians and what is presented in cultural art forms—even some of which deal with things we would never practice.

Any disparate belief can become a teaching tool for an alert parent willing to discuss it with their child. Children who are raised to understand the language and literature of their culture are also best prepared to understand God's will in contrast. This does not hinder their ability to stand firm in personal devotion to God and to choose to follow God's commands.

Discovering Glimmers of God's Truth in Almost Everything

Once children understand the basic themes of the Bible, these need to be reinforced and made relevant to something they already understand. This can be done by teaching them to discover glimmers of God's truth all around them. We can redeem the language and literature by finding themes in popular culture that correlate to Bible truths and pointing out the parallels. We started doing this with our children when they were very young. Before we rejected something popular straightaway, we prayerfully looked for ways to redeem it by finding analogies to Bible truths. The kids also learned to look at everything to discover glimmers of the gospel.

Here are some of these analogies our family has discovered over the last ten years. Some of these I found, some they found (which showed me that their minds were on God's truths, and that they were growing to view all of life through a Christian lens).

Power Rangers. Power Rangers reminded us of Romans 12:21: "Do not be overcome by evil, but overcome evil with good." The Power Rangers face evil forces bent on destroying the earth. The teens had to wrestle against Putties, who attacked them. Sometimes they were attacked by giant monsters. To overcome the monsters they had to turn into a Megazord (a powerful robot created when the individual Power Ranger connected with others to form one body). This came to represent how Christians must continually be on guard to fight off evil wherever they encounter it. We may occasionally fight off temptation alone, but the Megazord is similar to the body of Christ. The only sure way we overcome an evil attack is to band together with other Christians. When the teen Power Rangers were in trouble, they spoke into a wristband to communicate with the Big Head. Whenever we are in trouble, we can pray, and God in heaven hears us and sends help. (Now, I wish I had recorded my son, at age five, telling his friend from kindergarten how this worked. It was precious!)

Batman vs. the Joker. During the Batman phase, Taylor noted that the Joker is a deceiver and Batman knows it. Whenever Batman battles the Joker, he wins by thinking about the kinds of schemes he can expect because he knows the Joker's character. We know the devil is a deceiver who tries to trick us into disobeying God so he can hurt us. When tempted, we must remember the devil's schemes and determine not to fall into his traps "in order that Satan might not outwit us. For we are not unaware of his schemes" (2 Corinthians 2:11).

The Little Mermaid. At age seven, Casey discovered several gospel parallels in Disney's *The Little Mermaid.* King Triton banished the evil seawitch, Ursula, from the palace. She still had powers and offered to use them to help Ariel get what her father restricted. Ursula enticed Ariel to disobey her father's rules. In reality, she was trying to destroy Ariel to get back at King Triton. God banished Satan from heaven, but there are still satanic forces that entice people to pursue their heart's desires through the pleasures of sin. In reality, Satan is trying to destroy us to get back at our heavenly Father, who loves us dearly.

King Triton can also be seen as a type of God the Father and a type of Christ. We see his fatherly love in the way he gives Ariel rules that will protect her if she obeys them. When Ariel rebels and goes her own way (like all of us do sometimes), she is caught in the seawitch's evil plot. She loses the very things she hoped to gain: love of Prince Eric, freedom, even her voice and body. She ends up as a shriveled seaplant in Ursula's garden of captive souls. But King Triton loves her so much he makes a deal with Ursula. He will give his life for hers. He takes her punishment, becoming a shriveled seaplant to free her. This is like when God so loved the world that he gave his only Son, Jesus, to die for us. Jesus took our punishment to free us from death.

You can even see a type of the resurrection at the end of the story. Ariel and Prince Eric battle the seawitch and defeat her. Then King Triton is "resurrected" to his former strength. In the end he gives Ariel what she tried to get for herself through disobedience. Likewise, disobedience to God and rebellion, like we saw in Ariel at the beginning, resulted in disaster. After she was freed from the seawitch's clutches, she gained understanding of the dangers of turning away from her father's protection. It was her loving father who gave her that which her heart desired. Likewise, God wants to help us fulfill our heart's desires in legitimate ways. We are to live realizing that disobedience and rebellion against God, who loves us, will not give us the happiness we seek. But when we turn to God, trusting that his love for us is best, and praying to him for our heart's desires, he will bless us with that which is truly best when the time is right. When I heard Casey explaining this to me through a story she knew, I knew she was growing in a real understanding of what God has done for us.

Kids have fun searching for Bible-related truth in characters and stories familiar to them. It's like a scriptural scavenger hunt. Ask your kids to look for a specific Bible theme in whatever they see and hear. Give them a specific theme, such as good vs. evil, self-sacrifice to save another's life, death and res-urrection. Then have them report back about where they find illustrations of Bible themes. Assign a specific verse of Scripture to look for, or give extra points if they can find a specific verse of Scripture related to their metaphor. You'll be surprised to see them discover Bible truths on *Nickelodeon, Fox Kids Club,* Disney movies, even in commercials.

Some of these cultural encounters can be useful to draw attention to dif-ferences between a contrary belief system and Christianity as well as to find glimmers of God's truth. As long as we first draw the distinctions and clarify that the Bible is our basis for truth, then we can exercise our freedom to redeem the cultural images with our kids by pointing out biblical analogies.

Determining When to Take a Stand

While teaching our children to be respectful of those who hold differing reli-gious beliefs from ours, we firmly believe that there are times when we must be prepared to take a stand for our faith and help others understand the dif-ferences in what we believe. We engage our culture, but we do not become homogenized; nor can we sit in silence if the culture twists the truths of the Bible. We can be tolerant of people of other faiths, but not of anyone twisting the truth of God's Word. When that happens, we need to courageously speak the truth in love if we have the opportunity, yet with respect and kindness toward those involved.

We need God's wisdom to know when it's time to take a stand, and to have the courage to stand when the time comes. Usually, taking a stand for God means we may stand alone among our peers. Occasionally, we might have to stand up to someone in authority over us at personal risk. Daniel took a stand when he told King Nebuchadnezzar that there is a God in heaven who could do what none of his magicians could do. He stood again late in his life when he refused to stop praying to God three times a day, even though a new law decreed that he could only pray to King Darius. Daniel's three friends took a stand when they refused to bow to the golden statue the king set up and demanded all to worship.

Recently, Pat and I saw that Taylor has learned well how to engage his culture in such a situation and take a stand. His test came when his seventh-grade social studies teacher began to explain the teachings of Mohammed in class. She wasn't just teaching *about* Islam in a historical setting, or Mohammed as a real figure who shaped history. She was teaching from a California textbook that required her to teach the five pillars of Islam from the Koran. It even had exercises requiring kids to imagine they were on jihad with Mohammed! (This was before the topic became a national debate after 9/11/2001.) Taylor came home and told us what the teacher was teaching and why he objected to it.

You see, immediately after the terrorist attacks, Taylor wanted to understand the radical religious beliefs that prompted the attack. A man at our church (seminary trained, with two Ph.D. degrees) who teaches an adult Sunday-school class held a special class to address these issues. He explained which tenets of the Koran had been applied literally. He also taught about the historical background of the worship of Allah, and the distinctions between the God of the Bible and Allah in character and history. Taylor and I attended that class. He took notes and paid careful attention, studying the handouts afterward.

Therefore, when his teacher began teaching about Islam, he had a biblical and reliable historical frame of reference. His concern was that the textbook spun the lessons, presenting only a positive view of Islam that ignored much of history and any of the radical Islamic views that motivated the terrorist attacks. What disturbed him most was that she also taught things about the Lord our God that were not true. She said Allah and the God of the Bible were one and the same. Taylor knew that, although both religions are monotheistic now, Allah originated as one of over two hundred tribal deities. Allah, the moon god (thus the crescent moon as a symbol of Islam), had been the god of Mohammed's tribe. When Mohammed gained supremacy over the other tribes, his god became the Most High God. When his teacher unintentionally misled the class about the nature of the Lord our God, she crossed a line that prompted Taylor to address the teacher in front of the class.

When Taylor spoke up, his teacher brushed him off. So he brought the matter to his dad and me. Pat called the teacher, who was quite defensive and pointed out that she was just going by the California State Department of Education guidelines. She read him the passage. To our amazement, it decreed that she was to teach the life *and teachings* of Mohammed to her seventh-grade students. She couldn't help it if she wasn't well versed in world religions. She never expected to be teaching religion in a public school. She agreed to be more careful handling the subject.

We were not sure whether we should take up this battle on Taylor's behalf or encourage him to handle it. Taylor went off to school the next day with the matter still unsettled.

When we picked him up, he said the teacher was explaining how Abraham took *Ishmael* up the mountain (not Isaac, as the Bible says), and she was getting confused on several other points, so that the Bible story was not being told accurately. Taylor raised his hand. When she called on him, he said, "Excuse me, you're not getting the Bible part of the story quite right."

The teacher replied, "Taylor, I'm just saying what is in the textbook."

Taylor said, "I'm sorry, but that is not correct. If you are going to tell the story, I think the class needs to know that what you are telling them may be in the textbook, but it is not the same as the story in the original."

Then his teacher said, "Taylor, how would you know?"

That was the opening he'd been waiting for when he packed his Bible into his already overloaded backpack that morning!

Taylor replied respectfully, "I know because I have the original story here from the original text. May I read it to the class?"

The teacher agreed. (I'm sure that Taylor's respectful demeanor and his previous good reputation with her made her more agreeable to this than if he had been generally combative.) Taylor took out his Bible, turned to Genesis 22 and read the Bible account to his class. Given the charged atmosphere, his classmates were very attentive.

Taylor has learned how to engage his culture with respect for other views and an ability to discern the differences between other religious beliefs and those in the Bible. He is prepared to respectfully take a stand when that is necessary. His general friendliness toward his peers (he was just elected class representative), his involvement in his culture (at the performing arts academy with many art forms), and his reputation as a good student as well as a Christian show us that he is growing up to successfully engage his culture and love the lost. All three of our kids are growing progressively in these ways, not being swayed by the world, but becoming brighter lights in it; therefore, we are growing in our confidence that they will be able to go out *into all the world* with the same kind of positive impact as those who went out of Judah to walk tall in Babylon.

I realize that our family has taken a unique approach to parenting. Our kids have been eased into this way of thinking over the course of their lives. I don't think that we have a magic formula here. We've simply adopted some ways to deal creatively and biblically with the challenges of raising kids in today's culture.

Perhaps you're wondering how to incorporate some of these approaches if you are getting a late start. Maybe you're in the midst of culture wars in your own home, where your tweens and teens are insisting on partaking in parts of culture that are downright destructive or immoral. Maybe your family has opted to isolate from culture as much as possible, so these ideas are questionable to you at best. Maybe your kids are reluctant learners, or maybe you're realizing that you've let them take in far more than they were mature enough to handle and you don't know how to backtrack now.

If you abdicated your role to control their choices early on, it will be harder to reclaim it during the teen years. Consequently, I expect it will be somewhat more challenging to take this up as a new approach. Here are some brief notes that may help in general terms:

1. If you have taken the approach of isolating them from culture as much as possible, *you may find that your kids' desire to have more freedom to engage their culture can help motivate them* to let you redeem some of the things you see as redeemable to teach Bible truths.

2. If you have abdicated your responsibility to monitor your children's participation in their culture and find they are being adversely impacted by the sinfulness and worldliness that has crept into their lives, *start with considerable prayer.*

3. *Become familiar with your children's favorite cultural influences and choose your battles wisely.* At times you might be able to substitute a Christian alternative for the kind of music or books they like.

4. I strongly recommend *finding an excellent youth group for them to become part of,* even if that means that they go to a different church for youth group or that your family changes churches. Teens desperately need to belong to a peer group where they are accepted and fit in. If you try to rip them out of their current peer group before they have another to shift toward, they will fight as if their lives depend on it; to them it seems that it does.

5. *Don't overdo it by suddenly making everything into a Bible lesson,* but begin to engage culture with them as you guide them toward seeing culture from a biblical perspective.

Whatever situations we find ourselves in, we will always need to be open to negotiation. I do not mean we compromise with sinful behavior, but we will always have to grapple with questions and weigh shades of influence in our kids' lives. Most families find that even parents who have a shared commitment to biblical values may not see cultural influences the same way (hence the battles for the remote control).

I hope some of these ideas are helpful to you, or that you may find a fresh approach you can use or adapt to best help your own children engage their culture without being destroyed by it. Overall, we parents must continue trusting the grace of God, using common sense, praying about everything, partnering with our spouse (if possible), and following our conscience by the leading of the Holy Spirit.

NINE

RAISING CHILDREN
WITH COURAGE TO WITHSTAND
THE FIRES OF LIFE

The postscript to the note left by the D.C. sniper in the fall of 2002 was chilling: "Your children are not safe anywhere at any time." That same kind of threat could have been written of the children living in Judah during the years Daniel and his friends grew up. The nation's conflict with Babylon was escalating; the book of Deuteronomy warned of children being killed and eaten by their own parents. After King Josiah died, life got worse and culminated with Babylon's siege against Jerusalem.

Even in captivity, Jeremiah continued to warn God's people that if they did not turn away from evil, further judgment would surely come. He predicted that the city of Jerusalem, its walls, and even God's temple would be burned to the ground. Imagine the fear that would grip the heart of any parent or child who heard these words from Jeremiah during that time:

> But I am full of the wrath of the LORD,
>   and I cannot hold it in.

> "Pour it out on the children in the street
>   and on the young men gathered together;
> both husband and wife will be caught in it,
>   and the old, those weighed down with years."
>   (Jeremiah 6:11)

Now, O women, hear the word of the LORD;
    open your ears to the words of his mouth.
Teach your daughters how to wail;
    teach one another a lament.
Death has climbed in through our windows
    and has entered our fortresses;
it has cut off the children from the streets
    and the young men from the public squares. (Jeremiah 9:20-21)

Judah's sin is engraved with an iron tool,
    inscribed with a flint point,
on the tablets of their hearts
    and on the horns of their altars.
Even their children remember
    their altars and Asherah poles
beside the spreading trees
    and on the high hills.
My mountain in the land
    and your wealth and all your treasures
I will give away as plunder,
    together with your high places,
    because of sin throughout your country. (Jeremiah 17:1-3)

Even with such warnings the general population did not turn to God in repentance. Ashes of fires smoldered just outside the city gates, where babies had been burned alive, sacrificed to a foreign god. Evil seemed unrestrained, while godly people suffered persecution, some even execution, if they dared to oppose the wayward king and apostate priests. A few exhibited courage to withstand the fires of life faced in that generation. Are there lessons from their lives we can use to instill courage in the hearts of our children, courage that will empower them to withstand the fires of whatever may come to their generation? Yes. We see these exhibited clearly in what happened when Daniel's three friends literally had to face such fires. Generations change, but God's nature and intentions toward those who belong to him do not. Therefore, since God was the source of their courage and deliverance, we can draw applicable lessons from their lives to help our kids have courage in our own perilous times.

AN INSULATING PROMISE

One wonders what their parents said to Daniel and his friends the night before they parted. Most likely they encouraged one another with the Word of God. Perhaps they recalled Isaiah's prophecies and God's promise that could give them courage for their journey.

> But now, thus says the LORD, your Creator, O Jacob,
> And He who formed you, O Israel,
> "Do not fear, for I have redeemed you;
> I have called you by name, you are Mine!
> When you pass through the waters, I will be with you;
> And through the rivers, they will not overflow you. [They would have
>   to cross the great Euphrates River on their way to Babylon.]
> When you walk through the fire, you will not be scorched,
> Nor will the flame burn you.
> For I am the LORD your God,
> The Holy One of Israel, your Savior;
> I have given Egypt as your ransom,
> Cush and Seba in your place,
> Since you are precious in My sight,
> Since you are honored and I love you,
> I will give other men in your place and other peoples in exchange
>   for your life.
> Do not fear, for I am with you." (Isaiah 43:1-5, NASB)

God was true to this promise. He went with them through the rivers, showing the four young men his honor and love in Babylon. When Daniel interpreted King Nebuchadnezzar's dream, he and his three friends were promoted to high positions. Shadrach, Meshach, and Abednego became governors. Even so, a time came when their faith in and devotion to the Lord was severely tested.

In the dream Daniel interpreted (see Daniel 2:31-35), God showed the king a statue depicting the kingdoms that would rule the world in the course of human history. The head of gold represented Nebuchadnezzar as king of Babylon (which ruled the world); the chest and arms of silver represented an inferior kingdom to follow his (Medes/Persians); its belly and thighs of bronze (Greece), legs of iron (Rome), and feet partly of iron and partly of clay all represented world kingdoms that would arise after Babylon. The statue was struck on its feet by a rock that had been cut out of a mountain, but not by human hands. When this rock struck the statue, the figure became like chaff swept away by the wind. But the rock that struck the statue became a huge mountain and filled the whole earth.

Daniel gave Nebuchadnezzar this interpretation:

In the time of those kings, the God of heaven will set up a kingdom that will never be destroyed, nor will it be left to another people. It will crush all those kingdoms and bring them to an end, but it will itself endure forever. This is the meaning of the vision of the rock cut out of a mountain, but not by human hands—a rock that broke the iron, the bronze, the clay, the silver and the gold to pieces.

The great God has shown the king what will take place in the future. The dream is true and the interpretation is trustworthy. (Daniel 2:44-45)

For some time King Nebuchadnezzar acknowledged Daniel's God as supreme, but there came a time when he was not content to be *only* the head of gold. He wanted to be king of the world; he wanted his kingdom to last forever. He commissioned a statue of a man ninety feet tall and nine feet wide, similar in fashion to the one in his dream, but golden from head to foot. He called together all his officials and commanded them to come to the dedication of the statue he had set up. Then King Nebuchadnezzar commanded them all to bow to the ground to worship his gold statue. Anyone who refused to obey would be thrown immediately into a blazing furnace. Shadrach, Meshach, and Abednego had decided long before the king's pronouncement that they would never bow to an idol. While everyone else bowed before the golden idol, three men stood.

Someone reported them (in chapter 3, NLT), telling the king, "They have defied Your Majesty by refusing to serve your gods or to worship the gold statue you have set up" (Daniel 3:12, NLT). King Nebuchadnezzar flew into a rage and ordered them to be brought before him.

> When they were brought in, Nebuchadnezzar said to them, "Is it true, Shadrach, Meshach, and Abednego, that you refuse to serve my gods or to worship the gold statue I have set up? I will give you one more chance. If you bow down and worship the statue I have made when you hear the sound of the musical instruments, all will be well. But if you refuse, you will be thrown immediately into the blazing furnace. What god will be able to rescue you from my power then?"
>
> Shadrach, Meshach, and Abednego replied, "O Nebuchadnezzar, we do not need to defend ourselves before you. If we are thrown into the blazing furnace, the God whom we serve is able to save us. He will rescue us from your power, Your Majesty. But even if he doesn't, Your Majesty can be sure that we will never serve your gods or worship the gold statue you have set up." (verses 13-18)

Nebuchadnezzar was so furious his face distorted with rage.

> He commanded that the furnace be heated seven times hotter than usual. Then he ordered some of the strongest men of his army to bind Shadrach, Meshach, and Abednego and throw them into the blazing furnace. (verses 19-20)

The king's furnace was the size of a room, with an upper chamber at the ceiling level through which the condemned were thrown in. There was an opening in one wall and a viewing area at a safe distance where the king could watch as his enemies were burned alive. The king, still seething with anger, sat in the viewing chamber with his advisors. When the three young men refused to bow, their sentence was carried out immediately. Soldiers tied them up and threw them into the furnace, fully clothed. The furnace was so hot that flames leaped out and killed the soldiers who threw the three men in!

> So Shadrach, Meshach, and Abednego, securely tied, fell down into the roaring flames.
>
> But suddenly, as he was watching, Nebuchadnezzar jumped up in amazement and exclaimed to his advisers, "Didn't we tie up three men and throw them into the furnace?"
>
> "Yes," they said, "we did indeed, Your Majesty."
>
> "Look!" Nebuchadnezzar shouted. "I see four men, unbound, walking around in the fire. They aren't even hurt by the flames! And the fourth looks like a divine being!" (verses 23-25)

The one who came to set the captives free had used the fires to release them from the ropes that had bound them. The ropes were all that burned!

> Then Nebuchadnezzar came as close as he could to the door of the flaming furnace and shouted: "Shadrach, Meshach, and Abednego, servants of the Most High God, come out! Come here!" So Shadrach, Meshach, and Abednego stepped out of the fire. Then the princes, prefects, governors, and advisers crowded around them and saw that the fire had not touched them. Not a hair on their heads was singed, and their clothing was not scorched. They didn't even smell of smoke!
>
> Then Nebuchadnezzar said, "Praise to the God of Shadrach, Meshach, and Abednego! He sent his angel to rescue his servants who trusted in him. They defied the king's command and were willing to

die rather than serve or worship any god except their own God. Therefore, I make this decree: If any people, whatever their race or nation or language, speak a word against the God of Shadrach, Meshach, and Abednego, they will be torn limb from limb, and their houses will be crushed into heaps of rubble. There is no other god who can rescue like this!" Then the king promoted Shadrach, Meshach, and Abednego to even higher positions in the province of Babylon. (verses 26-30)

What can account for such courage, even in the face of death? What lessons can we draw from their example to help our children develop the courage they will need to withstand whatever may come to their generation? I believe there is enough in Scripture that was familiar to their generation to explain their courageous actions and God's powerful deliverance. Let's look carefully at God's Word to them in Isaiah 43:1-5 and consider how to communicate these beliefs to our own children.

"Do Not Fear, for I Have Redeemed You."
We need to impress on our children that they don't have to be afraid, because God has gone to great lengths to redeem them for himself. The book of 1 Peter was written to Christians who were suffering persecution under Roman Emperor Nero. Some of them were being burned alive as human torches to light Nero's festivities. Peter reminded them of the reality of heaven, the rich rewards awaiting those who were redeemed by God. Therefore, they were taught,

Prepare your minds for action; be self-controlled; set your hope fully on the grace to be given you when Jesus Christ is revealed. As obedient children, do not conform to the evil desires you had when you lived in ignorance. But just as he who called you is holy, so be holy in all you do; for it is written: "Be holy, because I am holy."

Since you call on a Father who judges each man's work impartially, live your lives as strangers here in reverent fear. (1 Peter 1:13-17)

Instead of being afraid of what might happen in this world, they were to have an eternal perspective that created a reverent fear of being held accountable to God one day. This fear of the Lord would give them courage in the face of truly fiery situations.

We who have been redeemed by God belong to him. He promises that he will take good care of us whether we live or die. We have the promise of eternal life, which can give us courage even in the face of physical death.

> If we live, we live to the Lord; and if we die, we die to the Lord.
> So, whether we live or die, we belong to the Lord.
> For this very reason, Christ died and returned to life so that he might be the Lord of both the dead and the living. (Romans 14:8-9)

"I Have Called You by Name; You Are Mine!"

God knows us personally and knows all we are going through because we are called by his name and belong to Christ.

"When You Pass Through the Waters, I Will Be with You; and Through the Rivers, They Will Not Overflow You."

God's Word predicts that he will bring his people through deep waters of difficulty. He also promises to keep us afloat and not let our circumstances overwhelm us. What gets us through such times is knowing that God is *with us* and that he is *upholding us* no matter how turbulent our circumstances. When we know God is with us, we gain courage to know we will make it through somehow. Also, God actually sends the grace and help we need during those times. Remembering this promise can give our kids courage.

I think of the rivers as being representative of the ultimate crossing over, of facing death—our own or that of someone we love. At those times we need reassurance that God is with us and will carry us through. Assure your children that no matter what happens, God will be with them and will give them the grace they need when they need it to face anything, even death. If you are not familiar with the story of *The Hiding Place,* get the book or movie. When your children are old enough, let them see this courageous tale of how God helped his people get through one of the darkest times of human history. As Christians, sisters Corrie and Betsy ten Boom suffered in a Nazi concentration camp. Yet, they learned that "There is no pit so deep that God's love is not deeper still." When Betsy faced death, the story shows how God gave each of them the grace they needed. Such stories can build our courage when we see how God was with others in harrowing circumstances.

God will be with you and your children when you or a loved one must go through the rivers. We saw this illustrated beautifully a few years ago when Sarah, a friend of our two younger children, was playing at our house and someone accidentally sat on Gus-Gus the hamster (named after the sweet mouse in Disney's *Cinderella*). The poor little rodent died, and the children (ages eight and ten) were devastated and terribly upset. It was the first time any of them held death in their hands. Sarah wanted to go home, but her parents, Tullie and Sue, were out to dinner. So she had to stay at our house while we talked about death—why there was death (which God didn't intend in the first place), how Jesus came to conquer death, how there is life after death, and how Jesus' resurrection gives us hope of everlasting life. We read Bible verses about life after death, including this promise:

> Do not let your hearts be troubled. Trust in God; trust also in me. In my Father's house are many rooms; if it were not so, I would have told you. I am going there to prepare a place for you. And if I go and prepare a place for you, I will come back and take you to be with me that you also may be where I am. (John 14:1-3)

I know this verse doesn't apply to hamsters, but the experience of being confronted with the finality of death—even that of a tiny pet—raised serious fears and questions about the nature of death overall. We began with the phrase, "Do not let your hearts be troubled," to comfort their troubled hearts. We considered whether a loving God who created such cute furry little creatures might let them into heaven. We noted that not one sparrow falls to the ground without the Father's notice and care. We looked forward to the day when God would wipe every tear from our eyes. Somehow we ended up talking about how Jesus is actively preparing a wonderful place for us to live eternally.

It was unusual for us to teach the Bible in such detail to one of our children's friends. Sarah didn't go to our church. We didn't know her family's religious beliefs or background and weren't in the habit of going over such sensitive issues with other people's children. But that day Sarah was stuck with us. We had a backyard funeral. It was drizzling as we laid our beloved hamster to rest. Then we had a big roast beef dinner with lots of comfort food. We continued talking about how God has overcome death and how we grieve, but not like those who have no hope. Although, the kids still struggled with guilt and questioning, "Why?"

Sarah's dad picked her up at the prearranged time that evening. In the middle of the night, we received a frantic call from Sarah. She needed one of us to come take her to the hospital. She said her mom had stopped breathing and her dad had rushed off to take her to the hospital. Sarah was alone and scared. Pat raced over to get her, while Haley and I prayed for Sue and their family, especially Sarah. While Pat and Sarah were on their way to the hospital, I called ahead. Sue had died of undiagnosed lung cancer. When Sarah heard the terrible news, she was taken in to see her dad. He was terribly shaken and quite worried over how Sarah would get through her mother's death. She actually began to reassure him, telling him much of what we had discussed that evening about God's promise of eternal life. Tullie thought that Pat had filled her in with this information on the drive over. That was not the case; God had prepared Sarah by allowing her to be part of the discussion begun that afternoon with the death of the hamster. We all realized that God had used those unusual events to let Sarah know that he was with her as she went through this difficult river. We didn't understand *why*, but we knew God was at work in the day's events. Knowing God was with her gave her assurance that he cared and would be with her in the days ahead. Our kids also took comfort in seeing that Gus-Gus's death, which had so disturbed them, even though he was just a hamster, somehow fit into God's plan and greater purpose. That, too, reassured them that God was with them and helping them make sense of things and helping them get through the loss of their beloved pet. So no matter what loss our children may experience, they need reassurance that "through the rivers" God will be with them.

We did not pry to know Sue's faith after she was gone. I had previously given her my book *Dancing in the Arms of God*, which shares my testimony and the gospel message. I had previously shared the gospel with Tullie (using Harry Potter as a parable). Our immediate concern was to love and care for Tullie and Sarah in their time of grief. As our church ministered to them through the funeral and season of transition that followed, Tullie decided to trust Christ as his Savior. We asked Sarah if she wanted to do likewise. She said Taylor and Haley had already led her to do that, but she asked to be baptized.

"When You Walk Through the Fire…"

We should make sure our kids don't get the mistaken idea that those who trust in God will be spared life's fiery trials. If we teach them to expect to go through dangers and difficulties, they will not be inclined to interpret such troubles as a lack of God's love. First Peter 4:12 says,

> Dear friends, do not be surprised at the painful trial you are suffering,
> as though something strange were happening to you.

Jesus himself promised his followers,

> I have told you these things, so that in me you may have peace. In this world you will have trouble. But take heart! I have overcome the world. (John 16:33)

So we should teach our kids to expect trouble in this world, but also God's peace.

God doesn't say that we won't have to go through such trials, only that he will be with us in the fires. We are promised his presence always, and also his protection. Daniel's friends believed God's promise, even if they didn't know for sure *how* he would keep it. They knew God was able to deliver them, but even if he didn't, they had set their hearts to be completely attuned to God. They had given their lives to him entirely and would not bow to the idol that represented the kingdoms of man rather than the kingdom of their God. As they were being tied up to be thrown into that fiery furnace, they had courage. We aren't told if any of them expected such a literal fulfillment of God's promise to deliver them from a fiery trial.

"You Will Not Be Scorched, Nor Will the Flame Burn You."

When Shadrach, Meshach, and Abednego passed the test, proving their complete devotion to God, something miraculous happened. The very same fires that killed the soldiers who trusted in Nebuchadnezzar and his gods did nothing to their bodies or their clothing. Only the ropes that had bound them were burned. Surely this was a miracle, although I recently saw a scientific demonstration of how something similar could happen as a result of applying scientific knowledge about electrical currents. I share the story because it's amazing, and also because it contains a spiritual metaphor that could prove useful to our children, encouraging them to completely trust in God alone.

I saw this demonstration at the Association of Christian Schools International by a man called "The Million Volt Man." This scientist set up an electrical current of a million volts and channeled it through a metal bowl. The effect looked like purple lightning bolts emanating from the bowl in a dramatic display. He assured us that if any person touched that current when it was tuned to that certain frequency, it would kill the person instantly. He also said that he could adjust the frequency of the electric current, as one would adjust the radio waves to differing frequencies for different radio channels. Then, he said, it would be possible for the same million volts of electrical current to pass through his body without hurting him, although it could set a piece of wood held in his hands on fire. To demonstrate, he stood on the bowl, had the frequency of the current adjusted, then with complete faith and calm, had his helpers switch on the electrical current. Within seconds, the stick he held in both hands burst into flames. He took one hand away from the flaming stick, and the purple lightning bolts emanated from his fingertips. Wow! It was a dramatic display.

Therein lies a lesson that can give our children courage. God calls us to figuratively set the dial of our heart, mind, and soul to be in tune with his kingdom and his righteousness. We are to be wholeheartedly set at the spiritual frequency of obedience to God, not moving our spiritual dial to dabble with or switch our faith to any other spiritual source of power, protection, or teaching. We are not to "tune in" to the ways of the world or think we can live a little to please God and a little to please the world around us. Those who are attuned to keeping the first great commandment and to seeking first the kingdom of God can take refuge in the Lord and find safety even in situations that would otherwise destroy people who have set their lives to please someone or worship something other than God.

This reminds me of a great scene in the movie *The Mummy*, where one of the explorer's servants wears necklaces bearing symbols of all religions. When he is in danger of being destroyed by the mummy, he holds them up frantically—one by one—but none of them save him. Even the Star of David and the Cross of Christ have no power for him, because he was not truly tuned in solely to the Lord. He had no access to God's protective power. Those who think they can just add the Lord to their spiritual collection will find no protection there. But the person who solely devotes his or her life to the living God, the one and only God, trusting him to save, will be powerfully saved.

"For I Am the LORD Your God, the Holy One of Israel, Your Savior."

The three young Hebrews knew God as I AM, the God who revealed himself to Moses in the burning bush. Surely they had heard the stories of the Hebrews standing at the foot of Mount Horeb as it burned with fire. Their memories held vivid imagery of their parents describing the rumbling darkness and gloom, flashes of lightning, and how the Lord spoke to their ancestors. Their parents would have recounted how King Josiah's voice had boomed, his words filled with emotion and pleading, as they heard him read God's command:

> You saw no form of any kind the day the LORD spoke to you at Horeb
> *out of the fire.* Therefore watch yourselves very carefully, so that you do
> not become corrupt and make for yourselves an idol, an image of any
> shape.... And when you look up to the sky and see the sun, the moon
> and the stars—all the heavenly array—do not be enticed into bowing
> down to them and worshiping things the LORD your God has appor-
> tioned to all the nations under heaven. But as for you, the LORD took
> you and *brought you out of the iron-smelting furnace,* out of Egypt, to be
> the people of his inheritance, as you now are. (Deuteronomy 4:15-20)

They believed their God was a consuming fire. But God had proven that he wanted them to escape the iron furnace of slavery in Egypt to give glory to his name. They didn't know how God would do it, but they trusted God to somehow take care of them even in the fires—if they stayed true to him. The great I AM revealed in the burning bush and the fires of Mount Horeb was more real to them than the threat of the fiery furnace of Nebuchadnezzar. They may have gained hope from thinking that the God who delivered their people from the furnace of Egypt wouldn't allow the few who remained standing for him to die in the furnace of an idolatrous king.

"Since You Are Precious in My Sight, Since You Are Honored and I Love You..."

They believed that God is good, that God loved them, that God wanted to bless and honor them if they would love him with all their hearts, so they proved that belief by trusting God rather than taking their chances by turning away from God to serve the idols of their world. They were richly rewarded with God's presence, and even with honors from King Nebuchadnezzar, as their faith brought glory to God before the watching world.

"I Will Give Other Men in Your Place and Other Peoples in Exchange for Your Life."

God was faithful to them even in this detail. They lived, but the men who threw them into the flames died. Today we have proof of God's love for us in that he gave his only Son in exchange for our lives to redeem us from death:

> For you know that it was not with perishable things such as silver
> or gold that you were redeemed from the empty way of life handed
> down to you from your forefathers, but with the precious blood of
> Christ, a lamb without blemish or defect. He was chosen before the
> creation of the world, but was revealed in these last times for your
> sake. Through him you believe in God, who raised him from the
> dead and glorified him, and so your faith and hope are in God.
> (1 Peter 1:18-21)

"Do Not Fear, for I Am with You."

We don't know what our children may have to face in the course of their lifetimes. We can't know, but we do know that they don't have to fear because the Lord their God will go with them. We do know *whom* we have believed and that he is *able* to keep our children safe here on earth and hereafter in eternity. We should teach our children what Paul taught his son in the faith, Timothy:

> Do not be ashamed to testify about our Lord, or ashamed of me his
> prisoner. But join with me in suffering for the gospel, by the power
> of God, who has saved us and called us to a holy life—not because of
> anything we have done but because of his own purpose and grace. This
> grace was given us in Christ Jesus before the beginning of time, but it
> has now been revealed through the appearing of our Savior, Christ
> Jesus, who has destroyed death and has brought life and immortality
> to light through the gospel. And of this gospel I was appointed a her-

ald and an apostle and a teacher. That is why I am suffering as I am. Yet I am not ashamed, *because I know whom I have believed, and am convinced that he is able to guard what I have entrusted to him for that day.*" (2 Timothy 1:8-12)

TEACHING COURAGE IN PERILOUS TIMES

Here are truths we can teach our kids to give them courage in perilous times:

1. Remind them that those who stand for God and take refuge in him alone are "fireproof" eternally; God will get us through life's fires of suffering, and we will also escape the fires of hell. Teach them about the sovereignty of God. Read promises given to those whose hearts are *wholly* devoted to God: 2 Chronicles 16:9; Psalm 32:6-11; Psalm 91; Isaiah 43.

2. Collect verses that are promises to those who take refuge in God. Remind your children of these and memorize them together to encourage one another during times of difficulty. Just the other day I was going through a hard time when I received an e-mail from Casey that read: "Mom, I hope this helps: 'So don't get tired of doing what is good. Don't get discouraged and give up, for we will reap a harvest of blessings at the appropriate time.'—Galatians 6:9, [NLT]." At other times my kids have burst into song, singing a verse memorized at Kid's Fest (our church's summer program). "Be strong and courageous! Do not be terrified! Do not be discouraged! For the Lord your God will be with you, wherever you go!" (see Joshua 1:9). Whenever we teach our kids to memorize Scripture, we not only help them gain courage, but they can also share it with us when we need it.

3. Read them stories from the Bible as well as extrabiblical stories that inspire courageousness in the face of life's trials. I recommend the stories of David being chased by Saul, and how God protected him (see 1 Samuel 18–29). Good books include *The Hiding Place, Joni, Jesus Freaks,* and stories of everyday heroes and missionaries such as those

retold by David and Neta Jackson. Ask your children's pastor or local
Christian bookstore for suggestions of stories of faith and courage.

4. Teach them to let the peace of God guard their hearts and minds.
    Practice experiencing the peace of God in the way God says to do
    so. Philippians 4:6-7 says,

> Do not be anxious about anything, but in everything, by
> prayer and petition, with thanksgiving, present your requests to
> God. And the peace of God, which transcends all understand-
> ing, will guard your hearts and your minds in Christ Jesus.

This is good to memorize but better to practice. We all feel anxiety occasionally. During truly perilous times, it's normal to feel
afraid and anxious. When we do, we need to practice obedience to
God's command. We can teach our children to turn their fears and
anxieties into prayer requests. Here's how: Have your child tell you
something in particular that he or she is feeling anxious about. Figure out how to turn that fear into a request for God's help to deal
with whatever is causing the anxiety. Submit these to God, asking
him to give you what you think you need, but also trusting him for
what you really need; he may be doing something in the larger picture you may not understand. Then have your child give thanks to
God. Help him or her think of all the things to thank God for,
including hearing our prayers, loving us, being with us through
whatever makes us anxious or afraid. Thank God for hearing your
prayers and answering in some way.

When you practice doing this with your children every time they
are anxious or afraid, they may not get all the requested help from
God as they requested it. They will, however, receive what God
promises: His peace that passes all understanding will guard their
hearts and minds as he takes them through whatever fiery trials they
must go through.

5. Remind them of rewards to come. Just as Shadrach, Meshach, and
    Abednego received their rewards *after* coming through the fires that
    tested their faith, teach your children that a day will come in heaven
    when we will all receive rewards and give God glory as a result of
    how our faith was sustained and purified us in life's fires. Perhaps
    you can teach them or help them memorize these encouraging
    verses:

> Praise be to the God and Father of our Lord Jesus Christ! In
> his great mercy he has given us new birth into a living hope
> through the resurrection of Jesus Christ from the dead, and
> into an inheritance that can never perish, spoil or fade—kept
> in heaven for you, who through faith are shielded by God's
> power until the coming of the salvation that is ready to be
> revealed in the last time. In this you greatly rejoice, though
> now for a little while you may have had to suffer grief in all
> kinds of trials. These have come so that your faith—of greater
> worth than gold, which perishes even though refined by fire—
> may be proved genuine and may result in praise, glory and
> honor when Jesus Christ is revealed. Though you have not
> seen him, you love him; and even though you do not see him
> now, you believe in him and are filled with an inexpressible
> and glorious joy, for you are receiving the goal of your faith,
> the salvation of your souls. (1 Peter 1:3-9)

TEN

TEACHING CHILDREN MORALITY AND GODLY LIVING

Before and after the death of King Josiah, the people of Judah proved themselves determined to disobey God. Even though King Josiah had read the Ten Commandments and the Book of the Law to them, they did not turn from their evil ways as Josiah had hoped. It is important to teach our children the Ten Commandments and to intentionally communicate the basics of God's moral training to them. However, *just* teaching them the Law along with providing good role models will not give them the power they need to walk in God's ways. This chapter will not only show you some of the biblical basics kids need to understand as a moral framework for life, but it will also address how we—as human beings—find the power to live out holy lives in keeping with God's commands.

THAT WHICH REMAINS UNCHANGED

Where the moral training of our children is concerned, God gives us both responsibility and assistance. His assistance comes through these avenues, which we need to access and teach our children to bear in mind:

1. *God Himself:* Father, Son, Holy Spirit, who is alive, loves us, and offers to empower all Christians, guide us, and give us his wisdom. He will also hold us accountable for our behavior.
2. *Moral Absolutes:* the Ten Commandments and other commands given in Scripture.

3. *Godly Principles:* godly principles to guide our moral decisions (for example: the Golden Rule, love, protecting life, opposing injustice, resisting evil, doing good). These general guidelines are in keeping with the Ten Commandments but also help us apply them.

4. *Rules and Authority:* applicable laws, statutes, and ordinances. Such rules are specific applications of godly principles and the Ten Commandments to a given situation. The Old Testament gives rules specific to every facet of Jewish life: dietary laws, civil ordinances, military rules of engagement, domestic law, community and property rights, sexual limitations, religious observances, and so on. Some of these rules change under the New Testament, but the "spirit of the law" (which is to love the Lord with all our heart, soul, mind, and strength and to love our neighbor as ourselves) remains upheld for all. Some are lifted (like the dietary laws regarding certain unclean animals), while others become more strict (like the laws regarding divorce, which were fairly lenient under the Law of Moses, but more strict under Jesus' command). When we are not sure how the rules apply, we look to proper authorities to guide or arbitrate. Children ask their parents, whom God has given authority over them. In other situations the proper authority may be government officials, employers, military commanders, pastors, and so on, depending on the setting and who has authority in any given situation.

5. *Consequences:* Some of the laws, statutes, and ordinances decreed certain punishments by way of consequence under Old Testament law—including capital punishment for offenses ranging from cursing one's father or mother; practicing adultery, homosexuality, or bestiality; being a medium; blaspheming the name of the Lord; committing murder; making an unauthorized approach to God's sanctuary in the temple; and idol worship. Some general declarations predicted the kind of natural consequences one could rightfully expect, such as, "The soul who sins is the one who will die" (Ezekiel 18:4), and "No harm befalls the righteous, but the

wicked have their fill of trouble" (Proverbs 12:21). Other decrees warned of inciting God's wrath and judgment by national disobedience and injustice in the courts. In the New Testament, consequences may be amended, but the assurance of consequences is still in place.

6. *Mercy and Grace:* Even under Old Testament law, God exercised mercy and grace toward those who were truly repentant. In simple terms, mercy means you do not get the punishment you deserve under the Law. Grace is receiving God's favor that is undeserved.

A FRAMEWORK FOR MORAL TRAINING FOR EVERY CULTURE AND EVERY AGE

These six elements will always be useful for moral training, although one does need to study the Bible to fully understand how each functions in the kingdom of God. We need to train our children to understand these elements, and we need to reinforce their understanding by helping them practice moral decision making. When we do, we give them a framework they can use to make wise and godly decisions when we are with them, when we're not, and on throughout their lives.

Bear in mind that this framework I am about to provide may require your own further study and practice before you feel comfortable teaching it consistently to your children. It requires understanding that many Christians have yet to acquire and practice. Our generation has been raised—generally speaking—on small helpings of spiritual truth that may be compared to milk. Some are not acquainted with teachings about righteousness, which doesn't just come from book learning, but also by constant use.

The book of Hebrews says:

We have much to say about this, but it is hard to explain because you are slow to learn. In fact, though by this time you ought to be teachers, you need someone to teach you the elementary truths of God's word all over again. You need milk, not solid food! Anyone who lives on milk, being still an infant, is not acquainted with the teaching about righteousness. But solid food is for the mature, who by constant use have trained themselves to distinguish good from evil. (Hebrews 5:11-14)

According to George Barna's research on morality in the church today, the majority of churchgoers seem unfamiliar with "solid food." So I hope you will not let any shame or feelings of inadequacy hold you back. We all become mature as we practice applying God's Word in the discernment of good and evil. When we choose to learn this and practice it with our children, we help them mature into godly adults while we mature spiritually ourselves.

Many parents may feel that they should already know this stuff because of their age, but our generation was not raised in a culture concerned with reinforcing biblical moral standards. Therefore, some of us will need to overcome our lack of instruction for the sake of instilling godly values and good moral behavior in our children. If we do, we will see benefits for generations to come and the added blessing of watching our children grow up to be both godly and wise.

All aspects of moral development work within the context of the first great commandment. It is only as we and our children have a personal love of God and desire to please him that the rest of the moral training will function as it should. Without this, we risk falling into mere moralism, self-righteousness, holier-than-thou attitudes, and sins of pride. Therefore, the experience of a love relationship with the living God needs to be reinforced simultaneously with teaching moral discernment of good and evil (see chapter 5.).

Teach Them the Ten Commandments
Don't assume that your kids have "picked up" the Ten Commandments along the way, or that they know them by heart just because they have seen the movie. When our family took a pop quiz on the Ten Commandments awhile back, no one could list them all at first try. We live in a culture that has minimized these and consciously deleted them from public life. Get a good book

for kids your children's age and teach them each commandment, what it means for life today, and how we apply it as Christians. Dr. Laura Schlessinger has a book on the subject simply titled *The Ten Commandments;* Christian homeschool or curriculum publishers have also covered this topic. Find a resource that you believe is scripturally sound (ask your children's minister or pastor) and use it to make the Ten Commandments understood and relevant to your children.

You can find the Ten Commandments in your Bible in Exodus 20 and Deuteronomy 5. In Deuteronomy 6:6-7, parents are commanded to teach these to their own children. Here they are in brief (based on the NASB):

1. You shall have no other gods before Me.
2. You shall not make for yourself an idol. You shall not worship them or serve them; for I, the LORD your God, am a jealous God, visiting the iniquity of the fathers on the children, and on the third and the fourth generations of those who hate Me, but showing lovingkindness to thousands, to those who love Me and keep My commandments.
3. You shall not take the name of the LORD your God in vain, for the LORD will not leave him unpunished who takes His name in vain.
4. Observe the sabbath day to keep it holy. The LORD decreed that six days you are to labor and do all your work, but the seventh day is to be a sabbath of the LORD your God; in it you are not to do any work, but to rest as he rested.
5. Honor your father and your mother, so that your days may be prolonged and that it may go well with you on the land which the LORD your God gives you.
6. You shall not murder.
7. You shall not commit adultery.
8. You shall not steal.
9. You shall not bear false witness against your neighbor.
10. You shall not covet anything that belongs to your neighbor.

Explain that these commandments encompass God's absolute moral standard. Even though this holy standard of righteous conduct will prove too high for anyone to obey fully and continually, and is impossible for us to live up to perfectly apart from the power of the Holy Spirit and Christ in us, we cannot lower the standard. Instead, our failure to measure up in these areas should drive us to God for the power and help we need to live holy lives. (Theologically, this is something you will need to understand on a deeper level if you have not yet learned it.[1])

Teach Them Principles They Can Use to Make Moral Decisions

Explain to your children that God has given us principles we can use in everyday life to help us make general decisions about what is right to do in almost any situation, even where they don't have a specific rule. Sometimes they must choose between upholding the spirit of the law that is found in a principle or following a lesser rule. For example, the law "Do not murder," sets forth the principle that we should protect human life, but God's Law also allows for self-defense and just warfare. The principle (only do to others what you would want them to do to you) shapes the school yard rules (keep your hands to yourself, and don't hit other kids). However, if a situation arises where my son sees a group of bullies beating up his sister, a conflict may arise between the rule (keep your hands to yourself) and the principle (protect life). In such cases, kids should be taught to first go to someone in authority over the situation (playground supervisor or teacher). If no one is available to help, they may need to break the lesser rule of "keep your hands to yourself" in order to uphold the greater principle of protecting life. This process requires sophisticated thinking, which is why younger children should never be left to fend for themselves, but as kids get older they need to be equipped to make such moral decisions. As they mature and take on ever more sophisticated moral decisions, the following principles may help them discern the right thing to do.

Principles to Help Kids Determine the Right Thing to Do

- *God Is Watching You.* God always wants us to do what is right because he loves us and other people. Teach kids to ask themselves: Would I do this if I knew God was watching? (He is.) Would I do this if my Grandma was watching? (Or someone else whom I know loves me and wants the best for me, and whom I want to please.)

- *Play the Golden Rule Game.* What's known as the Golden Rule has roots in both the Old and New Testament. It comes down to: "Love your neighbor as yourself" and "Only do to others what you would want them to do to you." Teach kids to ask themselves, *Would I want someone else to do this to me?* If the answer is yes, then it's probably okay to do it to someone else. Whenever they have a decision to make or mention a situation at school they are struggling with (perhaps because their conscience is bothering them), don't just tell them what's right. Say, "Well, play the Golden Rule Game," then let them answer it themselves by applying the principle.

- *Measure for Measure.* This is sort of a negative version of the Golden Rule Game. A Bible principle in the Old Testament and the New teaches, "An eye for an eye, a tooth for a tooth" and "For with the measure you use, it will be measured to you." Teach kids to ask themselves, *Would I want to get back exactly what I'm about to dish out to somebody else?* If not, don't do it.

Teach Them Clear Rules and Respect for Authority

Kids respond well to clear rules, clearly defined consequences for rule-breaking, and consistent enforcement of those rules without partiality. (Any parent who has had to referee a game where one player tries to change the rules midgame knows this well.) Kids come with a built-in desire and need for fairness and clear-cut rules. It makes them feel safer.

We can also help our children make sense of seeming inconsistencies by explaining early the role of authority in relationship to rules for various situations. There are rules at home, school rules, playground rules, and table manners for casual and formal occasions. Grownups, too, have to follow rules and submit to authorities or pay the consequences. In each situation, the rules are enforced by the persons in authority over that situation: At school it's the teacher and principal; on the playground it's the yard-duty officer; at home it's Dad and Mom; at work it's the boss; in the community it's the police; and in the military it's the officer with greater rank. Teaching this concept early will help children develop respect for authority and know how to behave in various situations.

A Grid for Teaching Kids to Make Moral Decisions

Once kids have a relationship with God, understand the moral absolutes, godly principles, rules and authority, consequences, mercy and grace, these can form a grid in which to consider all of life. Each category of decision making should spark the questions in the chart on the next page to help evaluate the possible choices.

Let me give you a few biblical examples to give you the hang of this as a basis for moral training and discussion with your older children while examining any story or situation. (Please see examples 1 and 2 on pages 165-167.)

By making the Bible the basis for all moral training and simply using stories and life experiences as springboards back to the Bible, parents can make God's moral training relevant to children because it is tied to their everyday lives.

Teach Them the Interplay Between Moral Absolutes, Consequences, Mercy, and Grace

Some adults have tendencies to look to the Law and demand absolute adherence, even to the point of insisting we expose ourselves only to stories about people and characters who behave in strict obedience to every ordinance. Of course, real people and real characters don't behave that way—not even legalists, according to Romans 2. Others may get so frustrated by their failure to keep the Law, even though they try, that they just give up the battle and give in to sin. Others may be rebellious and throw out God's Law. Still others may use God's mercy and grace as a license to sin as much as they want. Their lives are immoral; they pay only lip service to God's Law. These "types" pretty much cover the range of human moral efforts apart from God's power for holiness in life. They relate to morality, but none provides an adequate basis for holy living.

Children and adults who want moral maturity need to understand the

EXAMPLE CHART

	QUESTIONS TO ASK	STORY OR SITUATION
MORAL ABSOLUTES	What commandments come into play in this situation?	
	Would I be breaking any of God's commandments? (Review the TEN.)	
PRINCIPLES	What principles are being upheld or protected here?	
	Would I or the character do this if we really thought God was watching and was going to hold us accountable?	
	Play the "Golden Rule Game."	
	Would I want *this* measured back to me?	
RULES AND AUTHORITY	What rules are being, or might be, broken?	
	Are there principles to be upheld that are more important than the rules?	
	Who is in authority over this situation?	
	Can whoever is in authority help me here?	
	What is being risked by breaking the rules in this situation? Is it worth it?	
	Is the risk (overall) of abiding by the lesser rules greater than the risk of violating the higher principles?	
CONSEQUENCES	What specific consequences could naturally be expected?	
	What are the risks? What's the very worst that could happen as a consequence of the choices being made?	
	How could the person making the choice get hurt? Who else might get hurt? How?	
MERCY AND GRACE	Is mercy present in this situation?	
	What punishment was deserved that was not imposed?	
	Is grace present in this situation? What favor was shown that was not deserved?	

EXAMPLE 1: EVALUATING THE STORY OF DAVID AND GOLIATH

	QUESTIONS TO ASK	DAVID AND GOLIATH
MORAL ABSOLUTES	What commandments come into play in this situation?	You shall not murder.
	Would I be breaking any of God's commandments? (Review the TEN.)	Is killing a military soldier murder? No, or God wouldn't okay it.
PRINCIPLES	What principles are being upheld or protected here?	Self-defense, protecting weak from a bully, obeying authority of God and king (military authority).
	Would I or the character do this if we really thought God was watching and was going to hold us accountable?	Yes, David believed God saw him and would reward his courage.
	Play the "Golden Rule Game."	Wouldn't want it, but evil must be resisted to protect innocent lives of those threatened by Goliath.
	Would I want *this* measured back to me?	No, but it was a military contest where not acting would have made it happen to David and God's army.
RULES AND AUTHORITY	What rules are being, or might be, broken?	Did this break God's command "Do not murder"? No (military).
	Are there principles to be upheld that are more important than the rules?	Yes, protecting innocent lives of those threatened by Goliath.
	Who is in authority over this situation?	God and king in authority.
	Can whoever is in authority help me here?	Both agreed David should do this.
	What is being risked by breaking the rules in this situation? Is it worth it?	David's life, freedom of nation, innocent lives, God's honor.
	Is the risk (overall) of abiding by the lesser rules greater than the risk of violating the higher principles?	It was worth the risk because to do nothing posed a greater risk, and fighting evil was necessary to save all God's people and nation.
CONSEQUENCES	What specific consequences could naturally be expected?	He would please and honor God if he won.
	What are the risks? What's the very worst that could happen as a consequence of the choices being made?	He would die in disgrace if he lost. Israel would go on being humiliated if no one stepped up to the challenge. The future safety and freedom of the nation of Israel would be threatened if he did not fight.
	How could the person making the choice get hurt? Who else might get hurt? How?	David might die. Goliath might get hurt, but that was God's will to stop evil.
MERCY AND GRACE	Is mercy present in this situation? What punishment was deserved that was not imposed? Is grace present in this situation? What favor was shown that was not deserved?	David showed no mercy to the enemy who came to kill, steal, and destroy. God used David to deliver the punishment Goliath deserved. He saw God's grace in his victory with God's help.

concepts of legalism, lawlessness, and license. We can begin teaching these concepts to our children and aim to help our kids avoid them in the "new life" in Christ that God wants for them—and us. Avoiding them will result in holy living, but we cannot experience it by mere human effort; rather, we must experience Christ living in us (see Galatians 2:17-20).

EXAMPLE 2: EVALUATING THE STORY OF DAVID AND BATHSHEBA (IN WHICH DAVID DIDN'T DO SO WELL)

	QUESTIONS TO ASK	DAVID AND BATHSHEBA
MORAL ABSOLUTES	What commandments come into play in this situation?	Love the Lord your God. You shall not murder. You shall not commit adultery. You shall not covet anything that belongs to your neighbor.
	Would I be breaking any of God's commandments? (Review the TEN.)	Yes (duh)!
PRINCIPLES	What principles are being upheld or protected here?	No good principles.
	Would I or the character do this if we really thought God was watching and was going to hold us accountable? "Play the Golden Rule Game." Would I want *this* measured back to me?	Wouldn't do it if we thought God was watching, breaks Golden Rule, would not want that measured back to us.
RULES AND AUTHORITY	What rules are being, or might be, broken? Are there principles to be upheld that are more important than the rules? Who is in authority over this situation? Can whoever is in authority help me here?	In addition to God's commands, David was also breaking the rule of where he was supposed to be as a military commander. After committing adultery with Bathsheba, he tried to get her husband to break the rule of not sleeping with his wife while the men under his command had to be away from their wives. Uriah was a man of character and refused. (Side lesson: Sometimes doing what's right costs you in this world when others sin against you.)
	What is being risked by breaking the rules in this situation? Is it worth it? Is the risk (overall) of abiding by the lesser rules greater than the risk of violating the higher principles?	God's honor, the kingdom, David's reputation, pregnancy, the life of the possible unborn baby, unknown consequences as a result of God's judgment that is harsher for those in leadership.
CONSEQUENCES	What specific consequences could naturally be expected? What are the risks? What's the very worst that could happen as a consequence of the choices being made?	Pregnancy, death penalty for adultery and for murder, family complications, hurt to his wife/s, hurt of betrayal to Uriah (who was one of David's "mighty men" and a loyal soldier), could lose the throne and cause national disgrace.

(continued on the next page)

- *Legalism* "finds itself so preoccupied with the details and the regulations as to lose the primary sense of the meaning God had in the legislation in the first place." It is "an external adherence to the letter of the law while disregarding the internal spirit—the true divine intent—of the law."[2] Kids need to be reminded that God's Law was

EXAMPLE 2: EVALUATING THE STORY OF DAVID AND BATHSHEBA ...continued

	QUESTIONS TO ASK	DAVID AND BATHSHEBA
CONSEQUENCES (CONT.)	How could the person making the choice get hurt? Who else might get hurt? How?	The family and friends of both people involved in the sexual sin. David had no idea of the long-term consequences! As a result of his sin, all his children were hurt: The baby born of the adultery died; much later one of David's daughters was raped by her half-brother (David did nothing, perhaps because of his own shame over giving in to his own lusts); the daughter who was raped was avenged by her brother who killed their half-brother (carrying out the law his father refused to enforce); that son of David (Absalom) was estranged from his father; the family turmoil fulfilled the prophet's decree that because of this sin "the sword would never depart from David's family"; Absalom rebelled, forced David from the throne, had sex with his father's wives and concubines, and was killed by one of David's generals, thus breaking David's heart.
MERCY AND GRACE	Is mercy present in this situation?	God showed mercy in not giving David the death penalty prescribed by law.
	What punishment was deserved that was not imposed?	Death penalty.
	Is grace present in this situation? What favor was shown that was not deserved?	God's grace was shown in that David was allowed to remain king, the next son (Solomon) of Bathsheba became king after David, and Solomon was allowed to build God's temple in Jerusalem.

given because God loves people, and keeping his Law is good for people. It protects us from the hurt we could cause to ourselves and others, as well as the grief we could cause to God.

- *Lawlessness* is different from sin. Sin is breaking God's Law (even though we accept that God's Law is right). Lawlessness is rebellion against God and his moral authority. It says, "I don't have to keep God's Law; I can do whatever I want." Forgiveness can remedy sin because the one who sins will be convicted that he has broken God's Law, will confess the sin, and can receive forgiveness (see 1 John 1:8-9). There is no remedy for lawlessness, however, because the person refuses to submit to the authority of God's Law. Those who are lawless are in danger of condemnation and God's ultimate punishment.

- *License* refers to the practice of consciously abusing God's grace for the sake of living sinfully. Jude 1:4 refers to those who are godless "who change the grace of our God into a license for immorality and deny Jesus Christ our only Sovereign and Lord." Even though God is gracious and merciful, we are not to presume on His grace. License is committing sins while thinking, *Oh, God will forgive me, so it's no big deal.*

> What shall we say, then? Shall we go on sinning so that grace may increase? By no means! We died to sin; how can we live in it any longer? Or don't you know that all of us who were baptized into Christ Jesus were baptized into his death? We were therefore buried with him through baptism into death in order that, just as Christ was raised from the dead through the glory of the Father, we too may live a new life. (Romans 6:1-4)

Kids and adults alike who live by license lead lives that are basically the same as their non-Christian counterparts, but they think they are fine with God. Their immoral lives deny that they (a) really belong to Christ, or (b) understand the grace of God, or (c) have learned to walk by the power of the Holy Spirit.

We do not know specifically how the parents of Daniel, Hananiah, Mishael, and Azariah raised their kids, but we do know that we have access to the same tools God gave them to work with. We also have an added dimension to life that revolutionizes and empowers our moral training: the New Testament ministry of the Holy Spirit.

THAT WHICH REMAINS UNCHANGED AND THAT WHICH CHANGES EVERYTHING

Galatians 5:13–6:5 teaches the connection between upholding God's absolute moral standard, understanding God's purpose behind it, the inclinations of our sinful nature, and the way God designed for us to actually live in keeping with the Law, that is, by learning to "walk by the Spirit." Zondervan's *Study Bible* notes say, "Life by the Spirit is neither legalism nor license—nor a middle way between them. It is a life of faith and love that allows a person to be led by the Spirit."[3] The Law (which continually points out our fallen nature), working in tandem with our conscience and desire to please God, will continually lead us to see our ongoing need to depend on Jesus (see the parable of the vine in John 15:5). The only person who could fulfill the Law perfectly was Jesus. We must never give up God's absolute moral standard; instead, we must allow it to drive us to Jesus, who can live in and through us by the power of the Holy Spirit. As we do this and teach our children to do this, their behavior will become guided not by externally enforced moral behavior, but by the "law of the heart," which is what the New Covenant aims for us all to experience.

While we impart unchanging Old Testament truths and moral absolutes of the Ten Commandments, our goal is to get from the Old Covenant to the New Covenant prophesied by Jeremiah and ushered in by Jesus (see Luke 22:20).[4]

"The time is coming," declares the LORD,
  "when I will make a new covenant
with the house of Israel
  and with the house of Judah....

I will put my law in their minds
>   and write it on their hearts.
I will be their God,
>   and they will be my people.
No longer will a man teach his neighbor,
>   or a man his brother, saying, 'Know the LORD,'
because they will all know me,
>   from the least of them to the greatest,"
>   declares the LORD.
"For I will forgive their wickedness
>   and will remember their sins no more."
>   (Jeremiah 31:31,33-34)

MORALITY UNDER THE NEW COVENANT

Jesus did not come to abolish the Law and the Prophets, but to fulfill them (see Matthew 5:17). This is done as we learn to operate under the New Covenant. We have to move from just imposing external laws to having God's Word and commands written on our hearts. We have to stop just thinking about external perceptions (what Jesus called polishing the outside of the cup) in order to care about the purity within (cleaning the inside).

Our kids need to understand that living a holy life that is in keeping with God's commands will involve an inner battle described in Romans 7. Understanding that this struggle is normal, even for Christians, will encourage them not to give up or think there is something wrong with them just because they struggle. The fact that their heart's desire is to keep the Law, even though there is a battle within them, gives evidence that they actually have the Holy Spirit within them contending against their sinful nature.

This understanding is especially important when they reach puberty and have to deal with awakening sexual desires. Let them know to expect this kind of struggle, but to learn to walk by the Spirit to overcome the sinful nature.

So I say, live by the Spirit, and you will not gratify the desires of the sinful nature. For the sinful nature desires what is contrary to the Spirit, and the Spirit what is contrary to the sinful nature. They are in conflict with each other, so that you do not do what you want. But if you are led by the Spirit, you are not under law. (Galatians 5:16-18)

Therefore, there is now no condemnation for those who are in Christ Jesus, because through Christ Jesus the law of the Spirit of life set me free from the law of sin and death. For what the law was powerless to do in that it was weakened by the sinful nature, God did by sending his own Son in the likeness of sinful man to be a sin offering. And so he condemned sin in sinful man, in order that the righteous require-ments of the law might be fully met in us, who do not live according to the sinful nature but according to the Spirit.

Those who live according to the sinful nature have their minds set on what that nature desires; but those who live in accordance with the Spirit have their minds set on what the Spirit desires. The mind of sin-ful man is death, but the mind controlled by the Spirit is life and peace; the sinful mind is hostile to God. It does not submit to God's law, nor can it do so. Those controlled by the sinful nature *cannot* please God.

You, however, are controlled not by the sinful nature but by the Spirit, if the Spirit of God lives in you. And if anyone does not have the Spirit of Christ, he does not belong to Christ. But if Christ is in you, your body is dead because of sin, yet your spirit is alive because of righteousness. And if the Spirit of him who raised Jesus from the dead is living in you, he who raised Christ from the dead will also give life to your mortal bodies through his Spirit, who lives in you. (Romans 8:1-11)

This may seem like a lot to get a grip on. It is. However, our kids are worth the effort. The concepts I have presented in this chapter can be fully understood as you avail yourself of the ministry of those in your church called by God who are gifted and trained to teach you and help you put these into practice in your life, and in raising your children. This kind of moral instruction cannot be done in a day, a week, a semester, or a year. God gives us about eighteen years to equip our kids to live godly lives in a culture determined to disobey. We can prayerfully take on this project while they are growing up. In the next chapter we will take a look at how the intentional moral training of our children works out in a culture determined to disobey God.

ELEVEN

RAISING CHILDREN IN A CULTURE DETERMINED TO DISOBEY GOD

The parents of Daniel and Friends, living during the decline and fall of the kingdom of Judah, had to contend with a culture growing ever more determined to disobey God. They recognized that they were God's chosen people living in a hostile world that did not honor their God. They had to try to help their kids distinguish between their beliefs in God as he revealed himself in Scripture and the conflicting beliefs of the world's other religions. They built walls to try to keep them separate from that outside world; however, they also came to realize that part of the culture determined to disobey God was not outside their walls, but inside—not just inside their nation and city of Jerusalem, but actually inside the walls of the temple of God. Theirs were challenging times.

King Josiah, the true prophets, and people who sought to obey God did their best to rid the land of all sinful spiritual attractions left over from the times of their forefathers. These immoral practices were not just found in the secular community, but were rampant in the lives and culture of the religious. When Josiah turned his attention to the house of the Lord, he found that sin permeated even the heart of Jerusalem. There was only one significant difference between the moral behavior of the religious and the secular: Those who went to the temple used their sacrifices and God's provision of forgiveness as *license* for their continued immoral behavior.

As unlikely as it may seem, our moral and cultural climate is not so different from the one in which King Josiah's generation was trying to raise godly children. I will leave it to you to draw any comparisons you see between their culture and our own. Their politicians were oppressive, injustice in the courts was rampant, and false prophets were celebrated while true prophets were arrested or put to death. Those who should have taught God's Word in truth had revised it so much that it had no impact against sin. God said,

> Also among the prophets of Jerusalem I have seen a horrible thing:
> The committing of adultery and walking in falsehood;
> And they strengthen the hands of evildoers, so that no one has turned
>   back from his wickedness.
> All of them have become to Me like Sodom, and her inhabitants like
>   Gomorrah.
> Therefore thus says the LORD of hosts concerning the prophets,
> "Behold, I am going to feed them wormwood
> And make them drink poisonous water,
> For from the prophets of Jerusalem
> Pollution has gone forth into all the land." (Jeremiah 23:14-15, NASB).

Look at what Josiah found and destroyed *in the house of the Lord!* This is an abbreviated list:

- articles made for Baal and Asherah (fertility goddess)
- a rooftop place to worship all the starry hosts (astrology)
- the Asherah pole (associated with sexually immoral practices as forms of worship)
- living quarters for male shrine prostitutes (practicing homosexuality)
- a place where women did weaving for Asherah

And elsewhere in the city:

- a place just outside the city of Jerusalem regularly used for burning children in child sacrifices
- chariots dedicated to the sun (nature worship) at the gates of the temple

- high places to worship other gods built by King Solomon east of Jerusalem for his foreign wives

Josiah's people may not have had to contend with the bombardment of sexual imagery, vulgarity, violence, and "adult themes" coming at them through television, radio, the Internet, and video games; nevertheless, these same evil forces stood at the forefront of the culture of their day. And yet, there was hope! A few did grow up to be morally upright, wise enough to encounter the bombardment of enticements without letting their moral compass be reset away from that which is true. There was hope for them and their children; there is hope for us and ours. Their children did not succeed by hiding within the walls, but by being prepared to guard their hearts as they went out into a culture determined to disobey God; ours can too!

PRELIMINARY PRECAUTIONS

In the fall of 2002, the Public Agenda released the results of their parenting survey "A Lot Easier Said Than Done." The *Washington Times* reported, "American parents worry most about whether their children will have good character and values and they see America's popular culture as their adversary, according to a new survey." They quoted Deborah Wadsworth, president of Public Agenda, as saying, "Parents today are struggling very hard to raise respectful, responsible, well-behaved children.... My sense from this study, and it's really painful, is that parents just feel absolutely abandoned. They feel as if they are being sabotaged at every turn.... Nearly half, 47 percent, said they were most concerned about shielding their children from negative societal influences."[1]

The parenting survey noted above said parents are concerned about shielding their children from "negative societal influences." These include drugs and alcohol, pedophiles and abductors, antisocial peer groups, and media messages. "Television was blamed for its incessant vulgar language, violence, and 'adult' themes, especially between 8 P.M. and 10 P.M."[2] Initially, we need to take precautions to spare our children and ourselves unfiltered bombardment from such negative influences. This involves common sense, the willingness to say no to things we deem harmful, and the ability to set up boundaries that filter out blatant assaults on good morals. Each family needs to prayerfully consider where to draw the lines and how to put such safeguards into effect. However, for the sake of example I will offer a few.

Guard Your Children

Some people remove the television and Internet completely from their homes. For those who don't want to eliminate the possibility of gaining positive input from these sources, there are some ways to minimize negative influences and maximize positive influences that also come through these sources. You can take extra time with the person installing a television satellite system and customize it to be child-friendly. Not only can you block specific channels known to carry sexually explicit programming, you can block channels targeted to males seventeen to twenty-four years old. These channels routinely have commercials that are meant to be sexually stimulating, promote drinking alcohol, and glamorize the lifestyle that goes with it. A password can override the block if one wants to view a sporting event or child-appropriate program. However, a parent needs to be in the room to immediately switch channels during commercials until the kids learn to and prove they can do this on their own.

Bear in mind that many Christian men admit to having a serious proclivity toward sexually explicit programming. (Bill McCartney of Promise Keepers told me that the one year they brought this up on an anonymous exit poll of men leaving Promise Keeper events, over 60 percent of the men answering said they struggled weekly with sexual sin or using pornography.) Therefore, if this is the case for the man of your house, you may decide together to have the wife/mom be the keeper of the password. What is deemed "adult" in our culture is often deemed immoral by God regardless of age.

There are excellent Web sites and books that give up-to-date information on how to create a safer Internet experience for children. However, none of these filters is a substitute for parental supervision and training. For information on keeping kids safe online I recommend *Kids Online* by Donna Rice Hughes, and her Web site www.protectkids.com.

We need the moral courage to say no to that which is morally inappropriate, even if it's in vogue or you're the only parent who seems to object. For example, today's popular style of dress is highly sexually suggestive, even among preteens and preschoolers! Therefore, parents must exercise courage to say *no*. Our goal along the way is to instill in our children their own personal modesty and sense of morally appropriate dress, but until they consistently demonstrate that, we must enforce standards of decency.

Since bad company corrupts good morals, parents need to exercise control and influence over relationship building (facilitating and promoting fun experiences and healthy relationships) with kids who exhibit good morals. Take a firm stand, before junior high, that you will not let them develop close and continual relationships with kids who demonstrate bad morals. This becomes more difficult in junior high and high school, so lay the groundwork early. The best way is to facilitate the positive relationships and to resist caving in to pressure to let your child hang out with a group that is blatantly ungodly. It is one thing to be acquainted with and "in the world," but another to develop a close friendship with anyone whose general character and trend of moral behavior are contrary to God's Word. Subject your judgment in this area to the leading of the Holy Spirit. At times parents must step in and restrict time spent with friends who are a bad influence. For example, we would not let our children go to the mall with a child who was known to shoplift, nor spend the night at a home where the child uses a Ouija board or practices Wicca. We would encourage them to be friendly with that child at school but explain that their limited time to develop close friendships needs to be focused on relationships with kids who share our values. We let them choose from that group, so we're not picking their friends, but we also exercise parental controls to help protect them.

APPLYING THE GRID

In the previous chapter, I introduced a grid that parents can use to help their children practice moral decision making. Once you and your children learn how to use this tool, you can use it in all areas of life as you help your children look at what they see and hear with moral consideration and practice in discerning good from evil.

These might include:

- reading Bible stories (some are unsuitable for children of a certain age)
- looking at secular culture and considering the ways of the world
- discussing current events on the nightly news
- looking at Christian culture (for good and bad examples)
- reading stories (fiction and nonfiction, fairy tales, folklore, legends, mythology, fantasy, science fiction)
- experiencing the arts (visual arts, plays, music)
- reviewing their own experiences
- sharing personal experiences

Before choosing to expose your child to something in our culture, the Bible, or true-life experiences, parents must first weigh the risk/reward ratio and decide if there is more to be gained than risked in using a particular opportunity for moral instruction. This should be done with much prayer, discussion between Mom and Dad, and consideration of each individual child's sensitivities, inclinations, age, and so on. Take these concerns to the Lord and ask the Holy Spirit to give you the wisdom you need to make these decisions. We are responsible before God to determine if our child will gain more benefit than detriment from any given aspect of life. If you, together as parents, feel the risk is too high, shield your kids from it; if there is sufficient benefit to be gained, don't shy away from using even pop culture to raise moral issues as a basis of instruction.

MORE TIPS FOR RAISING MORALLY UPRIGHT KIDS IN A DISOBEDIENT CULTURE

Unfortunately, our current moral climate is not supportive of God's moral standards. We see this in changing laws that are shaking the nation "free" from the restraints of biblical moral decrees. We also see a high degree of immorality being practiced by those who bear the name of Christ. A recent study showed that while today's Christian youth are more inclined to take politically conservative stands in keeping with the Bible (anti-abortion, support for prayer in school), their tendency to lie, cheat, and steal is about the same as their non-Christian counterparts.

This really shouldn't come as a surprise; statistics also show that Christian adults have adopted the immoral standards of the world in many areas of their behavior while proclaiming outrage over the socially unacceptable "sins of the world." Christians' comfort level with "socially acceptable sin" is every bit as dangerous—perhaps more so—as the possibility that Christian kids will adopt an out-and-out promiscuous or homosexual lifestyle (for example) because they heard about it from a tolerant teacher in public school. Statistics bear out that our kids are at great risk of falling into the "socially acceptable sins." They may end up, for example, going through several marriages because they never learned to think of divorce as a "serious" sin; many pastors and Christian celebrities have divorced without much comment from the Christian community. The Bible condemns both homosexuality and adultery (which Jesus defines as including divorce without the grounds of "sexual immorality," derived from the Greek word *porneia*—see Matthew 19:9). However, while there is a concerted outcry against homosexuality, there is almost nothing said publicly across the board condemning divorce and remarriage without scriptural grounds.

Since we live in a culture that is morally confused, we parents need to help our kids try to make some sense out of the confusion and not just go with the flow of culture—even the Christian culture. In addition to mastering the grid I presented in the last chapter, these ideas can also help our kids:

1. Bring Them Back to the Greatest Sin of All

Pastor John MacArthur writes:

> One doesn't hear the Religious Right arguing with much enthusiasm
> against pride or materialism. I haven't seen them mounting any great

campaign against divorce. They rarely even decry the sin of adultery. They are vocal against sins like homosexuality, pedophilia, abortion, pornography, and other shocking or perverted forms of sin. But they don't even deal with the worst sin of all. What's that? Consider this: If the first and Great Commandment is Matthew 22:37, "You shall love the LORD your God with all your heart, with all your soul, and with all your mind" [NASB], then the greatest sin would be any violation of that commandment. You want to talk about morality? Let's talk about *that.* You want to talk about sin? Let's not pick out five we can most easily assault because we do not do those sins. Let's talk about the greatest of all commandments."[3]

We can stand where Jesus did by helping our kids focus on loving God and their neighbor. If they always judge their behavior by the question, *Will this show love for God and my fellow human being?* they will have a guide that covers every moral decision, regardless of whether some sins are more socially acceptable than others.

2. Help Kids Connect the Hurts They Feel to the Sin at the Source

If your family has been hurt by the sins of others, use that pain to help kids learn that sin hurts people. This can help them build compassion and empathy if you tie the pain they feel or negative consequences in their lives back to the source. You can later say, "Don't ever do ———. Think of the hurt you could cause innocent people."

Our family was severely hurt financially when a publisher broke a contract without paying me the money due. Our whole family suffered serious financial difficulties and ongoing consequences for several years. Many of these hurt our children indirectly. As we prayed about our needs and worked through issues of forgiveness, asking God to reprimand the people who had sinned against us, we also took care to clarify with our kids that even though such behavior was justified as "common business practice," there was still sin involved, and what we were suffering was partially a result of sin. We discussed the sins involved: using the Lord's name in vain (since we trusted these people because they called themselves Christians), bearing false witness (in order to justify what they did, they misconstrued facts and broke a contract that was signed and to which someone bore witness), and stealing (they kept money rightfully owed to me).

Our children saw the connections between the ways our whole family suffered and specific failures to keep specific commandments. As a result, they became keenly aware that they would never want to bring that kind of pain on others. Therefore, they have inner motivation not to go along with "common business practices" that involve sin and would hurt innocent people. That personal hurt will be a valuable lesson in business ethics for the rest of their lives. By tying it to specific commandments, we helped them clarify the meaning of God's commands and God's protective intention behind the commandments.

3. Cultivate Their Conscience and Warn Them of the Dangers of Dulling Their Conscience

God gives us each a conscience that can help us if we keep it clean. We must help our children practice keeping a clean conscience by teaching them to confess their sins to the Lord. Affirm them when they mind their conscience, and emphasize how dangerous it is when people dull their consciences to the point of having no restraint.

4. Frame Their Own Moral Struggles and Temptations in Personified Spiritual Terms

The Bible says that good and evil are tied to God, who is the ultimate source of goodness, and Satan, who is the evil one. Remind them that God and Satan are real spiritual and personal entities who have intentions toward them. John 10:10 says the evil one comes to kill, steal, and destroy. First Peter 5:8 says, "Your enemy the devil prowls around like a roaring lion looking for someone to devour." If they remember that God loves them and wants what's best for them, while *their enemy* wants to destroy them, and if they tie this personal battle to all temptation, they will be more inclined to resist temptation. It's sort of like knowing how Wiley Coyote tries to trick the Roadrunner into following signs for "Free Bird Seed," when, in fact, the sign points toward a cliff. If you frame your kids' moral temptations in such terms, they will naturally want to stay on the good side if only for self-preservation.

5. Practice Key Prayers with Them That Relate to Moral Uprightness

- The Lord's Prayer—see Matthew 6:9-13. ("And lead us not into temptation, but deliver us from the evil one.")
- The Prayer of Jabez—see 1 Chronicles 4:9-10, NKJV. ("Keep me from evil that I may not cause pain.")
- Prayers of repentance. (Personal prayers based on 1 John 1:9 and Bible examples such as Psalm 19:12-14; 51:1-14; 143:1-2; Jeremiah 3:25; and Luke 7:28.)

Here is a simple process to practice prayers of repentance with children based on the promise in 1 John 1:8-9:

> If we claim to be without sin, we deceive ourselves and the truth is not in us. If we confess our sins, he is faithful and just and *will forgive us our sins* and *purify us* from all unrighteousness.

We shouldn't pretend we don't sin, but practice repentance and receive God's purifying power to get rid of sin whenever we find it. The sentences in parentheses are prayer models for kids.

- Confess sin whenever you spot it. The word confess here means "to agree with God." Agree with God that what you have done is wrong, since God says it is wrong. ("Dear God, I lied about not breaking the lamp. I know that's wrong because you say not to lie.")
- Remember, Jesus paid for all your sins. Thank him. ("Thank you, Jesus, that you died to pay for this sin too.")
- Repeat God's promise. ("God, you promised that if we would confess our sins, you are faithful and just and will forgive us our sins and purify us from all unrighteousness.")

- Ask God to forgive this sin. ("Please forgive me for lying.")
- Ask God to clean up this area of sin in your life. ("Please clean my heart so I don't lie to try to get out of trouble.")
- Ask God to show you anyone who was hurt because of your sin and how you can undo any damage or hurt you caused. ("I know I hurt my mom's feelings by lying to her. Please help me show her how sorry I am. Please show me what I can do to help replace the lamp I broke.")
- Thank God for assurance that you are forgiven. ("Thank you, God, for always keeping your promises, so I know I am forgiven. In Jesus' name. Amen.")

When modeling and teaching cleansing from sin, also explain that God's forgiveness doesn't mean there won't be consequences. Good parents—even God—use consequences to discipline beloved children. As kids get older, explain this from Hebrews 12:5-11.

6. Teach Them to Flee Temptation and Youthful Lusts

(These can be evil desires or natural desires that are too much for them to control.) When the Bible says that every temptation comes with a way of escape (see 1 Corinthians 10:13), that escape exit can usually be found long before the actual act of sin. Teach them to exit any situation early that could predictably lead to temptation and sin. There is a television commercial that shows young adults out drinking alcohol at a club and "partying." One young man is getting ready to leave when several sexy young women show up. The commercial suggests that if he goes home, he will miss out on the "fun" to come. However, even such immorally suggestive messages can be used for training: "That is a picture of the kinds of situations where sin could be predicted if that young man stays any longer. He shouldn't have been there in the first place, but this is when he should flee his normal youthful lusts and desires (being pictured so attractively, as temptation truly is) because after one more drink, or one more seductive glance, he may not have the moral strength to resist."

7. Teach Them to Set Their Standards in Keeping with What the Bible Says About Any Topic

Teach them not to lower their standards just because some other Christians act as though some sin is okay. When a new topic of moral interest or questions of right or wrong arise, take them to the Bible to see what God's Word has to say about the subject. Teach them to make their moral decisions on the basis of what is right, not on the basis of who is in power or who is popular.

Recently, a discussion came up in our family about a Christian celebrity who had left her husband and family to marry another man, just as he left his wife and family to marry her. The media, in a feature on a national television news magazine show, made a big deal about how wonderful it was that she finally found her "true love" and married her "soul mate." They did not address the pain caused to her other children and first husband, or the damage to those looking to her as a Christian role model. Simultaneously, she happened to be having a concert in our town. The local Christian radio station ran enthusiastic ads for the concert, and the Christian bookstores featured her new CD.

In view of the subtle and not-so-subtle messages that her divorce and remarriage were not really a big deal, indeed may have been the best thing she's ever done, we felt compelled to take the question of what was right back to the Bible. We looked up everything Jesus had to say about divorce and remarriage and read that aloud after watching the news magazine feature about her new marriage. There was quite a difference in perspective. Then we raised the issue of the promotion in the Christian media. It turned into an emotion-packed conversation. However, because we live in a culture that gives morally confusing messages, we needed to raise the issues in light of God's Word. That had to be the starting point. We ended up discussing the grace and mercy of God to cover all manner of sin, but our conversation also covered the possible consequences of shaking off God's standards because they stand in the way of personal desires. We talked about God's grace to King David—he did get to marry Bathsheba and remain king; God even allowed the next son of their union to become David's successor. However, we showed our kids the long-term consequences to the rest of David's children and kingdom and future, showing how God's forgiveness and grace did not negate the terrible consequences of disobeying God. This leads to my next point.

8. When Appropriate, Let Them Learn from the Lessons You Learned the Hard Way

Tell them about your wrong choices and bad consequences, along with the grace and mercy God has shown you. After our family discussed the divorce and remarriage issue, we talked about some of the dangerous consequences our family faced many years ago when my husband had fallen into adultery (our children already knew about this) and how we consequently had to face the possibility of an unwanted divorce ourselves. Pat shared with our children how different all our lives would have been if he had refused to repent. He could have left our family to follow the desires of his sinful nature. If we were making decisions on the values of today's world, he could have tried to justify leaving our marriage because it was extremely painful to stay and resolve our problems. He could have relied on the grace of God to grant him forgiveness in advance.

If he had, what would have happened to our family as a result? Our youngest daughter wouldn't even have been conceived! Then he talked about how he repented, how we received the grace and mercy of God along with the supernatural strength needed to bear the consequences, but how we still paid a heavy price. He talked about how hard it was at the time to make the right choice, but how good the consequences turned out to be. He explained how the love we share and the blessings we know in our family relationships, his regained sense of self-respect, and his deepened love for God are all connected to that tough but right moral choice. You need to use discretion so you don't burden your children with shameful details they are not meant to bear. However, we all have plenty of appropriate lessons to share from our own moral failures and redemption. Hopefully some were wrong choices that were corrected by true repentance proved by godly behavior.

9. Point Out Hypocrisy Before They Do

Kids are keenly aware of hypocrisy. In a situation where hypocrisy is overt, use it for instruction as a bad example. Once when I was speaking at a conference along with several well-known Christian speakers, my sisters and mother attended, including one sister who was not yet a Christian. I was in the VIP dining room where some of the speakers were eating breakfast when my sisters came past the door, pushing my mom in a wheelchair. The speakers kindly introduced themselves and invited them to join us. My family declined, but my colleagues were kind, urging them to come in and feel welcomed. At that moment, the woman in charge of evangelism for the conference pushed her way past my sisters and the wheelchair without a word of greeting or acknowledgment. She briskly walked to the VIP table and said, "I hope she doesn't think *they* are going to come in here and eat with *us*." Before I could register the shock, my non-Christian sister turned Mom's wheelchair around and headed down the hall. The woman who'd made the statement showed no emotion. The others tried to cover up with humor. One kindly put her arm around me. You can imagine the conversation over dinner that evening among my sisters, my mom, my young teen daughter, and me.

I could have chosen to make light of the situation or make excuses for the woman's behavior. However, since hypocrisy has power to undermine someone's moral training or faith in Christ, I chose instead to use it as a Bible study object lesson with Casey. We talked about the verses in the book of James where it says,

> My brethren, do not hold your faith in our glorious Lord Jesus Christ
> with an attitude of personal favoritism. For if a man comes into your
> assembly with a gold ring and dressed in fine clothes, and there also
> comes in a poor man in dirty clothes, and you pay special attention
> to the one who is wearing the fine clothes, and say, "You sit here in a
> good place," and you say to the poor man, "You stand over there, or sit
> down by my footstool," have you not made distinctions among your-
> selves, and become judges with evil motives? Listen, my beloved
> brethren: did not God choose the poor of this world to be rich in faith
> and heirs of the kingdom which He promised to those who love Him?
> But you have dishonored the poor man.... If, however, you are fulfill-
> ing the royal law according to the Scripture, "YOU SHALL LOVE YOUR

NEIGHBOR AS YOURSELF," you are doing well. But if you show partiality, you are committing sin and are convicted by the law as transgressors. (James 2:1-9, NASB)

This woman's hypocrisy powered an important lesson for my kids. I was also able to contrast her words with the kindness of the speakers deemed VIPs who treated others respectfully. In this way, I used the example to help my children see why they'd never want to behave that way toward others. Also, they are all determined to be very careful of the impression they make by their actions because they don't ever want people to look at them and say, "Can you believe how so-and-so behaved? And she calls herself a Christian!"

OUR OWN SOCIALLY ACCEPTABLE SIN

I've given you a lot to think about here. I hope some of these suggestions and strategies will be useful to you as you raise your children in a culture that has been deeply influenced by the spirit of the age. Before closing, I need to raise another point for us as parents and as Christians in a morally compromised culture.

We, too, need to be very careful not to fall into the kind of moral relativism rampant in the religious establishment of Josiah's generation. The people of Judah were focused on the sins of Israel (their brethren whom God had judged by the Assyrian conquest and who were considered worse sinners than themselves). They were also focused on the fact that their enemies the Babylonians were *total pagans,* seeing themselves more righteous in comparison. As I've pointed out, they had legislated several forms of socially acceptable sins right in their own temple courts and the "holy" city of Jerusalem.

As I mentioned earlier, the Christian community has taken an active stand vocally and politically against the cultural assaults on God's moral law (most notably in pro-homosexual and pro-abortion legislation). We worry and resist these agendas, as we should, because we don't want them to become or remain the law of the land. We don't want our children to grow up thinking that behavior God condemns is actually acceptable. Yet we seem to miss the irony that our generation may have already accepted laws that God says are unacceptable, such as our attitudes toward divorce and remarriage, except in the case of sexual sin (which Jesus calls adultery), or abandonment by a non-Christian spouse (which Paul allows for in 1 Corinthians 7:15). Our culture and American jurisprudence accept divorce under the no-fault laws that were passed when we were children.

My aim is not to condemn those who have divorced. There are those who have been divorced when they wanted nothing to do with it. Because of the easy divorce laws, they could not avoid becoming unwilling victims of divorce after their husband or wife chose to divorce them against their will. There are many sad stories reflecting all the complexities of human relationships. My point here is not to single them out and heap more guilt on top of their heartbreak. Rather, I raise the issue because it shows that we may be in a religious culture so similar to that of ancient Judah that we—as a community of people known by God's name—may be living at risk of incurring a similar judgment beginning with the house of God. Today, that means the body of Christ. If so, our awakening to our own selectively sanctioned sins could be a turning point that will help avert such judgment.

I feel compelled to discuss this here, since it seems few others are willing and because this has a far-reaching negative impact on the lives of children in our culture. This kind of spiritual selectivity (targeting "worse sins" of those outside "the courts of God's temple") was one reason God brought judgment on the religious leaders of Judah. I'm sure most people in our culture are indirectly hurt by the rampant divorce and remarriage trends. Even if this issue does not directly impact your immediate family, the larger issue of church leaders and teachers of God's Word failing to clearly relate God's commands or avoiding this topic—a sin that God equated with the severity of the sins of Sodom and Gomorrah—could seriously impact us all.

I suggest that the divorce culture of our secular world has become so prevalent among Christians that we no longer have many who want to or dare to draw attention to God's definition of adultery, which is quite different from the definition most Christians hold. Is it any wonder that the divorce rate among Christians is the same as among non-Christians?

In her 1997 book, *The Divorce Culture,* Barbara Dafoe Whitehead writes,

As the sense of divorce as an individual freedom and entitlement grew, the sense of concern about divorce as a social problem diminished. Earlier in the century, each time the divorce rate increased sharply, it had inspired widespread public concern and debate about the harmful impact of divorce on families and the society. But in the last third of the century, as the divorce rate rose to once unthinkable levels, public anxiety about it all but vanished. At the very moment when divorce had its most profound impact on the society, weakening the institution of marriage, revolutionizing the structure of families and reorganizing parent-child relationships, it ceased to be a source of concern or debate.

The lack of attention to divorce became particularly striking after the 1980s, as a politically polarized debate over the state of the American family took shape. On one side, conservatives pointed to abortion, illegitimacy, and homosexuality as forces destroying the family. On the other, liberals cited domestic violence, economic insecurity, and inadequate public supports as the key problems afflicting the family. But politicians on both sides had almost nothing to say about divorce. Republicans did not want to alienate their upscale constituents or their libertarian wing, both of whom tended to favor easy divorce, nor did they want to call attention to the divorce among their own leadership. Democrats did not want to anger their large constituency among women who saw easy divorce as a hard-won freedom and prerogative, nor did they wish to seem unsympathetic to single mothers. Thus, except for the bipartisan calls to get tough with deadbeat dads, both Republicans and Democrats avoided the issue of divorce and its consequences as far too politically risky.[4]

Not only are Republicans and Democrats not speaking up on this issue, neither are many of the otherwise vocal Christian advocates lobbying to protect the family as an institution. I wonder how many kids are hurt by "no-fault" divorce and remarriage as compared to how many are directly hurt by some of the other issues our attention is drawn to incessantly by Christian activists. We probably don't wonder why because some of those shaping our opinions and answering our questions in the Christian subculture don't want to go there for the same reasons politicians want to avoid this issue. Too many among us have been divorced and remarried without scriptural grounds. Some Christian leaders who are remarried with scriptural grounds talk about that openly; some Christian leaders who are remarried avoid the issue altogether for various reasons.

Again, I am not suggesting we condemn Christians who have divorced and remarried. I consider the forgiveness of God priceless and rely on it often for my own sins. What troubles me is the approach the Christian community seems to have taken on the issue of divorce and remarriage without scriptural grounds. The grace we offer for this borders on license sometimes (see chapter 10), which definitely sends the wrong message to children directly hurt by this probably more than by any other sin or social problem. If God says that remarriage under certain conditions is allowed, but under other conditions is adultery, who are we to say, "Don't worry about it"?

I do believe the grace of God forgives all confessed sin. I am troubled, however, by Christian celebrities and leaders who enter into divorce and remarriage, then go on with public ministry without working through the seriousness of this prevalent type of sin. Their example sends a message to our kids that might influence their attitudes about marriage, that could contribute to their entering into marriage with insufficient seriousness, and that could give them reason to bail out of a marriage for any number of reasons. Treating divorce as a lesser issue or nonissue could leave them with the impression that God will let them disregard his commands about marriage and just trade up when marriage becomes difficult, or when they find their true "soul mate" after marrying "the wrong person."

As we focus on teaching our children how to be godly and wise in a culture determined to disobey God, let us also ask God to give us eyes to see the areas of sin that have become so accepted in our Christian culture that our attitudes may have already slipped away from God's standards without our even realizing it.

TWELVE

GREAT IS GOD'S FAITHFULNESS!

The faithfulness of God can be a source of blessed assurance, or it can be quite troubling, depending on whether we align our lives with God's promise of blessing. As the Bible and history reveal the entire story of Daniel's generation, we can see that God's prophecies, promises, and warnings all came true with startling accuracy. Those who aligned themselves and their children according to God's commands so that they could be blessed were blessed *just as God predicted.* Those who disregarded or disobeyed God's warnings and aligned themselves to receive the curses God warned them against received precisely what God had urged them to escape.

Josiah's sons and grandsons who ruled after him turned away from the Lord and did evil in his sight. Jehoahaz ruled only a few months before being taken captive to Egypt, where he died.

Next, King Jehoiakim trusted in the strength of Egypt instead of God, even though the Lord offered to relent of the judgment decreed against them through this prophecy:

> Now therefore amend your ways and your deeds and obey the
> voice of the LORD your God; and the LORD will change His mind
> about the misfortune which he has pronounced against you. (Jeremiah 26:13, NASB)

But King Jehoiakim, leaders, false prophets, priests, and the people would not. God spoke to them through Jeremiah again, saying,

"Woe to him who builds his house without righteousness
And his upper rooms without justice,
Who uses his neighbor's services without pay
And does not give him his wages,
Who says, 'I will build myself a roomy house
With spacious upper rooms,
And cut out its windows,
Paneling it with cedar and painting it bright red.'
Do you become a king because you are competing in cedar?
Did not your father eat and drink
And do justice and righteousness?
Then it was well with him.
He pled the cause of the afflicted and needy;
Then it was well.
Is not that what it means to know Me?"
declares the LORD.
"But your eyes and your heart
Are intent only upon your own dishonest gain,
And on shedding innocent blood
And on practicing oppression and extortion."

Therefore thus says the LORD in regard to Jehoiakim the son of Josiah,
    king of Judah,
"They will not lament for him:
'Alas, my brother!' or, 'Alas, sister!'
They will not lament for him:
'Alas for the master!' or, 'Alas for his splendor!'
He will be buried with a donkey's burial,
Dragged off and thrown out beyond the gates of Jerusalem....
I spoke to you in your prosperity;
but you said, 'I will not listen!'
This has been your practice from your youth,

That you have not obeyed My voice.

The wind will sweep away all your shepherds,

And your lovers will go into captivity;

Then you will surely be ashamed and humiliated because of all your
wickedness....

And I will give you over into the hand of those who are seeking your
life, yes, into the hand of those whom you dread, even into the hand of
Nebuchadnezzar king of Babylon and into the hand of the Chaldeans.
I will hurl you and your mother who bore you into another country
where you were not born, and there you will die." (Jeremiah 22:13-
19,21-22,25-26, NASB)

What was the response of King Jehoiakim and the religious and political
leaders who aligned themselves with him? This was the king who received
God's Word on a scroll and burned it piece by piece. What became of these
people? Every terrible thing God warned them of came true in their lives.
What does this have to do with us and our children? I suggest we need to read
these verses again—not just as ancient history—but to see where they might
apply to us today. It would behoove us to prayerfully consider if any of their
faults have crept into our own lives and into the practices of today's politicians,
priests, prophets, and scribes (political leaders who make public statements of
faith; ministers, preachers, and publishers who are entrusted with God's
Word). Wherever we are like them, we need to repent and pray for a spirit of
repentance among our leaders.

Jehoiachin—grandson of Josiah—was next on the throne. He was eighteen and he also did evil in the sight of the Lord. Jeremiah warned him that
unless he surrendered to Babylon, he and all who belonged to him would be
destroyed by the besieging armies. In the third month of his reign, the armies
of King Nebuchadnezzar besieged Jerusalem. King Jehoiachin believed the
warnings of God through Jeremiah, so he went out to the king of Babylon to
surrender. He went with his mother and his servants and his captains and his

officials. So the king of Babylon took him captive. Those in the royal family and about ten thousand of the people of Jerusalem prepared for departure, weeping as they saw the servants of Nebuchadnezzar carry out "all the treasures of the house of the LORD, and the treasures of the king's house, and cut in pieces all the vessels of gold which Solomon king of Israel had made in the temple of the LORD, *just as the LORD had said*" (2 Kings 24:13, NASB).

The Word of the Lord proved true to Jehoiachin. God said he would preserve those who surrendered to Babylon; those who surrendered with King Jehoiachin were spared death. They lived out their days in Babylon until the seventy years God had decreed were completed.

Jehoiachin—the only king of Judah to obey Jeremiah's warnings—was the only king of Judah who lived to one day be released from prison. He was the only king in the line of Josiah who turned from his evil ways to surrender. While in a Babylonian prison for thirty-seven years, he must have searched for God with a whole heart and found him, because the Lord allowed him to die a free man. This gave the exiles of Judah great hope and demonstrated that surrender to God had ultimate rewards, even though Jehoiachin paid a heavy price for his initial rebellion. So ends the book of 2 Kings:

> In the thirty-seventh year of King Jehoiachin's exile in Babylon,
> Evil-merodach ascended to the Babylonian throne. He was kind to
> Jehoiachin and released him from prison on April 2 of that year. He
> spoke pleasantly to Jehoiachin and gave him preferential treatment over
> all the other exiled kings in Babylon. He supplied Jehoiachin with new
> clothes to replace his prison garb and allowed him to dine at the king's
> table for the rest of his life. The Babylonian king also gave him a regu-
> lar allowance to cover his living expenses until the day of his death.
> (2 Kings 25:27-30, NLT)

> Among those left behind in Judah,

> All the leaders of the priests and the people became more and more
> unfaithful.... The LORD...repeatedly sent his prophets to warn them,

for he had compassion on his people and his Temple. But the people mocked these messengers of God and despised their words. They scoffed at the prophets until the LORD's anger could no longer be restrained and there was no remedy. (2 Chronicles 36:14-16, NLT)

After King Nebuchadnezzar exiled King Jehoiachin and the ten thousand to Babylon, Jeremiah received a vision in which he saw two baskets of figs placed in front of the Lord's temple in Jerusalem. One basket was filled with fresh ripe figs. The other was filled with rotten spoiled figs that were too gross to eat. Then the Lord said to Jeremiah,

"What do you see, Jeremiah?"

[Jeremiah] replied, "Figs, some very good and some very bad."

Then the LORD gave [Jeremiah] this message:... "The good figs represent the exiles I sent from Judah to the land of the Babylonians. I have sent them into captivity *for their own good.* I will see that they are well treated, and I will bring them back here again. I will build them up and not tear them down. I will plant them and not uproot them. I will give them hearts that will recognize me as the LORD. They will be my people, and I will be their God, for they will return to me wholeheart-edly." (Jeremiah 24:3-7, NLT)

God fulfilled this promise precisely for the "good figs." What are the implications for us today? There is great hope here. God sorts out those whose hearts are devoted to him and takes good care of them, even in times of judgment and overwhelming peril. God will protect, provide for, and keep his promises to anyone, or any small group of people, who turns to him wholeheartedly.

"But the rotten figs," the LORD said, "represent King Zedekiah of Judah [Judah's final king, who succeeded Jehoichin and did evil], his officials, all the people left in Jerusalem, and those who live in Egypt. [Remember King Jehoahaz, the first bad fig after King Josiah was taken captive to Egypt.] I will treat them like spoiled figs, too rotten to eat. I will make them an object of horror and evil to every nation on earth. They will be disgraced and mocked, taunted and cursed, wherever I send them. I will send war, famine, and disease until they have vanished from the land of Israel, which I gave to them and their ancestors." (Jeremiah 24:8-10, NLT)

The book of 2 Kings records the fulfillment of this prophecy against Zedekiah and those who sided with him against God:

So in the ninth year of Zedekiah's reign, on the tenth day of the tenth month, Nebuchadnezzar king of Babylon marched against Jerusalem with his whole army. He encamped outside the city and built siege works all around it. The city was kept under siege until the eleventh year of King Zedekiah. By the ninth day of the fourth month the famine in the city had become so severe that there was no food for the people to eat. Then the city wall was broken through, and the whole army fled at night through the gate between the two walls near the king's garden, though the Babylonians were surrounding the city. They fled toward the Arabah, but the Babylonian army pursued the king and overtook him in the plains of Jericho. All his soldiers were separated from him and scattered, and he was captured. He was taken to the king of Babylon at Riblah, where sentence was pronounced on him. They killed the sons of Zedekiah before his eyes. Then they put out his eyes, bound him with bronze shackles and took him to Babylon.

On the seventh day of the fifth month, in the nineteenth year of Nebuchadnezzar king of Babylon, Nebuzaradan commander of the imperial guard, an official of the king of Babylon, came to Jerusalem. He set fire to the temple of the LORD, the royal palace and all the houses of Jerusalem. Every important building he burned down. (2 Kings 25:1-9)

Every prophecy and promise came true precisely as God spoke through his holy prophets and as written in Scripture. The rotten figs were tossed out;

the good figs were protected and preserved through perilous times. Those who positioned themselves to be blessed were blessed and became a blessing to the whole world, none more than Daniel and Friends. They continued to serve God in Babylon, continually promoted through several different administrations. Daniel remained safe (even in a den of hungry lions, when once more God fulfilled his promise to give other men's lives in exchange for his). Daniel continued praying three times a day, looking toward Jerusalem, and looking forward to the day when the seventy years decreed for his people in Babylon would be completed. Therefore, we can rest assured that God will continue to be absolutely faithful to his Word. As we learn what God's Word teaches, we and our children, too, can walk in the ways that lead to blessing, avoid the ways that lead to curses, and look forward with full assurance to the rest of the promises and glorious prophecies to come true.

Daniel, by the grace of God, looked forward through visions to a time when God's anointed One would come to a rebuilt Jerusalem, enter a rebuilt temple, and by so doing bring the glory of God's presence back into his holy city. Daniel received visions in which he looked forward to a day when all the evil in the world will be put down. He was blessed to see a time when "the sovereignty, power and greatness of the kingdoms under the whole heaven will be handed over to the saints, the people of the Most High. His kingdom will be an everlasting kingdom, and all rulers will worship and obey him" (Daniel 7:27).

As the time of their release drew near, Daniel was not surprised when Cyrus, king of Persia, decreed the release of God's people and the rebuilding of the temple in Jerusalem. God had foretold these things over 150 years before through the mouth of the prophet Isaiah, calling Cyrus by name long before he was born. Consider the amazing nature of this prophecy; it's as if someone wrote in 1850 that terrorists were going to use two airplanes to destroy the World Trade Center towers—before airplanes or skyscrapers were invented—and then went on to comfort us by saying, "But don't worry, the towers will be rebuilt along with a monument," and then gave the first name of the architect and financier for the project.

This is what the LORD says to his anointed,
    to Cyrus, whose right hand I take hold of
to subdue nations before him
    and to strip kings of their armor,
to open doors before him
    so that gates will not be shut:
I will go before you
    and will level the mountains;
I will break down gates of bronze
    and cut through bars of iron.
I will give you the treasures of darkness,
    riches stored in secret places,
so that you may know that I am the LORD,
    the God of Israel, who summons you by name.
For the sake of Jacob my servant,
    of Israel my chosen,
I summon you by name
    and bestow on you a title of honor,
    though you do not acknowledge me.
I am the LORD, and there is no other;
    apart from me there is no God.
I will strengthen you,
    though you have not acknowledged me,
so that from the rising of the sun
    to the place of its setting
men may know there is none besides me.
    I am the LORD, and there is no other.
I form the light and create darkness,
    I bring prosperity and create disaster;
    I, the LORD, do all these things.
You heavens above, rain down righteousness;
    let the clouds shower it down.

Let the earth open wide,

> let salvation spring up,

let righteousness grow with it;

> I, the LORD, have created it....

This is what the LORD says—

> the Holy One of Israel, and its Maker:

Concerning things to come,

> do you question me about my children,

> or give me orders about the work of my hands?

It is I who made the earth

> and created mankind upon it.

My own hands stretched out the heavens;

> I marshaled their starry hosts.

I will raise up Cyrus in my righteousness:

> I will make all his ways straight.

He will rebuild my city

> and set my exiles free,

but not for a price or reward,

> says the LORD Almighty. (Isaiah 45:1-8,11-13)

Great is God's faithfulness! This came to pass precisely as God said that it would, even though Isaiah wrote these things long before Cyrus was born, before Persia was a world power, before Judah had been exiled to Babylon. You can read how this prophecy came to pass in Ezra 1:1-4 and 6:3-5. When we realize that God knew what was going to happen, the happy ending for his people, and even declared the name of the unbeliever through whom it would happen, we can rest assured that God knows how he is going to get us, our children, and our grandchildren yet to be born through whatever the next 150 years hold for us.

Daniel, his friends, and all the exiles of Judah who turned to the Lord, received the blessings promised in the Book of God's Law, which their parents had heard read aloud by King Josiah. They believed God's Word and were blessed. God set before them life or death, blessings or curses. They chose life, and God gave them life. They believed the words of the prophets and lived to see the fulfillment of those prophecies in amazing complexity and glorious specificity. Daniel was further blessed with a vision that foretold the establishment of Christ's kingdom (see Daniel 9:23-27). This can give us great hope! We serve the same living God! He loves us and our children!

HOPE FOR OUR CHILDREN

My husband and I are still actively engaged in parenting, seeking God to help us raise our own three children to be godly and wise. According to Philippians 2:15-16 (NASB), we pray that they may prove themselves to be "blameless and innocent, children of God above reproach in the midst of a crooked and perverse generation, among whom [they] will appear as lights in the world, holding fast the word of life, so that in the day of Christ [we] have reason to glory because [we] did not run in vain nor toil in vain." All parents who hope to raise kids today to be godly and wise must devote time to prayer and depend on God for the sake of their children. None of the parents I know— ourselves included—dare be self-assured about the daunting task of parenting in such perilous times, but we can be God-assured. That assurance comes as we seek first God's kingdom and his righteousness, then everything else we need will be added to us (see Matthew 6:33, NASB). God will cover us and even our mistakes to help our kids "walk tall in Babylon."

Our first daughter, Casey, went off to her first year of college last fall. She just turned eighteen and is now officially deemed an adult. Our son is in eighth grade, and our younger daughter is in sixth grade. We are very much aware of and living with the stresses and struggles of raising children in such challenging times. The past few years have been incredibly difficult for our family, and yet, we are grateful for seeing the blessings of God's promises to us and our children coming true. God has proved himself faithful to protect and provide for our children in miraculous ways. He has covered the important issues of life, like college tuition for Casey, and what might be deemed mundane issues, like getting us NBA playoff tickets for Taylor's thirteenth birthday. We are most grateful for what God is doing *in* our children's lives and *through* them.

One of our goals in raising our children was nicely summed up by Lindy Beam, youth culture analyst for Focus on the Family's *Plugged-In* magazine, as the obvious goal for parents today: "to grow kids who are wise, thoughtful, culturally literate, pure, God-fearing, and who can make a positive impact in their world."[1] That has been our heart's desire, our aim, and our prayer. We determined to raise our children in the fear of God, not in the fear of man, not even in the fear of offending some of our Christian friends.

Doing this as we have done has occasionally brought criticism, more often the raised eyebrow, from other Christians. We've been able to withstand the verbal and nonverbal disapproval from people because we have been clear from the beginning that we were checking in with God, staying true to the Bible, and keeping a clean conscience. I daresay that if you choose to employ some of the methods I recommend in this book, you, too, will encounter criticism. Here is what helps us to consider the input of well-meaning Christian friends, while not being continually swayed by varying opinions:

> So we make it our goal to please him [the Lord], whether we are at home in the body or away from it. For we must all appear before the judgment seat of Christ, that each one may receive what is due him for the things done while in the body, whether good or bad. (2 Corinthians 5:9-10)

As we look at the life of our daughter Casey as she stands on the threshold of adulthood, we have much for which we are grateful. She willingly attends a Christian college where she shares a dorm room with her friend Darcy. If you visited their dorm last Christmas, you would have entered a hallway decorated with variations on the theme "Walkin' in a Winter Wonderland"—a host of holiday decorations all with the slightly frightening face of actor Christopher Walkin. There was a Mr. and Mrs. Santa (both with a Walkin face), all eight reindeer (with Walkin faces), and a drawing of a Christmas choir (all with

Walkin's face). Why? Well, just because they thought it was funny and their suitemates agreed.

If you looked on their bookshelves, you would find a wide range of literature: Bibles, concordances, Walt Disney's *Treasury of Children's Classics,* art books, *Ancient Legends of Ireland,* The Golden Age of Children's Book Illustrations, Shakespeare's plays, *The Hiding Place,* Bunyan's *Pilgrim's Progress,* The Chronicles of Narnia, The Lord of the Rings trilogy, Harry Potter books (right next to my book *The Gospel According to Harry Potter*), A Treasury of Poems, *The Piggy in the Puddle* (one of our all-time favorite children's books) by Charlotte Pomerantz, along with books by Ray Bradbury, Dean Koontz, Michael Crichton, and Stephen King.

If you were given access to Casey's collection of music CDs you would find many Christian music artists alongside about twenty musical scores ranging from *My Fair Lady* (her favorite), *Thoroughly Modern Millie, The Music Man,* and *Godspell* to *Ragtime, Cabaret, Evita, Les Misérables,* and *Phantom of the Opera.* You'd find soundtracks for almost every Disney animated feature, plus *The Prince of Egypt,* and *Anastasia.* You might find the funny Christian satirical musings of *Relient K* tucked in with the operatic vocals of Audra MacDonald and Josh Grodin, next to her *Ella Fitzgerald Sings Gershwin.*

We enjoy all of these with Casey on our long drives to and from her campus. We are not the least bit put off that she enjoys a wide range of literary, musical, and theatrical selections. We know she does so from a heart and mind that is devoted to the Lord, grounded in Scripture, and biblically informed. We—in keeping with how God looks at a person—have always tried to deal with our children by looking on the heart. When we do that, we are overly pleased with the way Casey has turned out. If you'll pardon what may sound like a parent bursting at the seams with pleasure over what God has done in and for a child we love, I'd like to share some of the goodness of God we see working out in Casey's life. This is shared partly to validate the idea that the things we have applied and shared in this book actually work.

In eighth through twelfth grades, until she graduated in June 2002, Casey attended a public charter school that specialized in performing and fine arts. Mr. Silveira, one of her teachers (who does not publicly profess Christ) has taught her over several years in government, history, and social studies. In her college letter of recommendation he wrote:

> Casey has been one of the main participants in class debates on subjects ranging from drug legalization to homosexual marriage. I have been particularly impressed by her willingness to take positions that often go against those held by the majority of her classmates. Rather than simply remain silent (and thereby avoid possible repercussions of being in the minority) Casey has met these issues head on, and became a calm and rational advocate of her values and beliefs.... Casey is one of the finest people I have ever met.
>
> She is kind and considerate, the type of person who treats everyone well. She is helpful and giving, the kind of student who is always willing to help a classmate.

At graduation, Casey didn't get the award for most outstanding student in writing, nor in music, nor in art, nor in drama—which are her ardent areas of interest and pursuit. Instead, she received the award for outstanding student in social studies. Listen to how Mr. Silveira introduced this award:

> Social Studies is far more than the study of names, dates, and events. It is the study of human societies, thoughts, and actions. In short, it is the study of life. To succeed in this field, one needs to revel in the world of ideas. Although many students in the class of 2002 are worthy of this award, one stands out in particular. She is a young woman who encourages open and honest discussion, who connects thoughts to actions, and who excels in every task assigned to her. It is my pleasure to give the 2002 Social Studies Award to one of the finest students I have ever had the honor of teaching: Casey Neal.

Casey is friends with many people at school and has a closer small group of Christian friends near home and at church. However, we have always encouraged our kids to pray for and love their friends who are not yet believers. One of Casey's friends from school has shown interest in the Lord but has not committed her life to him. Some people are put off by her looks. She is a beautiful girl, slightly built, with pale skin, black eyes, and long black hair. When we first met her she only wore black, with the occasional bit of red as an accent color (and I think that was the flames on her thick-soled boots). Let's just say her appearance is not typical of most of the youth at our conservative suburban church.

Even at school, people joked that these two made an unlikely pair. One year on dress-up day Casey's friend dressed in black with horns and a tail, as a bad angel, and Casey dressed in white and gold with wings, as a good angel. One day her friend offered to dress in a pink poodle skirt outfit (á la the fifties) if Casey would wear all black and dress in what is commonly known as goth fashions. A picture of them together that day was in the yearbook. It's a testament to real friendship. Yes, Casey knows what is associated with being goth, and everyone who knows her *knows* that she is definitely *not* goth. When I chose photos of Casey's life for our church's graduation dinner, I included that photo. I think it may be one of the most "Christian" images I have of her. The caption reads: "She became all things to all friends, that by all means, she might save some."

Casey has not shied away from the world, but sought to develop her talents and use them to share her gifts and God's message of love through her art and music, which is distinct from her classmates. The reality of God's grace in Casey's life came through in all that she did, whether or not she was talking directly about God.

Casey's peers voted her Most Likely to Succeed. You can tell a lot by the impression one leaves on one's peers. A kid can put on the Christian act at home and church, but in the middle of a secular performing arts academy, the real person comes through. Casey's graduating class only had about thirty students, so their yearbook had few special features. One of these was that each senior was given a sheet with the name of the other seniors. They were asked to write the one word or phrase that comes to mind when they thought of that person. It was very interesting to read these peer reviews for Casey: smart, talented, great singer, friendly, songwriter, little angel, gifted, Christian, sweetheart, artistic, go-getter, 4.0, nice, Disney, sweet—then I love the last one—*going to heaven.*

What more can a parent ask for any of our children except that perhaps they will be used by God to bring others along too?

I hope you see that what I am sharing has little to do with recommending which form of schooling is best: homeschool, public, private, or parochial. It has little to do with whether your child or children excel in the arts, athletics, comedy, music, or mechanics. I hope that whoever God has created each of your children to be, and whatever circumstances you have to deal with in your family—single parent or partner-parent, blended family or broken family, rich or poor, newly churched or coming from a godly heritage that goes back generations—that some of what I have shared will help the children you love to grow up among the few who walk the narrow way of obedience to God, so that they will stand even if the whole world falls. My prayer is that they will be among those who are raised up to receive God's blessings, and that they will be a blessing to the dark world in days to come, no matter what those days bring.

I see many kids around our family who are shining examples of those whom I believe are well on their way to "walking tall in Babylon":

There's David James, a handsome young man Casey and Darcy declare to be the living expression of the animated character Milo from Disney's *Atlantis—the Lost Empire.* Casey cast him in that part for her musical, and he was brilliant. He has a tremendous voice and comic flair that won him many lead roles in community theater and at school. David was the object of affection for many girls at school, although he was either oblivious or just played the gentleman by not getting caught up in the flattery, which he could have used to romantic advantage but never did. He was always known among his peers as a Christian and lived up to that by his behavior, even though he could be very funny in improv. He sings on our worship team at church beside his mother, unashamedly with our congregation in praise to God. He's on the youth worship team, where he is admired by other youths. He is unassuming, although tremendously talented.

School studies were never David's forte, so college didn't interest him much. Upon graduating, he chose to enlist in the army, as our country seemed to teeter on the brink of war. The week before he left home, he sang a solo about the Father's care for us and protection over us. I stood at the back of the church next to his mother, Charlotte. We both watched him with wonder, pride, and tears streaming down our faces. We don't know what David may have to face as he goes out into this dangerous world at this dangerous time. We do know that the words he sang about the Father, sovereignly watching over him, are true. I trust that David will go forward as one who lives walking tall in Babylon.

There are others: Andy Bertolucci, who excels in athletics and academics, who attended a Christian high school and now a Christian college; Karen DiFillipo, who was a shining light of Christ at her public high school, and who is now studying Chinese because she has a heart for missions; Kyle Roberts, who has been homeschooled since kindergarten and is being trained in film editing by his father (who's a professional editor in Hollywood) to be able to contribute something to our world through the media; Briana Morris, who has already been on several missions trips to Mexico and Europe, even though she's not yet out of high school. These are all kids I know whose parents have differing backgrounds, differing income brackets, differing denominational affiliations, and have made differing educational choices. But these are all kids I know who are growing to be godly and wise in this perilous world, where they will shine like lights in the darkness, neither defiled nor destroyed. I pray this book will help in some small way to encourage you and help you raise your children also to live walking tall in Babylon.

OUR FUTURE AND OUR HOPE

In closing, I want to share a note of encouragement and a love letter from God that offers assurance to us and our children of a future and a hope, no matter what may come. I cannot escape the realization that what I write here will have to hold up to whatever the future may bring for our children, our nation, and our world. We know there are plenty of dangers. There are some in the Christian community who see us as being in danger of God's judgment. Consider the words of Pastor John MacArthur from his book *Can God Bless America?*

> Can God bless America? Yes, but if we are to be the recipients of His blessing, *we* must be humble and repentant over our own sin. God resists those who revel in pride and arrogance; He exalts those who humble themselves. Calamities such as those that have struck our nation could be harbingers of greater judgments to come, or they could be the prelude to divine blessing. The difference will be seen in how we respond....
>
> Numerous Christian leaders have warned repeatedly that if God does *not* judge America, He will have to apologize to Sodom and Gomorrah. Indeed, God plainly threatens judgment against nations that turn against His truth. "'If they do not obey, I will utterly pluck up and destroy that nation,' says the LORD" (Jeremiah 12:17, [NKJV]). Perhaps no society has ever taken a more dramatic turn against God than America did in the latter half of the twentieth century. Divine judgment seems inevitable if our nation continues down that road.

But judgment can still be averted and blessing regained through repentance and spiritual renewal. The word of the Lord through the prophet Jeremiah goes on to say, "The instant I speak concerning a nation and concerning a kingdom, to pluck up, to pull down, and to destroy it, if that nation against whom I have spoken turns from its evil, I will relent of the disaster that I thought to bring upon it" (18:7-8).

Certainly God can bless America, but the necessary prelude to national blessing is a sweeping spiritual renewal that begins with individual repentance and faith in the Lord Jesus Christ. Apart from such a profound spiritual awakening and a decisive return to the God of Scripture, we have no right as a nation to anticipate anything *but* God's judgment.[1]

We may already be seeing the beginnings of God's wrath being poured out on our nation, as Pastor MacArthur suggests. We may be on the verge of the greatest spiritual awakening ever, with God's miraculous protection about to be revealed on our behalf. I don't know what may happen next, or how our nation will respond to God's warnings. As Christian parents, we are keenly aware that our children are growing up amidst wars and rumors of war, nations rising against nations, ethnic groups taking up arms against other ethnic groups, false religions, false prophets, myriad "spiritual leaders" promoting a wide range of conflicting messages, and spiritual celebrities who are as well known for their moral failures as their message given in the name of God.

Paul warned the young pastor Timothy (and us):

But mark this: There will be terrible times in the last days. People will be lovers of themselves, lovers of money, boastful, proud, abusive, disobedient to their parents, ungrateful, unholy, without love, unforgiving, slanderous, without self-control, brutal, not lovers of the good, treacherous, rash, conceited, lovers of pleasure rather than lovers of God—having a form of godliness but denying its power. Have nothing to do with them. (2 Timothy 3:1-5)

As I think back to the reactions of those who heard King Josiah's message I recall that all gave lip service to God, but most lived out their lives by license or lawlessness. Very few listened to obey, turned from the errors of their ways, and lived to receive the blessings God longed for them to receive. I pray the same is not the case with us. However, as I studied in preparation for writing this book, I was struck by the similarities between the conditions of their hearts, their culture, their conduct, and our own. This has caused me serious reflection; I pray it does the same for you.

Given the perils of our time, we must also remind ourselves of the reassurance Jesus gave us:

You will hear of wars and rumors of wars, but *see to it that you are not alarmed.* Such things must happen, but the end is still to come. Nation will rise against nation, and kingdom against kingdom. There will be famines and earthquakes in various places. All these are the beginning of birth pains. (Matthew 24:6-8)

"See to it that you are not alarmed." As with many of the things Jesus said, at first glance this seems much easier said than done. How can we not be alarmed? How can we manage not to give in to fear or be dominated by worry? Here is how:

We have heard the sound of alarms in the past, but we have also seen that God took families through perilous times and empowered them to raise up their children to be blessed and protected. We have seen that there is much we can do as "Strategic Sources of Influence" in our children's lives to help ensure they are among the "good figs" whom God sorts out and protects during a time of severe trouble. Therefore, let us live every day we are granted to love God with all our heart, soul, mind, and strength, and love our children while we have them under our care. Let us make "the most of every opportunity because the days are evil" (Ephesians 5:16). But let us rest in the sure knowledge that our God is *good,* and *powerful,* and *sovereign* over all, and that he is intent on delivering those who are his during the most perilous times.

Habakkuk was another prophet in the nation of Judah during the times when Jeremiah prophesied, and while Daniel and his friends were growing up. Although the most likely date of his writings are between 609 and 597 B.C., his writings reflect a sense of what we parents may be feeling at this point in our history. He wasn't sure what would come. He wasn't sure what it all meant. He was deeply troubled by the violence, injustice, and immorality around him, and the powerful enemies amassing against them. He could see the truthful condemnation of the unrighteousness in Judah laid out in prophecies of Jeremiah, such as these:

I have listened attentively,
    but they do not say what is right.
No one repents of his wickedness,
    saying, "What have I done?"
Each pursues his own course
    like a horse charging into battle.
Even the stork in the sky
    knows her appointed seasons,
and the dove, the swift and the thrush
    observe the time of their migration.
But my people do not know
    the requirements of the LORD.

How can you say, "We are wise,
    for we have the law of the LORD,"
when actually the lying pen of the scribes
    has handled it falsely?
The wise will be put to shame;
    they will be dismayed and trapped.
Since they have rejected the word of the LORD,
    what kind of wisdom do they have?
Therefore I will give their wives to other men
    and their fields to new owners.

From the least to the greatest,
>   all are greedy for gain;
prophets and priests alike,
>   all practice deceit.
They dress the wound of my people
>   as though it were not serious.
"Peace, peace," they say,
>   when there is no peace.
Are they ashamed of their loathsome conduct?
>   No, they have no shame at all;
>   they do not even know how to blush. (Jeremiah 8:6-12)

But Habakkuk still maintained his presumption that God would never let the ruthless and utterly unrighteous Babylonians triumph over the relatively righteous people of Judah. Therefore, he had trouble believing that Jeremiah's prophecies were about to be literally fulfilled against Judah when he read,

So they will fall among the fallen;
>   they will be brought down when they are punished, says the LORD.

"I will take away their harvest," declares the LORD.
>   "There will be no grapes on the vine.
There will be no figs on the tree,
>   and their leaves will wither.
What I have given them
>   will be taken from them." (Jeremiah 8:12-18)

If you read the short book of Habakkuk in its entirety, you'll see that he begins by crying out for God to remedy the violence, injustice, and sinfulness that is rampant in Judah. God's reply called for him to brace himself for the judgment his nation was about to face at the hands of the Babylonians. Scripture records Habakkuk's reaction to God's shocking decree of impending judgment against God's people by Babylon:

I heard and my heart pounded,
> my lips quivered at the sound;
decay crept into my bones,
> and my legs trembled.
Yet I will wait patiently for the day of calamity
> to come on the nation invading us. (Habakkuk 3:16)

In Habakkuk's response, we hear an echo and acceptance of what Jeremiah prophesied would happen to Judah. However, he did not give up hope in God. Instead he held on to his faith, trusting that God's decision to allow judgment to befall his people by an ungodly enemy would be followed—as promised—by God's judgment on the Babylonians too. He grew to see the larger picture of God as Sovereign superintending over all world events, while still caring for those who would turn to him. He gives us a model for faith in perilous times. He wrote,

Though the fig tree does not bud
> and there are no grapes on the vines,
though the olive crop fails
> and the fields produce no food,
though there are no sheep in the pen
> and no cattle in the stalls,
yet I will rejoice in the LORD,
> I will be joyful in God my Savior.

The Sovereign LORD is my strength;
> *he makes my feet like the feet of a deer,*
> *he enables me to go on the heights.* (Habakkuk 3:17-19)

He went over the list of the worst he could imagine for their times and concluded, even though…even though…even though…, his life would not be determined by circumstances but by the Lord, his God and Savior.

We can do the same. We, too, can confidently say, "Even though…" Whatever may come, we will put our faith in God. We can say such a thing *because* the Sovereign Lord is our strength. He rules over all, and not one of us or our children escapes his providential care. We, too, can trust God to make our feet like the feet of a nimble deer so that we and our children can go on to the heights even if our whole world were to fall.

Life may become more challenging and more perilous. If it does, those of us who put our faith in our Sovereign Lord and instill that faith in our children can still look forward to rising above the turmoil in the world. How? The feet of the deer referred to in Habakkuk were able to scale the craggy heights where no other animal or human could go. God designed their feet to skip over and remain secure on terrain that would prove hazardous and deadly to any other creature. Those living in the valleys of Judah and Israel could look up and see these deer skipping on the heights.

Likewise, should life become more and more perilous, God promises to transform those of us who trust him, so that we can continue to have sure footing in situations that will prove too much for those who do not put their trust in God. In this way, God will use the rigors of life's difficulties to lift up those who are his, so that all will see that they are blessed and protected by God. Our children can rise above the perils of this world, bringing glory to God, even though the rest of the world may go down around them.

I saw this same kind of amazing view just a few weeks back, gazing up at the jagged cliffs of the Rocky Mountains of Colorado, where bighorn sheep ascended the heights with surefooted ease. Looking at the winding road made me a bit queasy, but looking up was amazing. As our road of life takes potentially frightening curves, let's obey Jesus and "see to it that we are not alarmed." Instead, let's point our children's gaze to the heavens and to the blessed hope we have in Jesus Christ:

> For the grace of God that brings salvation has appeared to all men. It teaches us to say "No" to ungodliness and worldly passions, and to live self-controlled, upright and godly lives in this present age, while we

wait for the blessed hope—the glorious appearing of our great God and Savior, Jesus Christ, who gave himself for us to redeem us from all wickedness and to purify for himself a people that are his very own, eager to do what is good. (Titus 2:11-14)

A Love Letter from God in Troubled Times

Many people know the promise of Jeremiah 29:11-13, but they are not aware of the context.

> This is the text of the letter that the prophet Jeremiah sent from Jerusalem to the surviving elders among the exiles and to the priests, the prophets and all the other people Nebuchadnezzar had carried into exile from Jerusalem to Babylon. (Jeremiah 29:1)

It was a letter to the good figs! The letter to them said,

> This is what the LORD Almighty, the God of Israel, says to all those I carried into exile from Jerusalem to Babylon: "Build houses and settle down; plant gardens and eat what they produce. Marry and have sons and daughters; find wives for your sons and give your daughters in marriage, so that they too may have sons and daughters. Increase in number there; do not decrease. Also, seek the peace and prosperity of the city to which I have carried you into exile. Pray to the LORD for it, because if it prospers, you too will prosper." Yes, this is what the LORD Almighty, the God of Israel, says: "Do not let the prophets and diviners among you deceive you. Do not listen to the dreams you encourage them to have. They are prophesying lies to you in my name. I have not sent them," declares the LORD.
>
>   This is what the LORD says: "When seventy years are completed for Babylon, I will come to you and fulfill my gracious promise to bring you back to this place. For I know the plans I have for you,"

declares the LORD, "plans to prosper you and not to harm you, plans to give you hope and a future. Then you will call upon me and come and pray to me, and I will listen to you. You will seek me and find me when you seek me with all your heart. I will be found by you," declares the LORD, "and will bring you back from captivity. I will gather you from all the nations and places where I have banished you," declares the LORD, "and will bring you back to the place from which I carried you into exile." (Jeremiah 29:4-14)

While we can't take all the mail addressed to others in the Bible and apply the promises to ourselves, God put this promise in the Bible for our sakes too. To those who qualify, the promises still apply. Whatever happens to our generation, we, too, can put our trust in God. We can trust him to take care of us and our families. We can settle down wherever we are and seek to be a blessing to those around us. We can pray to the Lord for the sake of our city and our nation, because as our nation prospers, so will the lives of our children. We can take care to study the Bible's prophecies that may apply to our times, and be careful not to let false prophets fool us. We can also receive the promise of God for ourselves and our children:

"For I know the plans I have for you," declares the LORD, "plans to prosper you and not to harm you, plans to give you hope and a future. Then you will call upon me and come and pray to me, and I will listen to you. You will seek me and find me when you seek me with all your heart. I will be found by you," declares the LORD. (Jeremiah 29:11-14)

GROUP STUDY AND DISCUSSION GUIDE

CHAPTER ONE: WHERE DO WE BEGIN TO KEEP LIFE SAFE AND GOOD FOR OUR CHILDREN?

Break up into pairs or small groups.

1. Share what you've done to try to keep life safe and good for your children in a recent two-week period. Describe your sense of anxiety with regard to your children.

2. Philippians 4:6-7 tells us what to do when we're anxious and gives us a promise. The command: "Do not be anxious about anything, but in everything, by prayer and petition, with thanksgiving, present your requests to God." The promise: "And the peace of God, which transcends all understanding, will guard your hearts and your minds in Christ Jesus."

   Obey the command to receive the promise of peace by using the model below to make a list with three columns to guide your prayers:

STUDY CHART 1

ANXIETIES	REQUESTS	THANKSGIVING

In personal notebooks or on a group flip chart, list your "Anxieties" in regard to your children at this stage in their lives. Turn each anxiety into a "Request" to God for help. For each anxiety and request, note something related for which you can give thanks to God (for example, some aspect of God's nature upon which you can rely or a promise). List that under "Thanksgiving." Practice doing this regularly.

3. Share your lists as you feel comfortable; look for ways to encourage one another. For example, point one another to scriptures that have been especially encouraging to you that speak of God's character and promises.

4. Pair up with your spouse or another parent and take turns praying through your list. End by thanking God that his peace will guard your hearts and minds as promised.

CHAPTER TWO: WHEN REFORMS AND LIMITS ARE NOT ENOUGH

1. As a group, come up with a combined list of social reforms that you believe are worth supporting for the sake of our children's future.

2. Divide into groups based on your children's ages (infants, toddlers, preschool/kindergarten, grade school, middle school, high school). If a family has kids in more than one group, have parents split up to cover two group discussions, or choose the most pressing age. In each group, list necessary limits and boundaries deemed most important to protect children's well-being during that stage. Then brainstorm ideas of what parents can do during that stage to nurture devotion to God in the hearts of children this age.

3. Have each parent create a sliding scale like the one on the next page for each of their children. These visually describe the balance of emphasis on external limits and proper external behavior as compared to development of a sincere heart of devotion to God. For each child, mark what represents your current focus of attention on

external limits, and compare that to attention on inner spiritual development. Use another color to mark what you think is needed during this stage of each child's life:

STUDY CHART 2

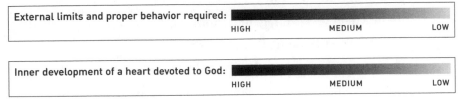

4. In parenting pairs, or during a few moments of personal reflection, use this chart to consider any adjustments you might need to make to ensure that while you keep necessary protective limits in place, you do not neglect your children's spiritual development for this stage of their lives. Write down one or two specific things you can do to maintain this balance.

5. Close in prayer (individual, partners, or group), asking God to help you find the right balance for each of your children to maintain safe limits, nurture their hearts for God, and still support needed, righteous societal reforms.

CHAPTER THREE: DUSTING OFF THE WORD OF GOD

A note for discussion leaders: Before your group discussion, write on posters each of the four typical reasons people don't dust off God's Word. Post each in one of the four corners of the room: (1) "Yeah, I already know it. I've heard it all my life." (2) "It's not relevant to me today; it's ancient history." (3) "I can't understand it; I'm too far behind to start learning it now." (4) "I don't like what I do understand of it. God's law is impossible to obey, so why torment us with threats of judgment when we are hopeless to measure up?" As people arrive, ask them to sit in the quadrant that best describes their general reasoning whenever they neglect dusting off the Word of God. In each quadrant, form discussion groups of up to six.

1. Have each small group look up the obstacles listed under their reason on pages 38-46. Then have them list what they can do (and hopefully are willing to do) to overcome whatever keeps them from dusting off the Word of God, whether occasionally or chronically.

2. Deuteronomy identifies ten things God said not to forget. Practice dusting off God's Word by assigning verses below to willing volunteers who can look them up. If time permits, have each group work together—with help if necessary—to find and share their discoveries. If time does not permit, assign and share next week.

   - The Lord is Creator (Deuteronomy 4:32; 1 Timothy 4:4; Genesis 1:1,21,27).
   - The Lord is the *only God;* beside him there is *no other* (Deuteronomy 4:35,39).
   - No idols! (Deuteronomy 4:16,23; 5:8).
   - What the people saw and heard when they stood before the Lord at Mount Horeb (Deuteronomy 5:1-5,22-32).
   - What God spoke to them out of the fire. Hint: There are ten of them (Deuteronomy 5:6-21).
   - All parts of the Exodus story and associated meanings (repeatedly), including what God did to Miriam on the way out of Egypt (Deuteronomy 24:9; Numbers 12:1-15).
   - How God brought them out of Egypt—with a mighty hand and great miracles, including specifically what God did to Pharaoh (Deuteronomy 7:18-21; Exodus 14).
   - How God provided a way of redemption for them (Deuteronomy 7:8; 9:26-27; 15:15).
   - How God provided for them during their forty years wandering in the desert; and *why* God allowed them to wander the way that they did (Deuteronomy 8:2-5).
   - What their hearts were like from the day God brought them out of Egypt until he settled them in the Promised Land (Deuteronomy 9:7,24).

3. Before closing, have one representative from each group share something good that happened in your group that motivates you to continue overcoming obstacles and dusting off the Word of God.

CHAPTER FOUR: HEAR THE WORD OF THE LORD AND PASS IT ON!

1. Circle the items that motivate you to want to hear the Word of God and pass it on to your children.

    Fear   Love and Hope   Rewards   Duty

2. What is the strongest factor that inhibits you from actually accomplishing the goal of passing on God's Word to each of your children? Discuss as a group ideas on how to overcome these obstacles.

3. Answer the following questions and share your answers with your parenting partner or someone in your group:

    *   Are you willing to accept God's command that you pass on his Word to each of your children as your personal duty (even though you may have the backup of another Christian parent, grandparents, and Christians ministering to your children)? If not, what keeps you from accepting this as your duty or from being willing to do it?

    *   What is the first step you need to take to hear God's Word yourself (and understand it) or to begin passing it on to your children, or both? Which child will you begin with?

    *   To whom are you willing to make yourself accountable to monitor your progress toward this goal?

    *   How will you measure your progress over time as your children grow up?

CHAPTER FIVE: FIRST AND LASTING IMPRESSIONS

1. How might you make changes in your current celebrations to keep the first great commandment at the forefront of all your biblical holidays and religious traditions?

2. Break up into small groups according to the general ages of your children, as you did with chapter 2. Have members of each group discuss and list things they can do, or methods that have worked to communicate God's love to children that age.

3. To celebrate Passover, God gave an example of how to make a biblical tradition a sensory experience. Prepare ahead of time to experience God's message of Passover—or another imminent celebration—with all your senses. (If you have someone of Jewish ancestry who can be a guest to share what is done during a Passover Seder, consider having him share.) In this way, the elements of a Passover meal can be experienced rather than just read about.

   • *Hearing:* Part of the Passover tradition is the retelling of the Exodus story. Find a storybook version of Exodus and ask your children questions about the story. To enhance the experience you could also add music—perhaps play the scene from *Prince of Egypt* where a song is playing as the Hebrews make their exodus from Egypt.

   • *Seeing:* Sometimes a candle or flashlight is used in a game to search out any leaven in the house and remove it. Beautiful sights also enhance the holiday and remind us of the beauty of the Lord and his creation (such as decorations, flowers, and the carefully laid table).

   • *Smelling:* Fragrance of cooking foods and herbs form lasting and evocative memories.

   • *Tasting:* "Taste and see that the Lord is good." In Exodus 12, God specifically commanded eating the lamb, unleavened bread, bitter herbs (horseradish), and salt water to use taste to convey figurative meaning (bitter herbs equal the bitterness of slavery; salt water equals tears; the lamb satisfies hunger and God's judgment against us). Talk about ways in which the foods you eat remind you of God's goodness (for example, the abundance of provision, the tenderness of meats, the sweetness of fruits and treats).

- *Touching:* Jewish families traditionally kept their Passover lamb as a *pet* before sacrificing it. Being "in touch" with it, literally and figuratively, added value to its sacrificial death.

  What can you do to make any holiday more meaningful and memorable by involving all the senses? Share ideas for an upcoming holiday.

CHAPTER SIX: RAISING SONS AND DAUGHTERS DETERMINED NOT TO DEFILE THEMSELVES

Below are the key points discussed in this chapter regarding what parents can do to help prepare kids to determine not to defile themselves.

- Help them establish their relationship with the true and living God (see page 88).
- Teach them that they each have a unique destiny to fulfill in keeping with God's dreams for their life (see page 90).
- Teach them that they have a path to choose as they venture out into life (see page 93).
- Teach them that they have an enemy to conquer (see page 94).
- As they enter their teen years, transfer personal accountability to them, even though you'll continue to be God's agents of discipline and some consequences (see page 97).
- Do all you can to encourage and facilitate relationships with "faith-full" friends who can be allies as they venture out into life (see page 100).

1. Break into small groups and review the section in the book corresponding with each item above. For each topic, have two to three people in the group address the points below.
   - what you have already done and how it's working
   - what you want to try from something you read or your ideas on that topic
   - one thing you feel you need to start doing soon

2. As a large group, discuss specific ways to help children prepare to deal with the kinds of temptations facing them today in your neighborhood and church culture.

CHAPTER SEVEN: RAISING CHILDREN TO GO INTO ALL THE WORLD WITHOUT BECOMING WORLDLY

1. Do you believe that Jesus' command to "Go into all the world" will one day apply to your children? Do you also accept that it is a parent's responsibility to protect young children from that which they are not prepared to face? What kind of tension does this cause you and your family when you try to protect them from being corrupted by the world at the same time you are supposed to be preparing them to go out into the world?

2. What ideas presented in this chapter run counter to your impressions or the direction you have already been pursuing within the subculture where you interact with other Christians? How has this challenged you?

3. This chapter suggested that there is a principle of progression at work in the lives of kids, a continuum, for example, between thrusting a toddler into a dark room without a night-light (which would be cruel) and sending a well-equipped young adult out into a dangerous world to be light to the world. What kinds of strategies are you employing or do you plan to employ to equip your children progressively as they grow so that eventually they can help fulfill the Great Commission?

CHAPTER EIGHT: RAISING CHILDREN TO ENGAGE THEIR CULTURE AND LOVE THE LOST

A note to discussion leaders: Before meeting, post three large sheets of paper with these headings at the front of the room:

- Isolate from Culture
- Give In to the Culture
- Engage and Translate Culture

1. Have the group share which category comes closest to describing what they tend to do with regard to cultural influences their children have to deal with (television, games, music, movies, books, fashions, trends popular with their friends). Explore why you tend to isolate from, give in to, or engage culture.

2. On another large sheet of paper, list specific challenges members of each category face in living with that particular approach to culture. Gather in your general categories and pray together for God to help you deal with the challenges unique to the approach. If you see areas where you need to change, also pray for God's help in making those changes.

3. How to engage culture and remain godly is not something that can be prescribed universally for every family. Each should be led by the Holy Spirit according to the sensitivities of each parent and the needs of each child. As a large group, share specific ideas from the chapter or from your own practices that you deem useful, have used successfully, or plan to use to help your children be in the world without becoming worldly.

Chapter Nine: Raising Children with Courage to Withstand the Fires of Life

1. Summarize the suggestions in this chapter on teaching God's Word to children to instill courage into their lives. Which of these have you already done? Which seem most appropriate for you to adopt now, given your children's ages? Choose at least one to focus on in the immediate future as you seek to build courage into your children's hearts and minds.

2. Just like Daniel's friends, your kids can expect persecution when they stand up for God's ways instead of bowing to the idols of this

world. In what situations can your children expect to experience some level of persecution if they refuse to go along with our culture? Share stories from your children's experiences and explore together ways in which parents in general can prepare their children for the kinds of confrontations they are likely to experience.

3. Pick one of God's promises given in this chapter and help your child memorize it as a way to gain courage in the face of life's trials, difficulties, and disappointments. How can you motivate your child or children to memorize it?

4. The study guide for chapter 1 offers guidelines for turning fears and anxieties into prayer requests. In the coming week, use this model with your children to help them pray through difficult situations they're experiencing. Share the results—including any challenges or obstacles you need help in overcoming—the next time you meet.

CHAPTER TEN: TEACHING CHILDREN MORALITY AND GODLY LIVING

A note for discussion leaders: Before meeting, make enough photocopies of the grid used to teach morality, located on page 164, so that small groups of three to four parents can each have one to work on.

1. Complete this "Checklist for Basic Training in Morality and Godly Living." Ask each of your children who are old enough to understand whether they know these basics (defined in the chapter):

STUDY CHART 3

What do you know?	Child 1	Child 2	Child 3	Child 4	Child 5
Ten Commandments					
God Is Watching You					
Play the "Golden Rule Game"					
Measure for Measure					
Rules Are Subject to Authority					

2. If they don't know these basics, plan to teach them as soon as you discern they are old enough. Praise them for gaining the knowledge as a preliminary for learning to discern right from wrong and living moral lives by the power of the Holy Spirit.

3. Break up into small groups and practice using the Grid for Teaching Kids to Make Moral Decisions. Using a Bible story, a current news event, an experience in family life, or pop-culture icon (stories, movies, plays, television), use the grid to help evaluate the morality of the issue at hand.

4. Discuss the inner struggle between the flesh and the Spirit (described in Romans 7) and how you've seen this battle play out in your children's lives. Pray for one another and your children to walk according to the power of the Holy Spirit so you do not fulfill the contrary desires of the sinful nature.

Chapter Eleven: Raising Children in a Culture Determined to Disobey God

1. What attempts do you make to shield your children from negative societal influences? How have your kids been hurt by the negative influence of living in an ungodly culture, and how has God worked in their lives to bring healing? Share any encouraging testimonies of how God can undo the negative societal influences our kids are subject to in this culture.

2. Share ideas that have proved successful as you've sought to protect children in your area from moral dangers: in the media, in games, on the Internet, at local parks and play areas. (These can be things you've done or resources you have found helpful for kids your children's ages.)

3. How do you find ways to build friendships with kids who are good influences? How do you limit friendships with kids whose bad morals have corrupting influences? Offer one another suggestions.

4. Review the section on socially acceptable sins within our Christian culture. Which of the points seems most immediately helpful to you as you alert your kids to deal with sins "in the courts of God's temple" in our generation?

CHAPTER TWELVE: GREAT IS GOD'S FAITHFULNESS!

1. Given the description of the "good figs," how can we qualify for the blessings and fulfilled promises of God in our generation? Write a list together.

2. How do the promises, protection, and provision afforded the "good figs" give you courage and hope for your children in our generation? Share the encouragement you have gathered from seeing God's faithfulness laid out in this chapter.

3. How does the comparison between the specific warnings given in Deuteronomy 27 and 28, along with the prophecies of Huldah and Jeremiah and what happened to those who were "rotten figs," affect your response to God's commands for us today? How does this story affirm that "the fear of the Lord" is the beginning of wisdom? Share your thoughts.

4. Daniel and his friends saw the prophecies of their generation come true before their very eyes. How might knowing Bible prophecies as they relate to current events help your children live to be godly and wise in perilous times?

5. Using Philippians 2:15-16 (NASB) as a guide, pray together that your children will be "blameless and innocent, children of God above reproach in the midst of a crooked and perverse generation, among whom [they] will appear as lights in the world, holding fast the word of life, so that in the day of Christ [you] will have reason to glory because [you] did not run in vain nor toil in vain."

NOTES

CHAPTER ONE

1. All excerpts in the chapter appeared in the Focus on the Family Letter of May 2002 by Dr. James Dobson, Colorado Springs, Colorado.
2. In 1989 my husband was removed from ministry because of sexual sin. I have written about this in several books: how we managed to keep our marriage intact, sexual addiction, and dealing with sexual sin in the church. Therefore, I am occasionally called on by churches for advice in such situations.
3. Statement from Al-Qaeda broadcast widely on all networks on 23 June 2002.

CHAPTER TWO

1. Tim Stafford, "The Third Coming of George Barna," *Christianity Today,* 5 August 2002, 34.
2. Stafford, "Third Coming," 38.

CHAPTER THREE

1. George Barna, *The State of the Church 2002* (Ventura, Calif.: Issachar Resources, 2002), 70.
2. Josh McDowell, *Beyond Belief to Convictions* (Carol Stream, Ill.: Tyndale, 2002). Found at BeyondBelief.com.
3. Larry Witham, "Bible Lessons Still Relevant," *Insight,* vol. 13, 30 June 1977, 39, as quoted by Leonard Sweet, *Soul Tsunami* (Grand Rapids, Mich.: Zondervan, 1999), 60.
4. Sweet, *Soul Tsunami,* 60.

CHAPTER SIX

1. Charles R. Swindoll, *You and Your Child* (Nashville, Tenn.: Thomas Nelson, 1977), 20.
2. For information on how to teach kids to avoid the influence of occult and evil spiritual forces, please see chapter 7 of my book *What's a Christian to Do with Harry Potter?* The information in this chapter is written at a second grade level so that it can be read directly to children.

CHAPTER SEVEN

1. John Fischer, *Fearless Faith* (Eugene, Oreg.: Harvest House, 2002), 10-2.
2. Dick Staub, *The Dick Staub Interview: Chris Seay.* Found at ChristianityToday.com, 24 September 2002, excerpted from the *Dick Staub Show.* Used by permission. Complete interviews may be found at www.dickstaub.com.
3. For those wishing to do this with anyone who knows and enjoys the Harry Potter stories, see my books *What's a Christian to Do with Harry Potter?* (WaterBrook) and *The Gospel According to Harry Potter* (Westminster John Knox).

CHAPTER TEN

1. See Galatians 2 and 3, Romans (particularly chapters 5 and 6), and talk these issues over with someone on your church staff.
2. *NIV Study Bible (CD-ROM),* notes on Numbers 9:3 (Grand Rapids, Mich.: Zondervan).
3. *NIV Study Bible (CD-ROM),* notes on Galatians 5:18 (Grand Rapids, Mich.: Zondervan).
4. For full understanding, study Hebrews 8, 9, and 12.

CHAPTER ELEVEN

1. Cheryl Wetzstein, "Parents See Tough Moral Rival in Popular Culture," *The Washington Times,* 31 October 2002). Found at www.washtimes.com.
2. Wetzstein, "Tough Moral Rival."
3. John MacArthur, *Can God Bless America?* (Nashville: W Publishing, 2002), 92.
4. Barbara Dafoe Whitehead, *The Divorce Culture* (New York: Knopf, 1996), 6-7.

CHAPTER TWELVE

1. Lindy Beam, found at www.pluggedinmag.com, July 2000.

AFTERWORD

1. MacArthur, *Bless America,* 27-9.